50 WALKS IN
West Yorkshire

50 Walks in West Yorkshire

Published by AA Publishing (a trading name of AA Media Limited, whose registered office is Grove House, Lutyens Close, Lychpit, Basingstoke, Hampshire RG24 8AG; registered number 06112600)

© AA Media Limited 2024
Fourth edition
First published 2001

Mapping in this book is derived from the following products:
OS Landranger 103 (walks 9, 14, 34, 42, 43, 46–48)
OS Landranger 104 (walks 4, 6–8, 11–13, 16, 17, 22, 23, 25–28, 30, 32, 33, 36, 37, 39, 40, 44, 45, 49, 50)
OS Landranger 105 (walks 1, 3, 6)
OS Landranger 109 (walk 41)
OS Landranger 110 (walks 18–21, 24, 29, 31, 35, 38, 41)
OS Landranger 111 (walks 2, 5, 10, 15)
OS Explorer 21 (walk 43)
OS Explorer 278 (walk 2)
OS Explorer 288 (walk 26)
OS Explorer 289 (walk 7)
OS Explorer 297 (walk 17)

© Crown copyright and database rights 2024 Ordnance Survey. 100021153.

Maps contain data available from openstreetmap.org © under the Open Database License found at opendatacommons.org

ISBN: 978-0-7495-8379-8
ISBN: 978-0-7495-8387-3 (SS)

A CIP catalogue record for this book is available from the British Library.

AA Media would like to thank the following contributors in the preparation of this guide:
Clare Ashton, Tracey Freestone, Lauren Havelock, Nicky Hillenbrand, Lin Hutton, Graham Jones, Ian Little, Richard Marchi, Nigel Phillips and Victoria Samways.

Cover design by
berkshire design company

Printed and bound in the UK by Oriental Press, Dubai.

A05851

We would like to thank the following photographers, companies and picture libraries for their assistance in the preparation of this book. Abbreviations for the picture credits are as follows:
Alamy = Alamy Stock Photo
Trade Cover, Andrew Smith/Alamy
Special Cover, Andrew Kearton/Alamy
Back Cover Advert, SolStock/istockphoto; 9, James Elkington/Alamy; 12/13, travellinglight/Alamy; 42/43, James Elkington/Alamy; 59, petejeff/Alamy; 72/73, Ian Dagnall/Alamy; 95, Andy Pearson / Stockimo/Alamy; 117, Andrew Smith/Alamy; 142/143, Stephen Dinsdale/Alamy; 153, Bailey-Cooper Photography/Alamy; 169, Andrew Smith/Alamy; 176, SolStock/istockphoto

The contents of this book are believed correct at the time of printing. Nevertheless, the publishers cannot be held responsible for any errors or omissions or for changes in the details given in this book or for the consequences of any reliance on the information it provides. This does not affect your statutory rights. We have tried to ensure accuracy in this book, but things do change and we would be grateful if readers would advise us of any inaccuracies they may encounter by emailing walks@aamediagroup.co.uk

We have done our best to make sure that these walks are safe and achievable by walkers with a basic level of fitness. However, we can accept no responsibility for any loss or injury incurred while following the walks. Advice on walking safely can be found on pages 10–11.

Some of the walks may appear in other AA books and publications.

Discover and book AA-rated places to stay at www.RatedTrips.com.

AA

50 WALKS IN
West Yorkshire

CONTENTS

How to use this book 6
Exploring the area 8
Walking in safety 10

The walks

WALK		GRADIENT	DISTANCE	PAGE
1	Fairburn Ings	▲	5 miles (8km)	14
2	Ackworth	▲	5.5 miles (8.8km)	17
3	Wetherby	▲	4 miles (6.4km)	20
4	White Wells	▲	3 miles (4.8km)	23
5	Upton	▲	3.5 miles (5.7km)	26
6	Barwick in Elmet	▲	10 miles (16.1km)	29
7	Stanley Ferry	▲	7.5 miles (12.1km)	32
8	Bardsey	▲	3 miles (4.8km)	35
9	Widdop Reservoir	▲	2.75 miles (4.4km)	39
10	Walton	▲	3.5 miles (5.7km)	44
11	Harewood	▲	7 miles (11.3km)	47
12	Meanwood Valley	▲	5.25 miles (8.4km)	50
13	Golden Acre Park	▲	6 miles (9.7km)	53
14	Stoodley Pike	▲▲▲	3.8 miles (6.1km)	56
15	Newmillerdam	▲	4.5 miles (7.2km)	60
16	Tong and Fulneck	▲	5 miles (8km)	63
17	Burley in Wharfedale	▲▲	5 miles (8km)	66
18	Farnley Tyas	▲▲	5.4 miles (8.7km)	69
19	Holme	▲▲	3.25 miles (5.3km)	74
20	Bretton Hall and YSP	▲	3 miles (4.8km)	77
21	Holmfirth	▲	4.5 miles (7.2km)	80
22	Addingham	▲	5.5 miles (8.8km)	83

WALK		GRADIENT	DISTANCE	PAGE
23	Shipley Glen	▲▲	4 miles (6.4km)	86
24	Digley Reservoir	▲▲	2.5 miles (4.4km)	89
25	Otley Chevin	▲	3.5 miles (5.6km)	92
26	Halifax	▲▲	5 miles (8km)	96
27	Norland Moor	▲	5 miles (8km)	99
28	Bingley	▲▲	6.25 miles (10.1km)	102
29	Meltham	▲▲	2.75 miles (4.4km)	105
30	Rodley	▲	3.5 miles (5.7km)	108
31	Marsden	▲▲	8.25 miles (13.3km)	111
32	Haworth	▲▲	8.1 miles (13km)	114
33	Ilkley Moor	▲▲	4.5 miles (7.2km)	118
34	Limers Gate	▲▲	4.8 miles (7.4km)	121
35	Holme Valley	▲▲	4 miles (6.4km)	124
36	Oxenhope	▲▲	6.75 miles (10.9km)	127
37	Laycock	▲▲	8 miles (12.9km)	130
38	Colne Valley	▲▲	7 miles (11.3km)	133
39	Temple Newsam	▲	1.5 miles (2.4km)	136
40	Judy Woods	▲	3.5 miles (5.7km)	139
41	Rishworth Moor	▲▲▲	7.5 miles (12.1km)	144
42	Stoodley Pike	▲▲	9 miles (14.5km)	147
43	Hardcastle Crags	▲▲	5 miles (8km)	150
44	Wade Wood	▲▲	1.5 miles (2.4km)	154
45	East Riddlesden Hall	▲▲	5 miles (8km)	157
46	Warland	▲▲	6 miles (9.7km)	160
47	Lydgate	▲▲	6.25 miles (10.1km)	163
48	Jumble Hole	▲▲	6 miles (9.7km)	166
49	Saltaire	▲	3 miles (4.8km)	170
50	Harden Beck	▲	2.5 miles (4km)	173

HOW TO USE THIS BOOK

Each walk starts with an information panel giving all the information you will need about the walk at a glance, including its relative difficulty, distance and total amount of ascent. Difficulty levels and gradients are as follows:

Difficulty of walk
- Easy
- Intermediate
- Hard

Gradient
▲ Some slopes

▲▲ Some steep slopes

▲▲▲ Several very steep slopes

Maps
Every walk has its own route map. We also suggest a relevant Ordnance Survey map to take with you, allowing you to view the area in more detail. The time suggested is the minimum for reasonably fit walkers and doesn't allow for stops.

Route map legend

--→--	Walk route	▨	Built-up area
❶	Route waypoint	▨	Woodland area
- - - -	Adjoining path	🚻	Toilet
•	Place of interest	🅿	Car park
⌒	Steep section	⛱	Picnic area
☀	Viewpoint	)(	Bridge
ⅲⅲⅲ	Embankment		

Start points
The start of each walk is given as a six-figure grid reference prefixed by two letters referring to a 100km square of the National Grid. More information on grid references can be found on most OS Walker's Maps.

Dogs
We have tried to give dog owners useful advice about how dog friendly each walk is. Please respect other countryside users. Keep your dog under control, especially around livestock, and obey local by-laws and other dog control notices.

Car parking

Many of the car parks suggested are public, but occasionally you may have to park on the roadside or in a lay-by. Please be considerate about where you leave your car, ensuring that you are not on private property or access roads, and that gates are not blocked and other vehicles can pass safely.

Walks locator map

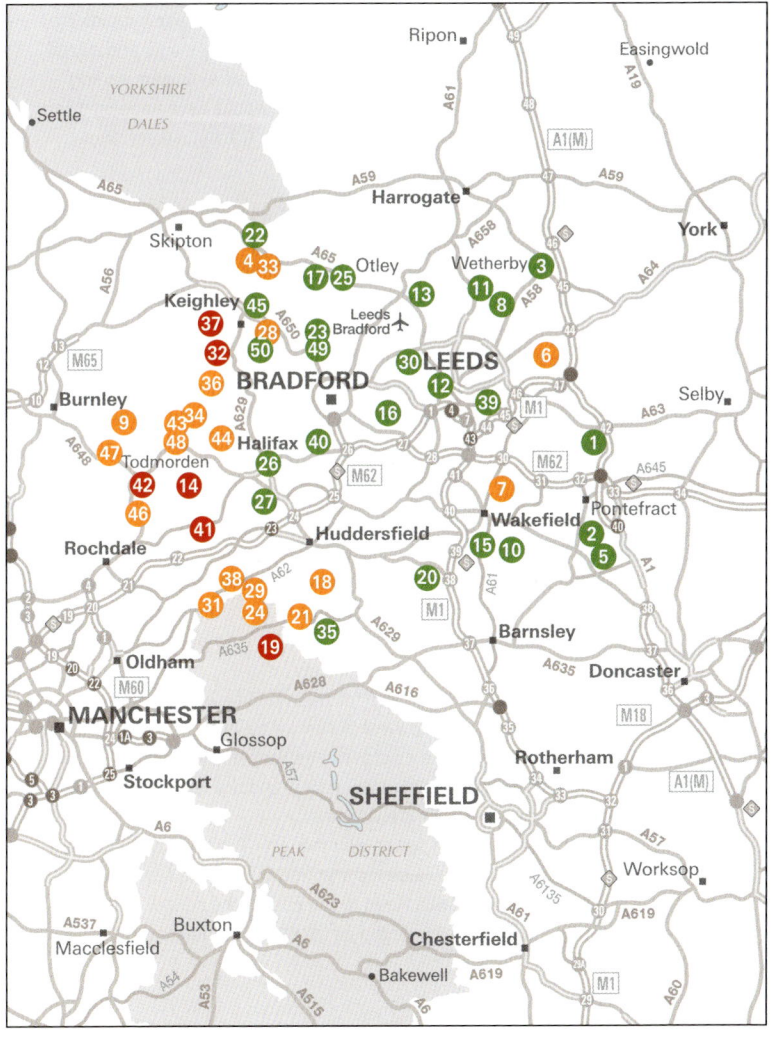

EXPLORING THE AREA

Everybody knows that Yorkshire has some special landscapes. Out in the Dales, the Moors, the Wolds and the Pennine hills, walkers can lengthen their stride, breathe fresh country air and be alone with their thoughts. But what about West Yorkshire? That's Leeds and Bradford isn't it, with their history of blackened mills? Well, this is true, and Hebden Bridge is a case in point. If you had stood on any of the surrounding hills a hundred years ago, and gazed down into the valley, all you would have seen was the pall of smoke issuing from the chimneys of 33 textile mills. The town itself would have appeared just once each year: during the Wakes Week holiday, when the mills were shut.

Wide open spaces

The expansion of industry forced a great many people off the land and into the towns. For generations, the open spaces on their doorsteps represented fresh air and freedom for those who laboured six days a week at the textile mills of Leeds, Bradford, Huddersfield, Batley and the other centres of industry along the valleys of the Colne, Aire and Calder rivers. When the textile trade went into terminal decline, the mills shut down forever. Hebden Bridge changed from being a place that people wanted to leave, to a place that people wanted to visit. The countryside around Hebden Bridge offers walking every bit as good as the more celebrated Yorkshire Dales; within minutes, you can be tramping across the moors, and this is repeated all across West Yorkshire.

Town and country

You'll find a truly wild landscape to the west, where the Pennine hills create a natural barrier between the old foes of Yorkshire and Lancashire. This is where Pennine Way-farers get into their stride. Here are heather moors, riven by steep-sided wooded valleys known as cloughs. Here are empty acres, sheep-cropped grass and the evocative cry of the curlew.

The Pennine moors are rightly valued for their wild beauty but take time to cherish the rural oases nearer to the West Yorkshire towns. These walks are valuable precisely because they are so close to centres of population. You will find beautiful deciduous woodlands, country parks, and the wildlife corridors provided by canal tow paths and old railway lines.

There'll be plenty of wildlife to spot along the way. The Pennine moors are home to birds such as red grouse, kestrels and ring ouzels; the fast-flowing rivers support dippers and wagtails. Head to the east of the county where opencast coal mines have been reinvented as lakes and wetlands, providing more wildlife habitat.

A Wealth of Choice

There's such diversity in the area that you can find yourself in quite unfamiliar surroundings, even close to places you may know very well. Take time to explore this rich county on foot and you will be thrilled at what you find to shatter preconceptions.

PUBLIC TRANSPORT
Most of these walks are within easy reach of frequent and relatively cheap buses and trains. For timetable information call West Yorkshire Metroline on 0113 245 7676 or visit www.wymetro.com. You can also find bus and train information at www.traveline.info.

Walk 32

WALKING IN SAFETY

All these walks are suitable for any reasonably fit person, but less experienced walkers should try the easier walks first. Route-finding is usually straightforward, but you will find that an Ordnance Survey walking map is a useful addition to the route maps and descriptions; recommendations can be found in the information panels.

Risks

Although each walk here has been researched with a view to minimising the risks to the walkers who follow its route, no walk in the countryside can be considered to be completely free from risk. Walking in the outdoors will always require a degree of common sense and judgement to ensure that it is as safe as possible.

- Be particularly careful on cliff paths and in upland terrain, where the consequences of a slip can be very serious.
- Remember to check tidal conditions before walking on the seashore.
- Some sections of route are by, or cross, busy roads. Take care, and remember that traffic is a danger even on minor country lanes.
- Be careful around farmyard machinery and livestock, especially if you have children with you.
- Be aware of the consequences of changes in the weather, and check the forecast before you set out. Carry spare clothing and a torch if you are walking in the winter months. Remember that the weather can change very quickly at any time of the year, and in moorland and heathland areas, mist and fog can make route-finding much harder. Don't set out in these conditions unless you are confident of your navigation skills in poor visibility.
- In summer remember to take account of the heat and sun; wear a hat and carry water.
- On walks away from centres of population you should carry a whistle and survival bag. If you do have an accident that means you require help from the emergency services, make a note of your position as accurately as possible and dial 999.

Countryside Code
Respect other people:

- Consider the local community and other people enjoying the outdoors.
- Co-operate with people at work in the countryside. For example, keep out of the way when farm animals are being gathered or moved, and follow directions from the farmer.

- Don't block gateways, driveways or other paths with your vehicle.
- Leave gates and property as you find them, and follow paths unless wider access is available, such as on open country or registered common land (known as 'open access land').
- Leave machinery and farm animals alone – don't interfere with animals, even if you think they're in distress. Try to alert the farmer instead.
- Use gates, stiles or gaps in field boundaries if you can – climbing over walls, hedges and fences can damage them and increase the risk of farm animals escaping.
- Our heritage matters to all of us – be careful not to disturb ruins and historic sites.

Protect the natural environment:

- Take your litter home. Litter and leftover food don't just spoil the beauty of the countryside; they can be dangerous to wildlife and farm animals. Dropping litter and dumping rubbish are criminal offences.
- Leave no trace of your visit, and take special care not to damage, destroy or remove features such as rocks, plants and trees.
- Keep dogs under effective control, making sure they are not a danger or nuisance to farm animals, horses, wildlife or other people.
- If cattle or horses chase you and your dog, it is safer to let your dog off the lead – don't risk getting hurt by trying to protect it. Your dog will be much safer if you let it run away from a farm animal in these circumstances, and so will you.
- Everyone knows how unpleasant dog mess is and it can cause infections, so always clean up after your dog and get rid of the mess responsibly – bag it and bin it.
- Fires can be as devastating to wildlife and habitats as they are to people and property – so be careful with naked flames and cigarettes at any time of the year.

Enjoy the outdoors:

- Plan ahead and be prepared for natural hazards, changes in weather and other events.
- Wild animals, farm animals and horses can behave unpredictably if you get too close, especially if they're with their young – so give them plenty of space.
- Follow advice and local signs.

For more information visit www.gov.uk/government/publications/the-countryside-code

1 FAIRBURN INGS AND LEDSHAM

DISTANCE/TIME	5 miles (8km) / 1hrs 45min
ASCENT/GRADIENT	262ft (80m) / ▲
PATHS	Good paths and tracks, several stiles
LANDSCAPE	Lakes, riverside and reclaimed colliery spoil heaps
SUGGESTED MAP	OS Explorer 289 Leeds
START/FINISH	Grid reference: SE470278
DOG FRIENDLINESS	Keep on lead around main lake due to wildlife
PARKING	Small parking area at the top of Cut Road, Fairburn, in the direction of Fairburn Ings
PUBLIC TOILETS	RSPB Fairburn Ings Visitor Centre

The coalfields of West Yorkshire were most concentrated in the borough of Wakefield. Towns and villages grew up around the mines and came to represent the epitome of northern industrial life. Mining was always a dangerous and dirty occupation, and it changed the landscape dramatically. Opencast mines swallowed up huge tracts of land, and the extensive spoil heaps were all-too-visible evidence of industry.

For the men of these communities, mining was almost the only work available. When the industry went into decline, these communities were hit especially hard. The mining industry was decimated and thousands of miners lost their livelihoods. The death of the industry was emphasised by the closing down of Caphouse Colliery and its subsequent conversion into the National Coal Mining Museum for England. The spoil heaps that scarred the landscape are going back to nature, a process hastened by tree planting and other reclamation schemes. Opencast workings have been transformed into lakes and wetlands – valuable havens for wildfowl and migrating birds. Within a single generation, West and South Yorkshire has achieved a network of lakes to rival the Norfolk Broads, surrounded by wild plants and woodland that attracts many insects, small animals and birds.

Fairburn Ings, now under the stewardship of the Royal Society for the Protection of Birds (RSPB), was one of the earliest examples of colliery reclamation – being designated a Local Nature Reserve in 1957. The result is arguably the most important nature reserve in West Yorkshire. Superficially, the site might seem unpromising; in proximity to the A1(M), the conurbation of Castleford, the River Aire, a railway and former spoil heaps. Nevertheless, the stark outlines of the spoil heaps are now softened by banks of silver birch, and mining subsidence has created a broad expanse of water near the village of Fairburn, as well as smaller pools and flashes.

There are plenty of birds to be seen at all times of the year, though the numbers of ducks, geese, swans and gulls are at their highest during the winter months. The 600 acres (243ha) of wetlands are a magnet for birds during the spring and autumn migration. In summer, there are many species of wildlife nesting on the scrapes and islands – including terns and a large, noisy colony of black-headed gulls. The best places from which to view all this activity are the public hides that overlook the lake.

Hidden away from the traffic hammering up and down the nearby motorway, the estate village of Ledsham is a tranquil little backwater. Behind the Saxon church – one of the oldest in West Yorkshire – is a row of picturesque almshouses and the village has an old and character country pub, the Chequers Inn.

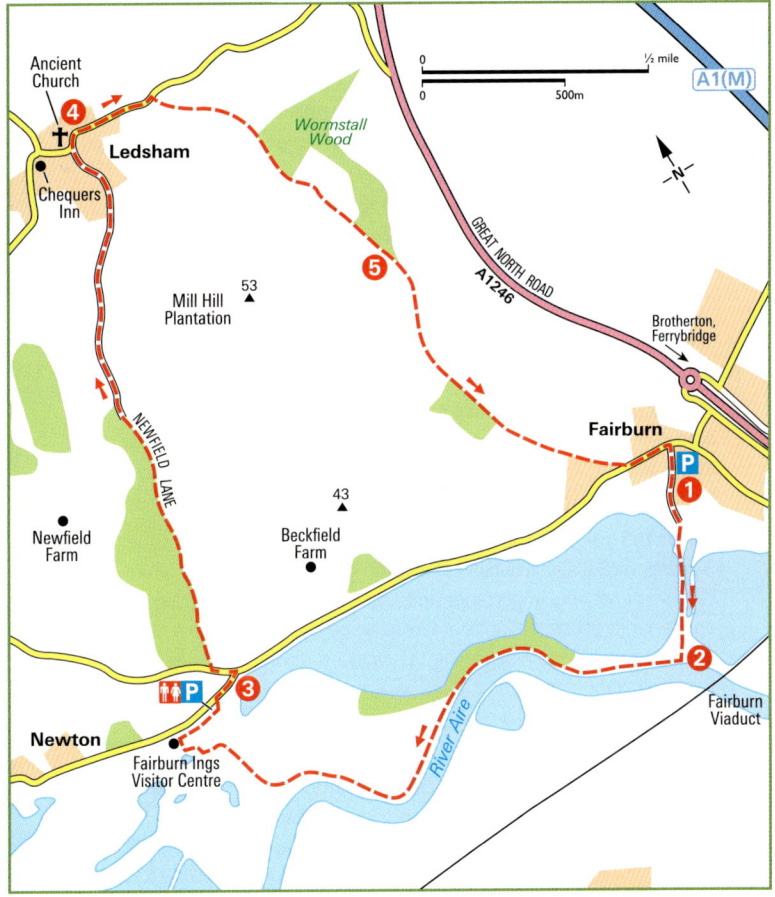

1. Walk down Cut Road. After passing through a gate, the way narrows to a wooded causeway between the lakes, from which a short detour leads to a bird hide over on the left. The route, however, remains with the main path, crossing a bridge and eventually leading to a junction overlooking the River Aire.

2. Go right through a kissing gate along the top of a wooded ridge (actually an old spoil heap), which separates the river from the lake. Look out for a couple of other bird hides before you lose sight of the lake. As the ridge broadens, the path diverges from the river. Later falling, it curves to join a track above a

smaller lake. Follow it down right to a metal gate and go left in front of it through a kissing gate. After 100yds (91m), opposite a sculpted frog, turn right on a walkway that winds across a marsh to the visitor centre. Swing right through the car park to a lane.

3. Go right to a junction and turn left towards Ledston and Kippax. However, after just 100yds (91m), take a path on your right that hugs the right-hand fringe of a wood. Beyond the trees, the way continues between fields, broadening to a track as it nears Ledsham. Emerging onto Manor Garth, go right to the main lane in front of the church.

4. The Chequers Inn lies a short distance to the left. The return route, however, winds to the right around the church and through the village. After 200yds (183m), on a left bend, leave ahead through a gate onto an undulating track. Over a stile, walk towards woodland and continue within its periphery. Beyond another stile, keep going beside the trees and then at the bottom of a pasture. A stile left of the corner takes the way through a narrow spur of woodland.

5. Head slightly left, uphill, across the next field, to follow a fence and hedgerow bounding the top. Keep ahead through kissing gates, remaining at the field edge and passing barns that stand over to the left. Through a final gate, a developing track leads downhill. Go left, when you eventually meet the road, back into the village of Fairburn.

Where to eat and drink

The Chequers Inn in Ledsham harks back to the past in more ways than one. The exposed beams and open fires give the pub a homely atmosphere. Excellent food makes the place popular for lunches with walkers and locals.

What to look out for

Be sure to take a pair of binoculars with you. Fairburn Ings is a bird reserve of national importance and, especially during the spring and autumn migrations, all kinds of birds can be seen. There are a number of strategically sited hides along this walk, from which you can watch the birds without disturbing them. Watch especially for the rare but inconspicuous gadwall, pochard and golden plover.

While you're there

Old and new coexist at Ferrybridge, gateway to West Yorkshire from the south and east. A sprawling interchange joins the M62 and A1(M) beside the huge cooling towers of the Ferrybridge Power Station, but nearby, alongside the modern span carrying the A162 (formerly A1) across the River Aire is an 18th-century bridge by the Yorkshire architect John Carr, better known for his work on Harewood House.

HIGH ACKWORTH AND EAST HARDWICK

DISTANCE/TIME	5.5 miles (8.8km) / 2hrs
ASCENT/GRADIENT	180ft (55m) / ▲
PATHS	Mostly field paths, many stiles
LANDSCAPE	Gently rolling, arable country
SUGGESTED MAP	OS Explorer 278 Sheffield & Barnsley
START/FINISH	Grid reference: SE440180
DOG FRIENDLINESS	Dogs on leads in villages and through farmyards
PARKING	A few parking places in middle of High Ackworth, near church and village green
PUBLIC TOILETS	None on route

With its village green acting as the centrepiece for some fine old houses, High Ackworth has a pleasantly old-fashioned air and is now designated a conservation area. Today, the village is best known for its school, founded by a prominent Quaker, John Fothergill, to teach the children of 'Friends not in affluence'. Ackworth Quaker School opened its doors on 18 October 1779, a day still commemorated by the pupils as Founder's Day. Opposite the village green are almshouses, built in 1741 to house 'a schoolmaster and six poor women'.

Nearby Ackworth Old Hall, dating from the early 17th century, is supposed to be haunted by John Nevison, a notorious robber and highwayman. His most famous act of daring was in 1676 when he rode from Rochester to York in just 15 hours. The story goes that he committed a robbery and then was afraid his victim might have recognised him. Fleeing the scene, he put the 230 miles (373km) behind him in record time. On his arrival in York, Nevison was seen asking the Lord Mayor the time. After his arrest he used the Mayor as his alibi and was acquitted. No one believed the journey could be made in so short a time. This amazing feat of speed and horsemanship is often wrongly attributed to another well-known highwayman, Dick Turpin, who was not yet born.

Until the Reformation, the stone plinth on the village green was topped by a cross. It was knocked off by Cromwell's troops, whose puritanical dislike of religious ornament led them to destroy the church font too. The cross had been erected in memory of Father Thomas Balne of nearby Nostell Priory, who once preached from here. During a pilgrimage to Rome, he succumbed to the plague. When his body was being brought back to the priory, mourners insisted on opening the coffin here in High Ackworth. As a result, the plague was inflicted upon the community, with devastating results. The Plague Stone, at the junction of the A628 Pontefract Road and Sandy Gate Lane, dates from a second outbreak in 1645, killing more than 150 villagers. The hollow in the stone was filled with vinegar to disinfect coins left in payment for food brought from outside the village while it was in quarantine.

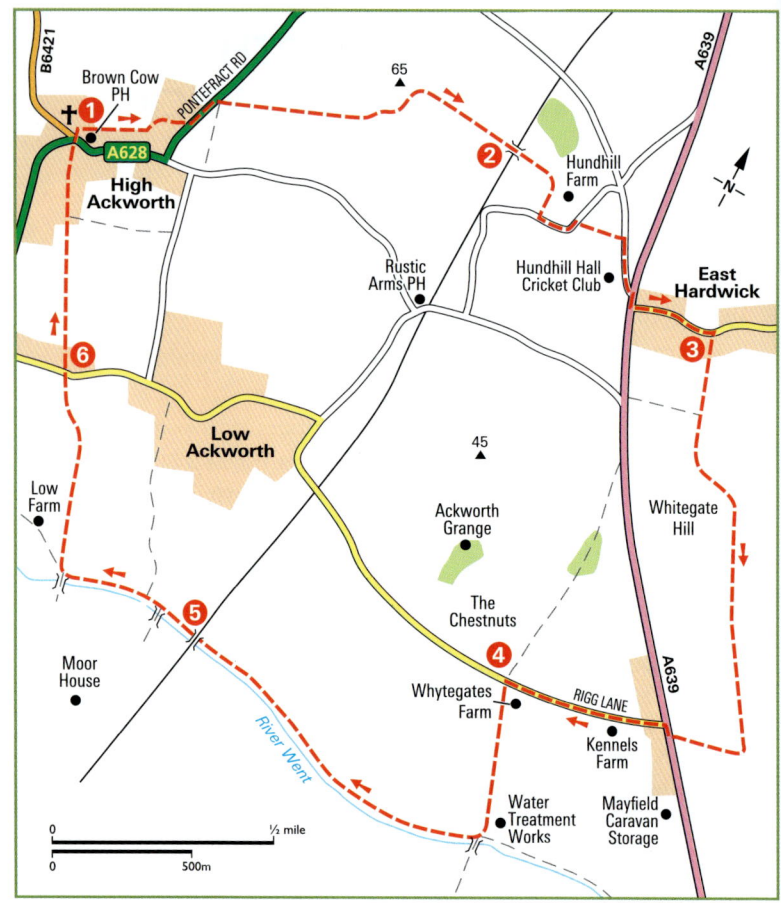

1. From the top of the village green, take a narrow alley immediately to the right of Manor House. Beyond a stile made of stone slabs, keep by the right-hand edge of a field to another stile. Another passage leads out into Woodland Grove; walk left then first right to meet the A628, Pontefract Road. Go left for just 100yds (91m), crossing to a signed gap in the hedgerow (opposite a house called Tall Trees). Guided by the left-most finger, head across to a tiny footbridge over a beck at the far side. Continue along the right-hand edge of the next two fields. In the third, dogleg left and right to continue beside the hedge, which then curves left. After some 150yds (137m), watch for a waymarked path striking right, due east across the open field. Continue across a second field to a bridge spanning a railway.

2. Continue between fields towards Hundhill Farm. By the farm, turn within the field corner along its bottom edge to a stile. Emerging on to a lane, go left, walking 100yds (91m) to round a bend. Immediately after, go over a stile on the right to follow an enclosed path. Beyond the next stile, turn right along a minor road that soon meets the A639. Cross to Darrington Road opposite, and walk into the village of East Hardwick. Where the road swings left, look out for a bridleway sign on your right, just before a house fittingly called Bridleways.

3. The track leads away between the fields behind, shortly bending sharply left. Carry on for a further 100yds (91m) then swing off into a narrow field on the right. Accompany the right-hand hedge to the top of the strip, there dog-legging right and left to continue between open fields. Meeting a crossing track at the end, go right to come out on the main road by a junction. Cross and follow Rigg Lane opposite for some 650yds (0.6km) to Whytegates Farm, where a concrete bridle track on the left is signed to Burnhill Bridge.

4. Follow this track past a water treatment works to a concrete bridge over the River Went (notice the old packhorse bridge next to it). Without crossing either bridge, turn right, on a field-edge path, to accompany the river. A little plank bridge takes you across a side-beck. Now walk beneath a six-arched railway viaduct.

5. Ignoring a field access bridge, continue to a waymarked junction just a little beyond. Bear left through a hedge gap and over a bridged ditch to remain with the main river. Reaching a stone bridge near Low Farm, swing right to a gate beside barns. Walk on at the edge of a large crop field and then a playing field to emerge in Low Ackworth.

6. Diagonally cross the road to a path between houses. Beyond a stile at the far end, bear half left across a field. Keep going across another field towards more houses, emerging over a stile between them. Walk forward along Hill Drive and then turn right down a cul-de-sac. At the bottom, take another passage on the left to arrive back in High Ackworth near the village green.

Where to eat and drink
The Brown Cow in High Ackworth serves evening meals from Tuesday to Saturday and lunches on Sunday. Otherwise, try the nearby Rustic Arms on Long Lane in Low Ackworth. It serves food daily and is set within its own grounds with a garden overlooking a lake.

What to look out for
Village greens are uncommon features in West Yorkshire, a county in which even the smallest community can feel like a town. But the Industrial Revolution passed Ackworth by; no mill chimneys ever disturbed the symmetry. Surrounded by buildings of character – including the parish church, Manor House and a row of almshouses – Ackworth has managed to retain its village atmosphere.

While you're there
The victims of the outbreak of the Black Death in 1645 are thought to have been buried in the 'Burial Field' a few hundred paces to the east of the Plague Stone. The year before, the same fields had witnessed bloody skirmishing between the Parliamentarian troops and Royalists, and may have already been used for mass burials.

WETHERBY AND THE RIVER WHARFE

DISTANCE/TIME	4 miles (6.4km) / 1hr 30min
ASCENT/GRADIENT	252ft (77m) / ▲
PATHS	Field paths and good tracks, a little road walking
LANDSCAPE	Arable land, mostly on the flat
SUGGESTED MAP	OS Explorer 289 Leeds
START/FINISH	Grid reference: SE404480
DOG FRIENDLINESS	Keep on leads along roads and by racecourse
PARKING	Wilderness car park, on right immediately over bridge when approaching Wetherby from the south
PUBLIC TOILETS	Wetherby

Wetherby, at the northeast corner of the county, is not your typical West Yorkshire town. Most of the houses are built of pale stone, topped with red-tiled roofs – a type of architecture more usually found in North Yorkshire. With its riverside developments and air of prosperity, the Wetherby of today is a favoured place to live. The flat, arable landscape, too, is very different from Pennine Yorkshire. Here, on the fringes of the Vale of York, the soil is rich and dark and productive, and the fields divided up by fences and hedgerows rather than dry-stone walls.

The town has a long history. A brief glance at an Ordnance Survey map reveals that Wetherby grew up around a tight curve in the River Wharfe. Its importance as a river crossing was recognised by the building of a castle, possibly in the 12th century, of which only the foundations remain. The first mention of a bridge was in 1233. A few years later, in 1240, the Knights Templar were granted a royal charter to hold a market in Wetherby. At Flint Mill, passed on this walk, flints were ground for use in the pottery industry of Leeds. The town also had two corn mills, powered by water from the River Wharfe. The distinctive, restored weir helped to maintain a good head of water to turn the waterwheels.

In general though, the Industrial Revolution made little impression on Wetherby. The town grew in importance not from what it made, but from where it was situated. In the days of coach travel, the 400-mile (643km) trip between London and Edinburgh was quite an ordeal for passengers and horses alike. And Wetherby, at the halfway point of the journey, became a convenient stop for mail and passenger coaches. The trade was busiest during the second half of the 18th century, when the town had upwards of 40 inns and alehouses. Coaching inns catered for weary travellers and provided stabling for the horses. The Angel, known as 'the Halfway House', had stables for more than 100 horses. The Great North Road ran across the town's splendid arched bridge, and right through the middle of the town. When the railway arrived in the 1840s, Wetherby's role as a staging post went into decline. The Great North

Road was eventually rerouted around the town, and became known simply as the A1 and now the A1(M). In 1964, Wetherby lost its railway too. Ironically, a town that had once been synonymous with coach travel is now a peaceful place, reinventing itself once again as an upmarket commuter town.

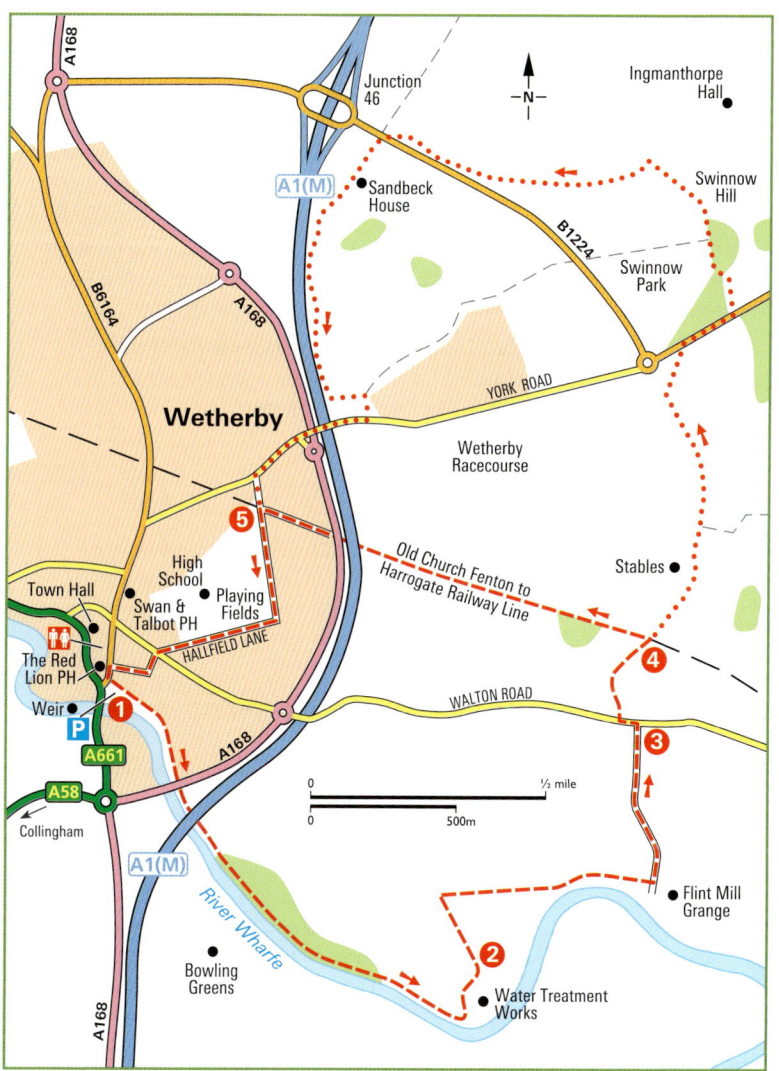

1. Walk to the far end of the car park, to follow a path at the foot of low cliffs beside the River Wharfe. You pass in quick succession beneath the shallow spans of three modern bridges, carrying the A168 and A1(M) roads across the Wharfe. Emerging beyond, walk the length of a narrow pasture, passing through a kissing gate at the far end by the water treatment works.

2. Turn left beside the perimeter fence to the plant entrance and go left again along a metalled drive. After 300yds (274m), meeting a junction of tracks at the top of a rise, turn off right along a field track. Carry on along the top of a

wooded bank that falls to the River Wharfe, emerging onto the bend of another drive at Flint Mill Grange. Go left and walk out to the main road.

3. Turn left along Walton Road. After 75yds (69m), cross to a gated drive on the right, an entrance to Wetherby Racecourse and a bridleway through to York Road. Walk for 0.25 miles (400m) to meet a crossing track. The longer walk continues along the drive ahead.

4. To return directly to Wetherby, however, turn left, dropping onto the trackbed of the old Church Fenton-to-Harrogate railway line, which carried its last train in 1964. A mile's (1.6km) easy walking takes you to the A1(M) motorway, raised up on an embankment as it skirts around Wetherby. Take the underpass beneath the road, and keep ahead along Freemans Way, until you meet Hallfield Lane.

5. Walk left, along Hallfield Lane, following it right around the playing fields of Wetherby High School towards the town centre. At the end, bear left into Nags Lane, right along Victoria Street and then go left back to the river.

Extending the walk You can extend the walk to see more of Wetherby's famous racecourse by leaving the main walk at Point 4 and following firstly a waymarked bridleway and then Sandbeck Lane, before crossing the motorway bridge to return to the main walk at Point 5.

Where to eat and drink

As a market town and a staging post on the Great North Road, Wetherby is well provided with a choice of pubs, cafés and old coaching inns. For example, The Red Lion on the High Street near the start of the walk serves traditional bar meals at very reasonable prices.

What to see

Unlike many towns in West Yorkshire, Wetherby still holds its general market every Thursday, with the stalls arranged around the handsome little town hall. Nearby are the Shambles, a row of colonnaded stalls built in 1811 to house a dozen butchers' shops.

While you're there

Wetherby's nearest neighbour is Boston Spa which, like Ilkley, became a prosperous spa town on the River Wharfe. It was the accidental discovery, in 1744, of a mineral spring that changed the town's fortunes. The salty taste and sulphurous smell were enough to convince people that the spring water had health-giving properties, and a pump room and bathhouse were built to cater for well-heeled visitors. The town's great days as a spa town are over but, with some splendid Georgian buildings, it has retained an air of elegance.

WHITE WELLS AND THE SWASTIKA STONE

DISTANCE/TIME	3 miles (4.8km) / 1hr 10min
ASCENT/GRADIENT	450ft (137m) / ▲
PATHS	Quiet lanes, peaty paths and good moorland tracks
LANDSCAPE	Urban fringe and open moor
SUGGESTED MAP	OS Explorer 297 Lower Wharfedale & the Washburn Valley
START/FINISH	Grid reference: SE117471
DOG FRIENDLINESS	Dogs should be on leads near grazing sheep on the moor
PARKING	Darwin Gardens Millennium Green car park, Wells Road, Ilkley
PUBLIC TOILETS	White Wells Spa Cottage

Today, we associate the swastika with the German Nazi party and the horrors of World War II, but for millennia before then, the swastika was a symbol of peace. In Hindu culture, it is a symbol that occurs in holy texts, standing for luck or rebirth. It occurs in Buddhism and the Indian Jainism religion, as well as other Asian and European cultures. So, what is a 3,000 to 4,000-year-old swastika doing carved into a gritstone rock above the town of Ilkley? The answer is, of course, that no-one has a clue.

The Swastika Stone is the best known of Ilkley Moor's hundreds of examples of prehistoric rock art, though it is thought to be slightly more recent than the majority of cup and ring markings carved into rocks all over the moor. The artist who carved it had probably never seen the Camunian rose, carved into a rock in Sellero, Italy, or the other rose designs in Val Camonica, but his work is virtually identical. The rose has been traditionally held to be a 'good luck' symbol but has also been interpreted as an image of the sun radiating life. Similar carvings are found elsewhere in Europe, including Sweden and Portugal, and one has even been reported in Australia, near Brisbane. Perhaps Ilkley's Swastika Stone is an international symbol of good luck, perhaps it illustrates the heavens revolving around the sun. Perhaps it's 3,000-year-old graffiti. Note that the one close to the railings on Woodhouse Moor isn't the original but is a modern reproduction, provided to offer clarity to the design; the real Swastika Stone lies directly behind it and is slightly less distinguishable thanks to its exposure to the elements.

There has been a spa in White Wells since the 18th century. The cottages were built in 1756 by the landowner, Squire Middleton, to provide plunge baths for visitors. It is the particularly cold nature of these mineral springs, believed to enhance their curative effect, that makes them famous. Today, when the cottages are open, you can see the chilly stone plunge pool and displays on Victorian ailments and cures.

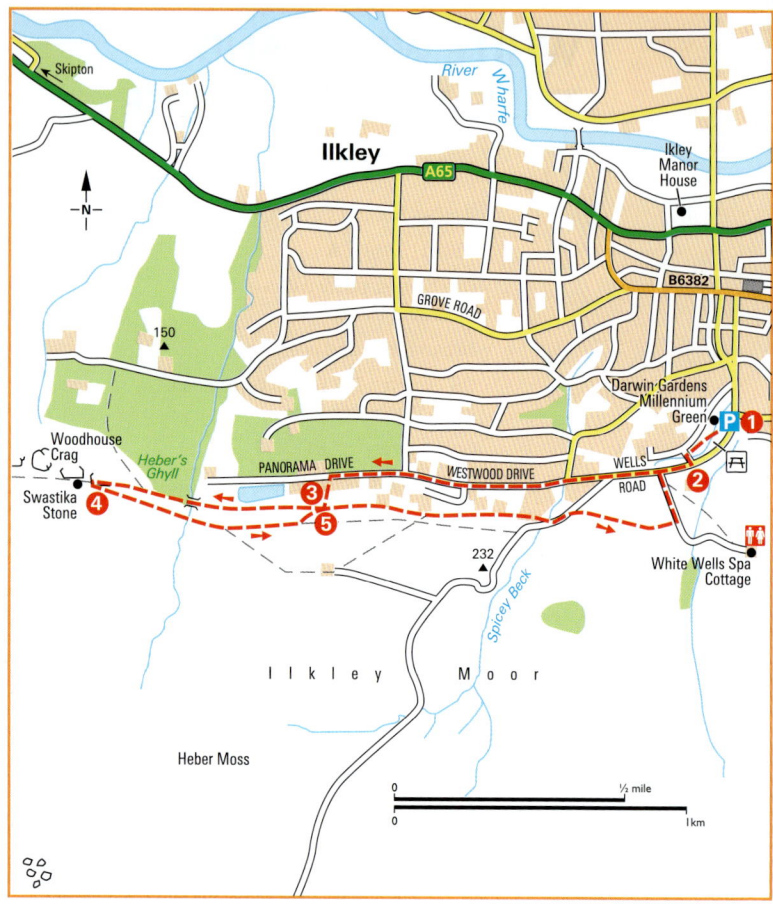

1. Take the ascending path from the uppermost corner of the car park, heading right at a fork, over a footbridge, then left at the subsequent three junctions to a driveway. Cross the grassy area in front of you to Wells Road.

2. Turn right along the pavement, keeping ahead into Westwood Drive when the road forks by Westwood Lodge. Maintain direction when the road bends off to the right, to enter quiet Westwood Drive, which in turn becomes Panorama Drive. Some 385yds (352m) later, by a house named Shambles Corner, take a walled path, signed 'Hebers Ghyll', to a wooden gate.

3. Pass through this into open country, turning right, past a small reservoir. A footbridge carries the path over waterfalls at Heber's Ghyll. The less distinct moorside path beyond soon passes through a latched metal gate and crosses a second stream. Bear left at a junction encountered after 30yds (27m) to follow a moor-edge track right, to a small fenced enclosure on Woodhouse Crag, within which lies the Swastika Stone.

4. Stepping away from the crag edge you'll find a broad track. Take this, heading back in the direction you came from, enjoying fine views towards the Cow and Calf rocks far ahead and, to your left, Wharfedale. After passing through a gate and crossing a beck, the trail brings you to the gate that you encountered at the end of Point 2.

5. Don't go through the gate this time. Turn right and 700yds (640m) later fork left, below a small car park, to cross Spicey Beck and meet a road beyond. Cross and hop up the bank opposite to find the path's continuation. Turn left for 550yds (503m) to its intersection with the driveway for White Wells Spa Cottage. If you're in need of refreshment and a flag is flying, turn right. Otherwise, turn left, down to Wells Road, and bear right there to return to the car park.

Where to eat and drink
White Wells Spa Cottage is something of a walkers' institution on Ilkley Moor. When the flags is flying you'll find snacks and drinks available – that's usually weekends, bank holidays (except Christmas Day) and school holidays. When the flag isn't flying, you'll find a variety of pubs, restaurants, bistros and sandwich bars in Ilkley.

What to look out for
The prehistoric artist who carved the Swastika Stone would have enjoyed a tremendous view from his perch on the edge of Woodhouse Crag. Gazing directly north across Wharfedale and the town of Ilkley, his eyes would have alighted on Barden Moor and Simon's Seat, Beamsley Beacon and Blubberhouses Moor, Stainburn Moor and Almscliffe Crag.

While you're there
Prehistoric artefacts from Ilkley Moor, along with items from other periods in the town's history, form a fascinating display at Ilkley Manor House. Parts of the house itself date from the 14th-century building, but it was built on the site of the Roman fort of Olicana – one of its treasured exhibits is a Roman triple vase. The museum is open at weekends 11am–4pm and admission is free.

UPTON'S RECLAIMED COUNTRY

DISTANCE/TIME	3.5 miles (5.7km) / 1hr 15min
ASCENT/GRADIENT	197ft (60m) / ▲
PATHS	Disused railway line and good tracks, several stiles
LANDSCAPE	Reclaimed colliery land
SUGGESTED MAP	OS Explorer 278 Sheffield & Barnsley
START/FINISH	Grid reference: SE478132
DOG FRIENDLINESS	Keep on lead near roads
PARKING	Car park off Waggon Lane, Upton Country Park, next to fishing lake
PUBLIC TOILETS	None on route

The scenery of the southeastern corner of West Yorkshire contrasts markedly with the high moorlands to the west. Breaking from the hills, the rivers writhe and twist across a flatter landscape more suited to agriculture than the abrupt slopes and bleak tops of the Pennines. Further west, the towns had grown out of narrow valleys, where fast-flowing streams had powered the beginnings of the Industrial Revolution, but here, it was what lay below the ground that would make the difference.

Although Yorkshire's coal has probably been dug since Roman times, it was not until the end of the 18th century that mining was developed on any significant scale. The change came with the development of river navigations, canals and subsequent railways, which, for the first time, created a cheap and effective network for transportation. Towns and villages sprang up around the pitheads, housing close-knit communities that depended upon the mines for their livelihood. The burgeoning steam age brought an almost insatiable demand, and in the early years of the 20th century, mines were sunk ever deeper in pursuit of seams far beneath the surface. The area became one of the largest coal producers in the country, but wholesale closures from the mid-1980s finished the industry.

Undertaken on a limited scale, traces of the early coal industry are often only revealed in the small craters of collapsed bell pits hidden amongst old woodland. But the mines of the industrial age changed the landscape irrevocably, in places creating barren moonscapes of mountainous tips and vast craters. Equally dramatic are the changes of the last 30 years. Great heaps of spoil have been planted with grasses, shrubs and trees, water has flooded opencast workings and subsidence flashes to create lakes, while disused railway lines now serve as footpaths and cycle routes. All have become havens for insects, birds, animals and wildflowers.

Beginning at a fishing lake on the site of the former Upton colliery, which was sunk in 1924 and operated for 40 years, the first half of this walk follows the course of the Hull and Barnsley Railway. Opened in 1885, it survived into the middle of the 20th century, but was progressively closed during the 1960s to leave just a remnant servicing the docks at Hull. Along the way are the remains of Upton Station, as well as embankments and cuttings, now cloaked in shrubwood that attracts birds and butterflies. At the halfway point is Johnny Brown's Common, a former tip at the foot of which is a large lake offering refuge to wildfowl.

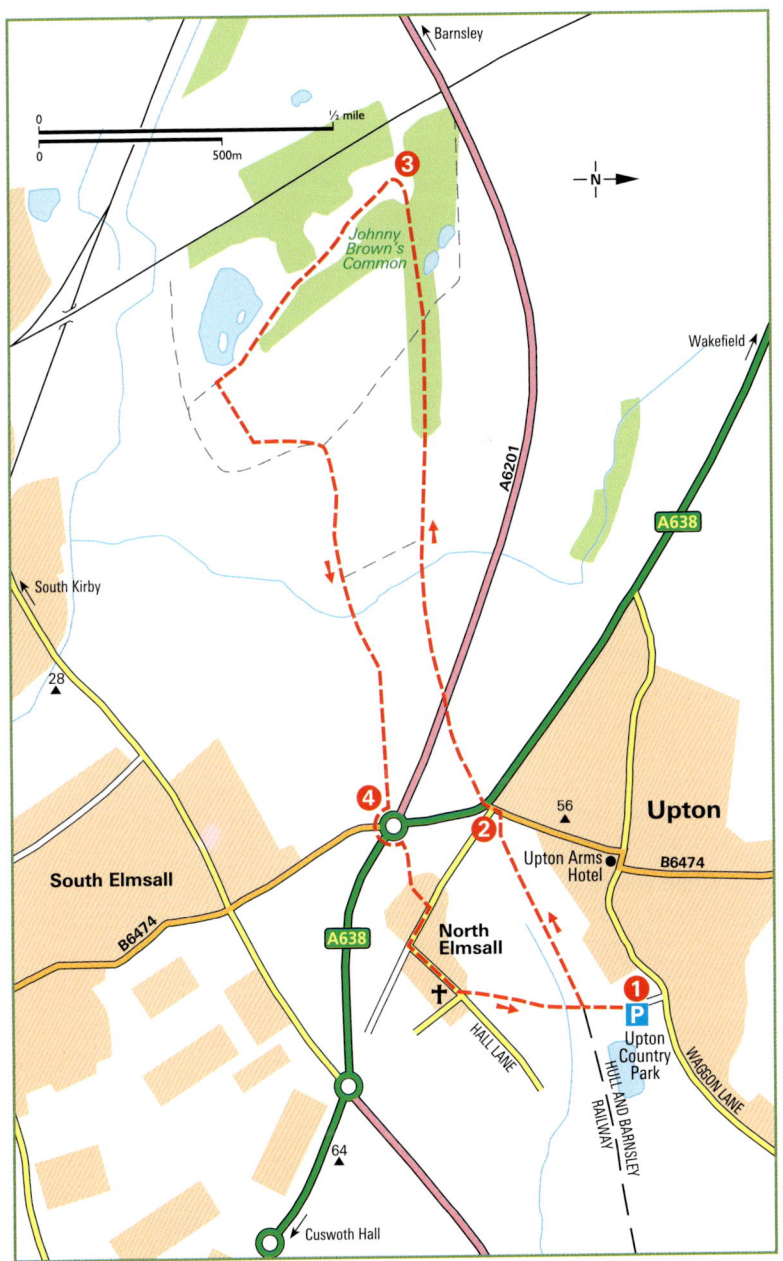

1. Leave the car park through a kissing gate by a fishing pond. Turn right to a second kissing gate and follow the cinder track bed of the former Hull and Barnsley Railway to the right. Keep to the main path, passing a tree-fringed pond and then later, the overgrown platform of Upton and North Elmsall Station. Finally, emerge through a gate beside a junction of roads with the A638.

2. Carefully cross the main road to pick up the ongoing track opposite. Signed as a bridleway, it runs within a wooded cutting to a second main road (A6201). Again cross and continue along the former railway line, which alternates between embankment and cutting across the rolling countryside. The path eventually rises onto more open ground, shortly meeting a broad trail near the crest of the hill.

3. Turning sharp left, descend between the trees towards a lake that soon appears ahead. Bear left at a fork to pass around the eastern bank. Meeting a crossing track at its far end, go left. Keep with it as it subsequently swings left and then right. Continue for another 0.75 miles (1.2km) before ultimately coming out at a large roundabout.

4. Following bridleway signs anticlockwise around the roundabout, cross the B6474 and then the A638 before turning off down a truncated minor road into North Elmsall. At the end go right and then left into Hall Lane. Walk up to a junction just beyond the church. There, leave over a stone stile on the left. A sign to Upton points a diagonal line across a couple of fields. At the far side, cross a drainage ditch and walk forward to a final stile. Rejoining the course of the railway, go right and then left back to the car park.

Where to eat and drink
The Upton Arms Hotel, on Upton High Street, is conveniently placed near the start of this walk for refreshments.

What to look out for
The trains are long gone old from the Hull and Barnsley Railway, but this narrow corridor, between the fields that stretch away on either side, is now a haven for wildlife. Judicious planting has created an excellent habitat for butterflies; look out for such colourful summer sights as the orange tip, the peacock, the painted lady and the red admiral.

While you're there
Close by, off the A638 towards Doncaster, is Cusworth Hall, a splendid mid-18th-century mansion, which houses permanent displays revealing the area's social history as well as a varied programme of occasional exhibits and events. The extensive grounds are managed as a country park and support a wealth of wildlife including Daubenton's bat, which flies low over the lakes at dusk feeding on insects.

BARWICK IN ELMET

DISTANCE/TIME	10 miles (16.1km) / 3hrs 30min
ASCENT/GRADIENT	508ft (155m) / ▲
PATHS	Field paths, good track through Parlington Estate, several stiles
LANDSCAPE	Arable, parkland, woods
SUGGESTED MAP	OS Explorer 289 Leeds
START/FINISH	Grid reference: SE399374
DOG FRIENDLINESS	Keep on lead through villages and past golf course
PARKING	Roadside parking in Barwick in Elmet, along Main Street
PUBLIC TOILETS	None on route

Elmet was one of a number of small, independent British kingdoms to emerge during the Dark Ages, between the end of Roman rule and the conquering of southern Britain, in AD 560, by the Saxon King Edwin. At the height of its powers, the kingdom included most of present-day West Yorkshire, and extended from the River Humber to the Pennine hills. Whilst it is known that Elmet was a realm of some importance, there is little solid archaeological evidence for its existence, apart from a series of defensive earthworks.

Barwick in Elmet is one of West Yorkshire's most ancient settlements. Before the Roman invasion, it was a town of some size, and after the Romans had left the area it became the capital of the local kingdom of Elmet. A road, 'The Boyle', bends around the castle mound, which was a 12th-century Norman fortification, built on the site of an Iron Age hill fort. Barwick boasts the second tallest maypole in the country. Every three years it is taken down, given a new coat of paint and hoisted back up to its full height again. It's a job requiring plenty of local labour, who come armed with ropes and ladders.

The road that runs through Aberford is of Roman origin, built around AD 70. On an Ordnance Survey map, you can trace its ruler-straight orientation from Aberford down to Castleford. Even the name survives on the map: Roman Bridge Road. Aberford was once an important stopping point for travellers up and down the Great North Road. There were coaching inns on the roadside where horses and passengers could be fed and watered.

Black Horse Farm, to the north of the town, was once the Black Horse Inn, a favourite haunt of John Nevison, a famous local highwayman. When he rode from London to York in a single day, he changed horses at the Black Horse. The great road of today, better known as the A1(M), makes the smallest of detours around the town, to allow the juggernauts to hurry past at speed. This leaves Aberford pleasantly quiet and free from the roar of traffic.

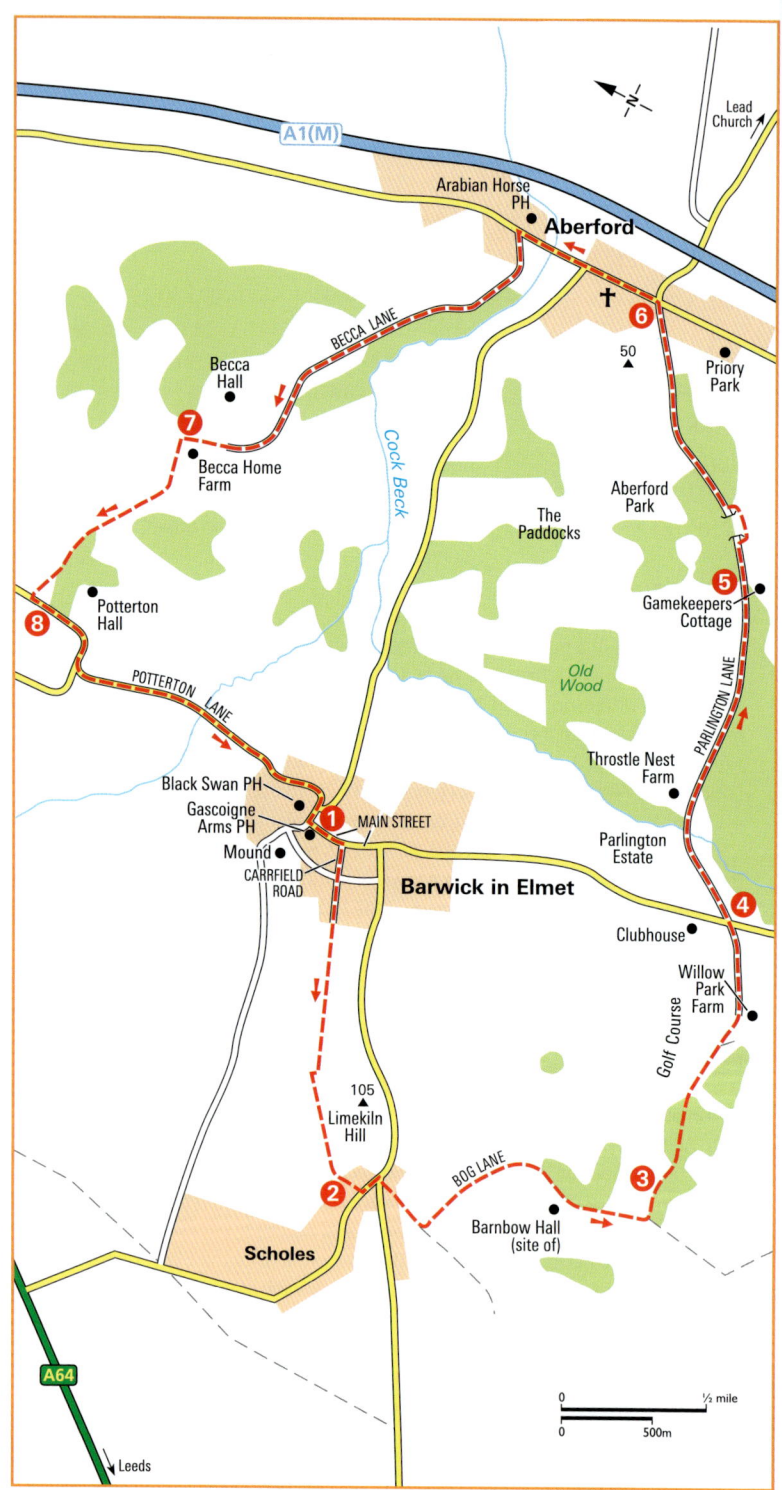

1. Walk south along Main Street, then right into Carrfield Road. At the end, keep ahead along a grass track and then a field path. Entering the third field, swing right to pass through a gap in the corner and then left beside the hedge. Cross back through further on, eventually coming out onto a lane at Scholes.

2. Go left for 100yds (91m) to a road off right, signed to Leeds. Cross to a stony bridleway beside the intersection, soon leaving Scholes behind. At a junction, keep left on the most obvious track. When another track comes in from the left, keep ahead past a barrier. Walk a further 0.5 miles (800m) to a junction. There, go left with the bridleway beside a small wood.

3. Passing through a golf course, walk straight along the main path, ignoring two footpaths subsequently signed off on the right. Leave the far end of the course along a track that soon passes Willow Park Farm. Keep straight ahead to meet a road near the golfers' clubhouse.

4. Cross the road and continue on a farm track into the Parlington Estate. Carry on for 0.75 miles (1.2km) beyond Throstle Nest Farm to a junction beside Gamekeepers Cottage, a curious-looking house with a wall around it.

5. Keep straight ahead along the bridleway through woodland. Bear right, just before a tunnel, to avoid walking through the gloom. The path rejoins your original route at the far end of the tunnel. Pass a gatehouse to arrive in the village of Aberford.

6. Walk left, along the road, crossing a bridge over Cock Beck and then passing the Arabian Horse. Go left, opposite this pub, along Becca Lane. Keep left when it forks past Cufforth House and continue beyond a gatehouse into the parkland surrounding Becca Hall. After another 0.25 miles (400m), look for a waymark signing the path off left at the edge of the pasture. Later developing as a track, it leads to Becca Farm.

7. Continue ahead on the farm track but, just after the barns, turn left at a discrete waymarker post and strike out over the field to a second marker post. Beyond a solitary tree, swing right towards the corner of woodland ahead and follow the ongoing boundary to another belt of trees. Over a stile, bear left to emerge in the next field and keep left along its edge. Passing into pasture, head half right to a final stile in the far corner to come out on to a lane.

8. Go left and then right by the entrance to Potterton Park to reach another junction. Turn left down Potterton Lane, which leads back to Barwick.

Where to eat and drink
The Gascoigne Arms and the Black Swan lie in the centre of Barwick. The Arabian Horse in Aberford is another good place for lunch.

What to look out for
Just south of Aberford is Priory Park, a Grade II* listed building dating from 1843. Although not open to the public, there is a clear view of this beautiful building from the road.

While you're there
On the other side of the A1(M) from Aberford, just off the B1217, is Lead Church. Lead is one of Yorkshire's 'lost' villages, and all that's left is this 14th-century church and nearby Lead Hall Farm.

STANLEY FERRY AND ITS WATERWAYS

DISTANCE/TIME	7.5 miles (12.1km) / 2hrs 30min
ASCENT/GRADIENT	279ft (85m) / ▲
PATHS	Canal tow path and other good paths
LANDSCAPE	Flat land and reclaimed colliery works
SUGGESTED MAP	OS Explorer 289 Leeds
START/FINISH	Grid reference: SE354230
DOG FRIENDLINESS	Can be off lead on tow path
PARKING	Large car park at Stanley Ferry Marina
PUBLIC TOILETS	None on route

The Yorkshire coal mining industry developed during medieval times. As productive as the coal seams were, the industry was held back by the high costs of transport. The same problem faced the woollen industry. Only very small craft could carry cloth along the Aire to Goole and Hull, where it was transferred to ships bound for European markets.

The River Calder meandered circuitously through the flat landscape to the east of Wakefield. In 1699, William III authorised the Aire and Calder rivers to be made navigable to the tidal Ouse. Leeds and Wakefield wool merchants paid for the canalising and deepening of parts of the rivers. The Aire and Calder Navigation took a more direct route, with comparatively few locks, so both costs and journey times were cut significantly.

The Aire and Calder Navigation proved to be a profitable investment for all concerned and continued to be upgraded to allow ever-larger vessels to negotiate the locks. Unlike most other canals, it is still used for commercial traffic. With the decline of the Yorkshire coal industry, however, the loads are mostly bulk deliveries of sand and gravel.

About 1860, a new system was invented for bulk transportation of coal by canal. Floating tubs, each one capable of holding up to 10 tons of coal, were linked together and pulled by steam tugs. Having reached the port, these tubs were lifted out of the water by primitive hoists and their contents swiftly emptied into ships' holds. This idea was refined by hauliers on the Aire and Calder Navigation, who developed tubs capable of carrying 40 tons of coal, and hydraulic machines for loading and unloading them. These tubs became known, affectionately, as Tom Puddings. They were a common sight on the waterway, with as many as 30 joined together in a line.

There are two aqueducts, side by side, at Stanley Ferry. The older aqueduct, built between 1836 and 1839 for the Aire and Calder Navigation Company, is believed to have been the first such suspension bridge in the world. It's an impressive structure, carrying the canal across the River Calder in a cast iron trough, suspended from cast-iron arches. The new aqueduct, a more prosaic concrete structure, dates from 1981.

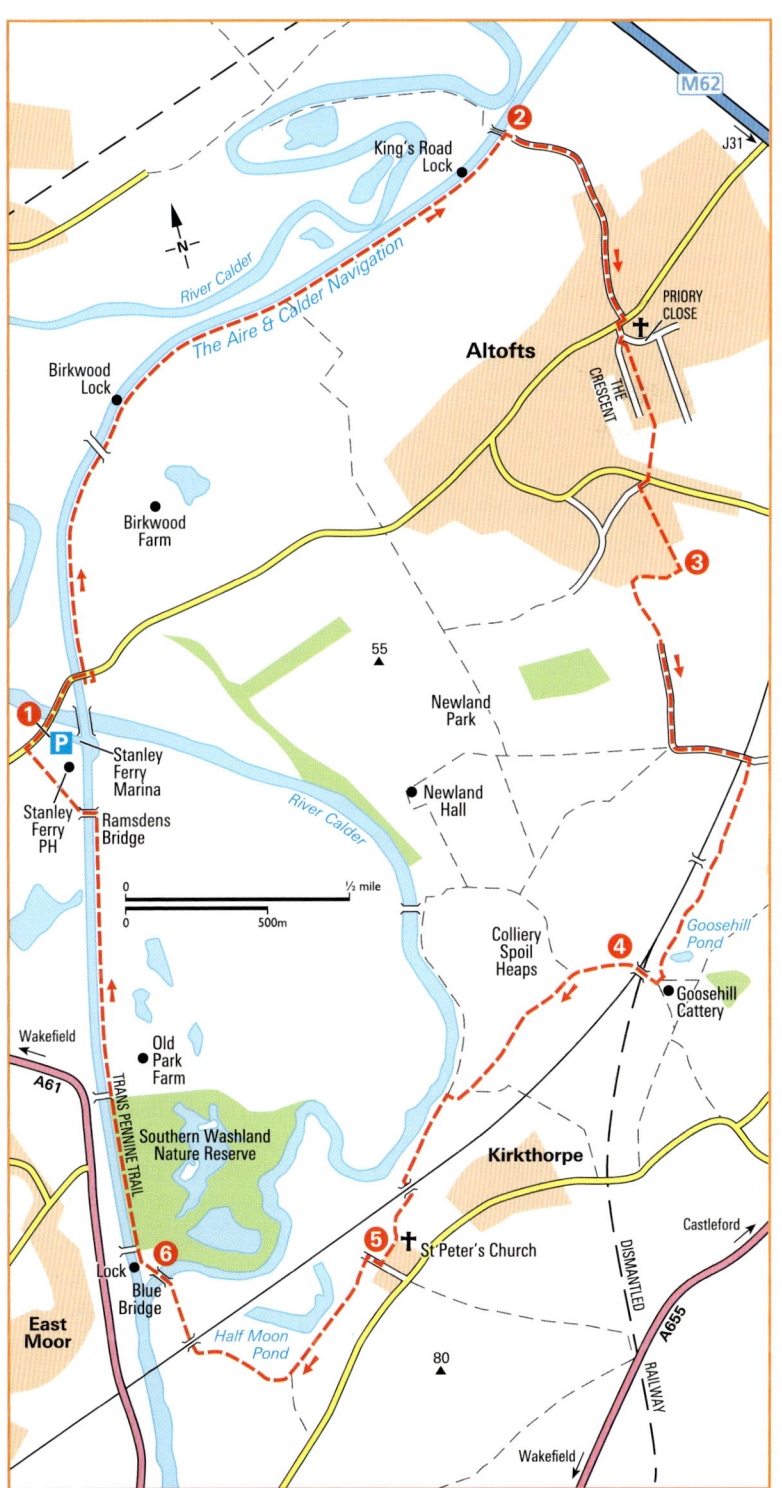

1. Park at the Stanley Ferry Marina. Turn right along the road, which crosses first the River Calder, then the canal. Take a few steps to the right, immediately after the canal, to follow the tow path to the right, back under the road bridge. Walk beneath another bridge just before Birkwood Locks; from here the tow path is metalled. Beyond King's Road Lock you come to a canal bridge and a lane to the right.

2. Follow the lane right for 0.5 miles (800m) to the main road at Altofts opposite St Mary's Church. Go right and left into The Crescent. After 50yds (46m), at the junction with Priory Close, take an alley between the houses opposite. At the end, bear right across a playing field and follow a street out to a junction. Take the street diagonally opposite beside a chemist, leaving left after only a few yards down another passage between house backs. Keep ahead beyond its end to emerge into a field.

3. Go right to the corner and swing left opposite a cul-de-sac through a kissing gate onto a path between the fields. Beyond a stream, continue beside another field and keep ahead over a rise to meet a rough track. Follow it forward and then left across a railway line. Immediately after the bridge, turn right onto a grass path, passing beneath an electricity pylon. Over an access road, carry on to pick up a developing path that winds into trees. Passing the reed-filled Goosehill Pond, fork up right to emerge onto a drive. Turn right, walking through gateposts at Goosehill Cattery to cross a couple of railway bridges.

4. Keep ahead along a broad gravel track, signed 'Pennine Trail', which leads across the landscaped slopes of former spoil heaps. When the track later fragments by a gate, bear left, then later on fork right, the onward path contouring the scrubby hillside and eventually reaching a junction overlooking the River Calder. Swing left, dropping to a small stone bridge across a stream. Carry on, going left again on a track that then leads beneath a railway bridge. Soon passing through a gate, carry on behind houses and past the church, forking right to emerge onto the lane at Kirkthorpe.

5. Turn right, but then after 50yds (46m), go left on a track that soon narrows to a woodland path. Remain with the main path above Half Moon Pond to a fork by an information board. Bear right through a gate (signed 'Stanley Ferry'), negotiating a wooded dip to gain the top of an embankment. Go right, walking for 0.25 miles (400m) before dropping right to pass beneath the railway again. A good track leads to the Blue Bridge, which spans the River Calder beside a lock that begins the Aire and Calder Navigation.

6. Walk on to a junction by a canal bridge and fork down left to follow the tow path away to the north. At the next bridge, the track above leads into the Southern Washland Nature Reserve, an area of reclaimed gravel pits noted for it's wonderful pink orchids, dragonflies and birds. Continue beside the canal to Ramsdens Bridge, crossing to return past The Stanley Ferry pub to the car park.

Where to eat and drink

You can watch the boats go by, enjoy good food and a relaxing drink, all in a splendid canal-side setting at The Stanley Ferry. It's a great place to take the children for a meal, it's easy-going and hospitable.

BARDSEY AND POMPOCALI

DISTANCE/TIME	3 miles (4.8km) / 1hr 15min
ASCENT/GRADIENT	246ft (75m) / ▲
PATHS	Good paths and tracks (though some, being bridleways, may be muddy)
LANDSCAPE	Arable and woodland
SUGGESTED MAP	OS Explorer 289 Leeds
START/FINISH	Grid reference: SE368432
DOG FRIENDLINESS	Keep on lead by roads and in fields near livestock
PARKING	Street parking off A58 at southern end of Bardsey
PUBLIC TOILETS	None on route

The Romans built a network of important roads across Yorkshire. They provided good transport links between their most important forts, such as Ilkley (probably their Olicana), Tadcaster (Calcaria) and York (Eboracum). And one of these roads, marked on old maps as Ryknield Street, passed close to the village of Bardsey, continuing west to a small Roman camp established at Adel. You walk a short stretch of the old Roman road when you take the track from Hetchell Wood, a local nature reserve.

Adjacent to these woods are a set of intriguing earthworks, known as Pompocali. Though rather overgrown, they still have the power to stir the imagination, not least because they are unencumbered by signs and information panels. A number of Roman finds have been unearthed here, including a quern for grinding corn and a stone altar dedicated to the god Apollo. A couple of miles away (3.2km), at Dalton Parlours, the site of a large Roman villa has been discovered.

Once the Romans had abandoned this northern outpost of their empire, Bardsey became part of the kingdom of Elmet, and was later mentioned in the Domesday Book. By the 13th century, the village had been given to the monks of Kirkstall Abbey. After the Dissolution of Monasteries, in 1539, Bardsey came under the control of powerful local families – notably the Lords Bingley. The Parish Church of All Hallows, visited towards the end of this walk, is another antiquity – the core of the building is Anglo Saxon.

Above the church is a grassy mound, where a castle once stood. Pottery found on the site indicates it was occupied during the 12th and 13th centuries, and then abandoned. Some of the stonework from the castle was incorporated into the fabric of Bardsey Grange, whose most notable inhabitant was William Congreve. Born here in 1670, Congreve went on to write a number of Restoration comedies, such as *The Way of the World*.

So close to the city, yet retaining its own identity, Bardsey has expanded beyond its ancient centre to become a popular commuter village for people who work in Leeds. It joins that elite group of places that lay claim to having the country's oldest pub. The Bingley Arms has better claims than most; there is documentary evidence of brewers and innkeepers going back a thousand years. Bardsey is, in short, a historic little spot.

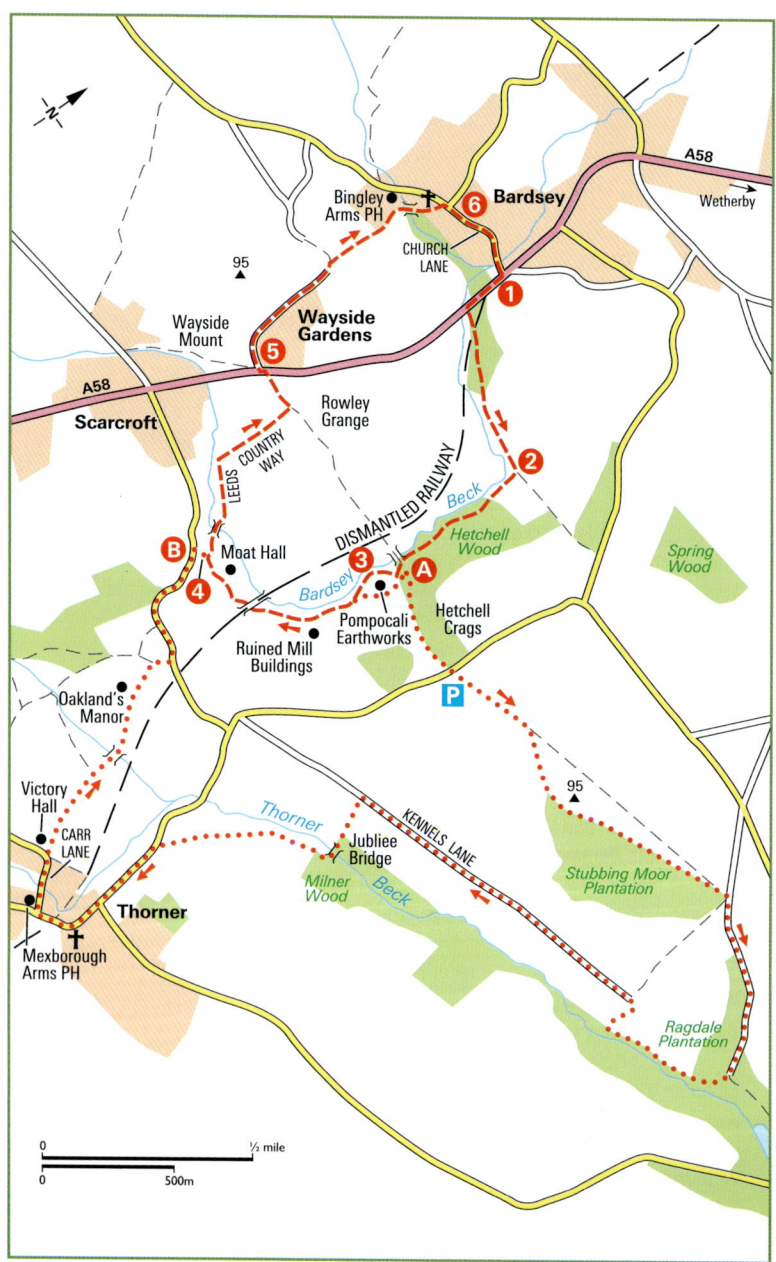

1. Begin from the junction of Church Lane with the A58 and head south along the main road. After 150yds (137m), take a path off left beside a gate into a wood where there is a small lay-by. It rises to the overgrown embankment of the former Leeds–Wetherby Railway, which opened in 1876 and operated until 1964, when it fell victim to Dr Beeching's cuts. Go right and almost immediately left through a gap. Soon emerging into a field, continue beside the perimeter. Passing into a second field, keep with the boundary as it swings right down to more trees.

2. Pass through a kissing gate into Hetchell Wood Nature Reserve. Keep right where the path later forks, soon passing beneath Hetchell Crags, whose soft gritstone façade offers a challenge to local climbers. Leave the reserve through another kissing gate at a junction by a footbridge spanning Bardsey Beck. Turn left along a climbing track that was once part of a Roman road. Look for a bridleway signed off through a gate, a short distance along on the right.

3. Through the gate, a path leads away above the stream, skirting the Roman earthworks (Pompocali). Beyond an overhanging rock, the path rises to a junction (to the left, you can wander back to investigate these intriguing mounds). The onward path, however, keeps to the right, joining a track that shortly leads past ruined mill buildings. Carry on beneath an old railway bridge and across a stream. Wind around two sides of a paddock and then swing left along a drive coming from Moat Hall. Look for a stile breaking the right-hand wall, a few paces along on the right.

4. Take a field-edge path, with a hedge to the right (from here back to Bardsey you are walking the Leeds Country Way). Towards the far end of the field, your path turns right into a copse. Cross a beck on a little wooden footbridge and swing left through scrub above the stream. Shortly wind right to emerge into the corner of a field. Climb away beside the right-hand hedge, dropping beyond the crest of the hill to a junction. Go left here on a track that follows a broken wall to meet the A58 road.

5. Walk left for just 20yds (18m) and turn right into Wayside Mount, an unsurfaced road that serves a collection of detached houses. Beyond the last house go through a gateway and follow the track ahead, a tall hedge on your left. When the track later swings left, leave and walk ahead, ignoring a stile to follow the field edge downhill. Approaching the bottom, bear right across the field corner to find a path dropping into the trees below. Cross a stream and climb to a gate into the churchyard. Keep right of the church to meet a road.

6. Go right on Church Lane to return to the start point.

Extending the walk This walk can be extended by another 4.5 miles (7.2km) to pass through the picturesque village of Thorner. Keep an eye out for the Church of St Peter, with a tower dating from the 15th century. The rest of the church was largely rebuilt in the mid-1800s. From Point A, walk east, cross a minor road, continue along the field edge. Bear left to go through a plantation. At the end, turn right onto a farm track, keep left through another plantation, then right at a junction to follow a stream. Turn right along a bridlepath, then left onto a lane. After 0.5 miles (800m) turn left, signposted Thorner via Jubilee Bridge. Cross the bridge and follow the path right towards Thorner. Turn left into Thorner, then right up Carr Lane. Continue straight on past Victory Hall following the path between fields. Cross a beck, continue through a field to meet a minor road. Turn left. Just before the gate to Moat Hall, cross a stile on your left to rejoin the walk at Point B.

Where to eat and drink
The Bingley Arms, in Bardsey, is a contender for the title of the oldest pub in England. Parts of the pub are supposed to date back to the year 950, when it was known as the Priests Inn. It has excellent food and, in summer, barbecues on the terrace.

What to look out for
Bardsey's church began life as a small Anglo-Saxon church, and just the nave is all that's left. Over the next thousand years, the old Saxon porch was extended into a bell tower, aisles were added in Norman times and, in the 19th century, the nave walls were heightened to support a new roof.

While you're there
Bramham Park has a splendid Queen Anne mansion and gardens laid out by Robert Benson, the first Lord Bingley, with grand vistas in the manner of Versailles. You can visit the house and gardens on most weekdays by appointment throughout the year.

WIDDOP RESERVOIR AND THE GRITSTONE CRAGS

DISTANCE/TIME	2.75 miles (4.4km) / 1hr
ASCENT/GRADIENT	305ft (93m) / ▲
PATHS	Good tracks and paths, some potentially boggy moorland
LANDSCAPE	Reservoir set in crag-surrounded moorland bowl
SUGGESTED MAP	OS Explorer OL21 South Pennines
START/FINISH	Grid reference: SD937327
DOG FRIENDLINESS	Sheep graze the moors around Widdop so dogs should be on leads
PARKING	Widdop Reservoir car park, Widdop
PUBLIC TOILETS	None on route

Of all the moorland reservoirs that stud West Yorkshire's peaty uplands, Widdop is the shining jewel, a glittering pool set in a wide, crag-rimmed hollow surrounded by mile-after-mile of rolling peaty moorland. Poet Laureate Ted Hughes, who was born just a few miles away in Mytholmroyd in 1930, described it as a 'frightened lake' in *Remains of Elmet*, the famous volume of poems about his vanishing South Pennine boyhood.

Widdop was, between 1871 and 1878, the first of the reservoirs to be built on the moors above Heptonstall to supply drinking water for the people of Halifax. With a capacity of 633 million gallons (2,880 million litres) it's also the largest. During construction a small, temporary village of wooden huts, with its own bake house and store, was built at Widdop. At its peak, around 200 men lived there.

Materials for the dam that couldn't be found on site were brought along a horse-drawn tramway that ran from Shackleton, above the National Trust's main car park at Hardcastle Crags, along the edge of the Hebden valley to Holme End, Clough Foot and then Widdop. Materials were pulled up the hillside to Shackleton by a stationary engine on an inclined tramway, the huge ramp for which can be seen in the lower reaches of Crimsworth Dean. The tramline can still be traced on foot from Shackleton.

The valve house at the far end of Widdop's dam wall looks slightly incongruous – an Egyptian-looking building made from Pennine gritstone. John Frederick Bateman, the engineer employed by Halifax Corporation to oversee the reservoir's construction, had attended the opening of the Suez Canal in 1869. He was so impressed by the architecture he saw there, that he incorporated elements of it in the design of the reservoir's valve house. Bateman, regarded as one of the greatest dam-builder of his generation, was responsible for overseeing the water supplies for Manchester, Glasgow, Dublin and many other cities and his work formed the basis of the water supply network still used today.

The impressive gritstone crags that frame the southern edge of the reservoir are The Cludders, more commonly known as Widdop Rocks. They're very popular with climbers; renowned climber Don Whillans did the first ascent of a route known as Ceiling Crack here in 1955. Other rocks nearby have equally evocative names Clattering Stones, Boggart Stones, Slack Stones, Raven Stones and Frock Holes.

The boulders scattered beneath Cludders have also attracted celebrity. John Wesley, the Methodist preacher, is said to have delivered a sermon to Widdop's isolated population from one of them in 1766 – one is inscribed with his initials and the date.

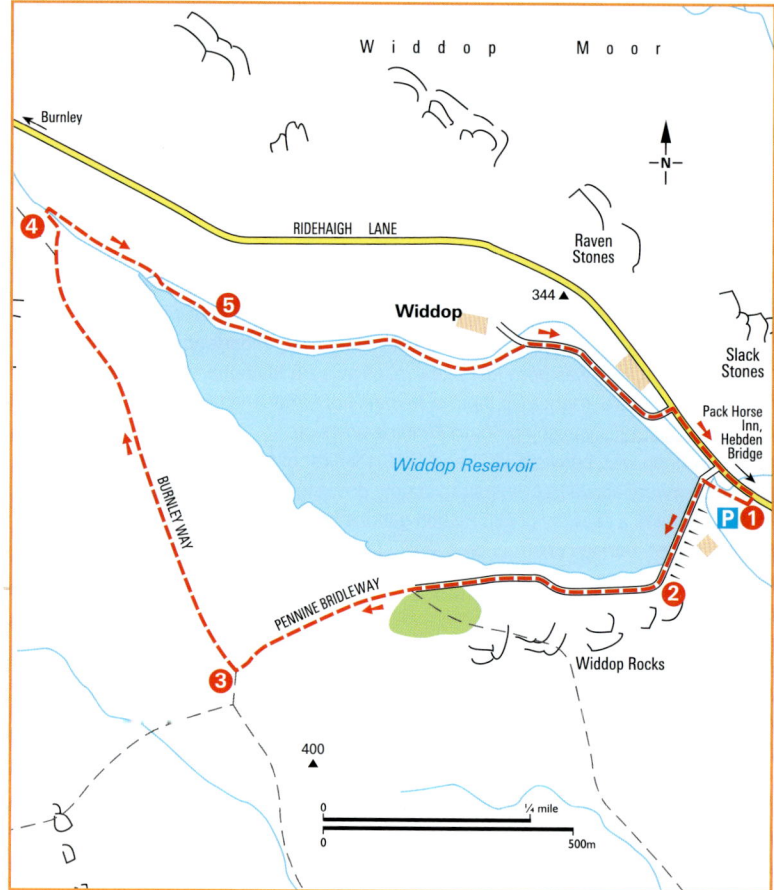

1. Follow the track from the car park towards the reservoir wall. Cross a metal footbridge over the dam's spill channel and turn left to cross the embankment.

2. Bear right at the end of the dam wall, along a track known as Gorple Gate, actually an old packhorse route that climbs from Worsthorne to Heptonstall and now forms part of the Pennine Bridleway National Trail. After passing a small plantation, the trail climbs gently away from the reservoir up a small clough and bears right, across the small stream near the top.

3. At a junction just above you'll find a marker post; leave the Pennine Bridleway to turn right down a rough path, which is muddy in places, as it follows a crumbled wall.

4. At the foot of the path, a fingerpost directs you back towards the dam, over a wooden footbridge to a second fingerpost; bear right. By a silt trap pond, where Old Hay Dyke's waters flow into the dam, the path runs to the right of a wall for a few paces, then carries you right over another footbridge, to turn left, between the water course and the reservoir.

5. Ignore the first metal footbridge on the left and continue along what is now a track, past the former reservoir keeper's house on your left, to cross the water course on a short vehicle track, which leads, through a metal gate, on to the road. Turn right down the tarmac for a short distance to return to the car park.

Where to eat and drink
Known locally as The Ridge, the walker-friendly Pack Horse Inn stands just yards from the Pennine Way and a mile's (1.6km) drive from the start of the walk. The isolated 500-year-old former farmhouse offers excellent food, fine real ales and a connoisseur's selection of around 130 whiskies. It is open Wednesday to Sunday all year but this is subject to change due to weather.

What to look out for
The moorland road above Widdop Reservoir was once a packhorse route between Heptonstall and Colne. Pasture House, on the roadside, was for many years an inn known as the Old Traveller's Rest, but doubled as the moorland base for a gang of robbers who raided homes across the nearby Lancashire border. The inn itself was raided and closed in 1891 for hosting an illegal gambling school.

While you're there
From the Stubbing Wharf Inn in Hebden Bridge, about 5 miles (8km) from Widdop, you can enjoy a traditional canal boat journey along the Rochdale Canal. This once-derelict 32-mile (52km) canal was re-opened in 2002.

THE LAKES AROUND WALTON

DISTANCE/TIME	3.5 miles (5.7km) / 1hr 15min
ASCENT/GRADIENT	197ft (60m) / ▲
PATHS	Good paths and tracks throughout, canal tow path
LANDSCAPE	Country park, lakes, woodland and canal
SUGGESTED MAP	OS Explorer 278 Sheffield & Barnsley
START/FINISH	Grid reference: SE375153
DOG FRIENDLINESS	Good, but care should be taken when near wildfowl
PARKING	Anglers Country Park on Haw Park Lane, between Crofton and Ryehill
PUBLIC TOILETS	At the visitor centre, at start of walk

Few houses are situated as delightfully as Walton Hall, isolated upon a little lake island with just a cast iron bridge for access. It was the ancestral home of Charles Waterton, who deserves wider acclaim, for although then regarded as an eccentric, his environmental interests would have put him in the vanguard of climate-friendly thinking today.

Born in 1782, Charles Waterton developed a childhood interest in wildlife, but his passion flourished when he went to British Guyana. During his time there he made several expeditions into the interior and neighbouring Brazil, becoming fascinated by South America's unusual wildlife. He returned home with many exotic specimens, many of which are now displayed in the Wakefield Museum, and turned his attention to studying and protecting his local wildlife.

At a time when shooting parties were an intrinsic part of landed gentry society, he created what was perhaps the world's first nature reserve, building a high wall around his estate to keep the poachers out. However, he opened the grounds for the peaceful enjoyment of local people. Over the next 40 years he fought against pollution, planted countless trees, managed his woodland for the benefit of the wildlife and built hides from which to watch the wild birds. He also experimented in encouraging breeding. One success was the establishment of herons on the estate; their descendants still around today. He spent over £9,000 (the equivalent £2.5 million today) on his project, funding it, he said, 'from the wine I do not drink'. When he died after a fall in 1865, he was buried in the woods he loved, a linnet supposedly singing as his coffin was lowered into the ground.

Ironically, his son Edmund subsequently resorted to hosting shooting parties to help to pay off his own debts. But the estate survived and today is split between a country park, nature reserve and a golf club, with the house forming the centrepiece of the four-star Waterton Park Hotel.

Beyond the wood and parkland of Waterton's estate, areas of the country park have been reclaimed from industry. The main lake was once a vast, opencast coal pit surrounded by spoil heaps, while the two reservoirs to the south supplied the Barnsley Canal. Opened in 1799 to carry coal, the waterway later lost traffic to the railways and was plagued by subsidence from the mines it served. Closed since 1953, it too has reverted to nature, adding yet another dimension to the habitats of the area. At the country park visitor centre, you will find exhibitions illustrating Squire Waterton's work and highlighting the local wildlife.

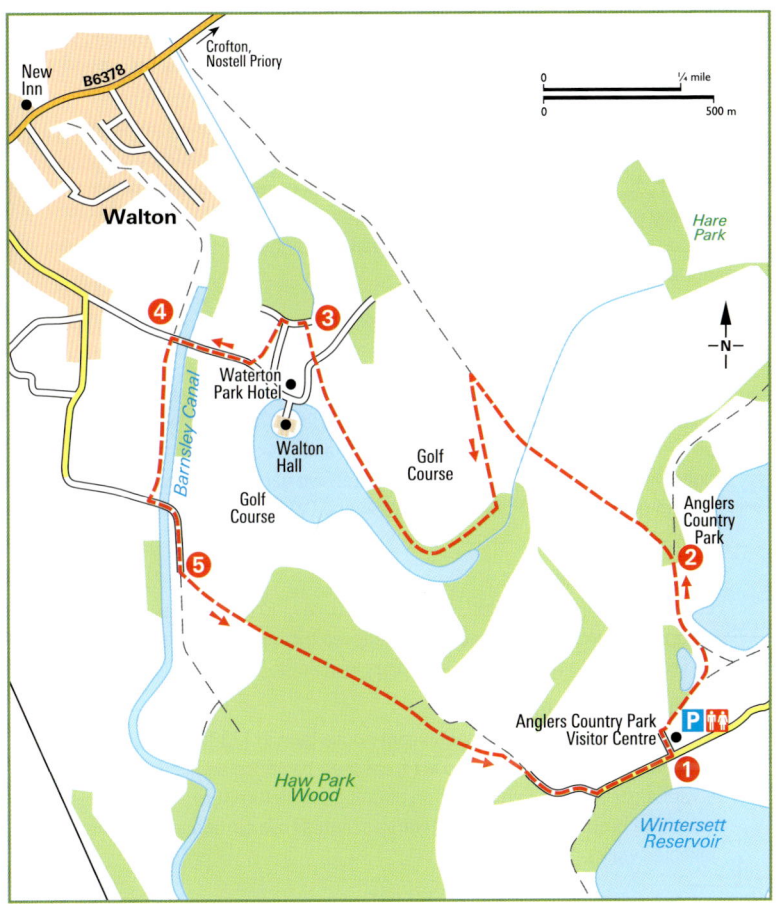

1. From the car park, take the track past the visitor centre towards the main lake, signed 'Lakeside Walk'. At a fork, bear left towards the bird hides. Keep to the main path for some 300yds (274m), looking for a gap in the left hedge from which a path is signed to Walton.

2. Through a kissing gate, walk at the edge of two fields towards the distant golf course. Cross a footbridge into a third field and keep ahead to another kissing gate in the far corner. Turn sharp left on a path fringing the golf course, passing a small pond to enter woodland. Ignoring a crossing path, keep to the obvious trail, which shortly curves right past the tail of a lake. Beyond the trees, continue forward as golfers' paths merge to reach a junction.

Take the waymarked grass path ahead to a three-way fingerpost and carry on towards the Barnsley Canal, descending behind the hotel complex to meet a gravel drive.

3. Go left, but leave after 50yds (46m), going left again on a waymarked path that climbs beside a fence. At the top, pass through an opening in a high brick wall and swing left again to emerge onto the hotel's main drive. Follow it up to the right, rising to a bridge over the Barnsley Canal near the golf clubhouse.

4. Immediately over the bridge, drop left to the tow path and follow it away beside the disused waterway. After 0.25 miles (400m) bear off right, rising to another bridge over the canal. Cross and swing right in front of a gate on a broad track running above the opposite bank.

5. When it later forks, keep left beside the boundary wall of the Walton Estate into woodland. Eventually reaching a junction at the end of the wall, bear right with the main track. Walk on to a second junction by an information board and go left towards Anglers Country Park. Leaving Haw Wood behind, the track later develops as a lane, eventually leading back to the car park and visitor centre.

Where to eat and drink
The New Inn at nearby Walton welcomes walkers. The regular menu and daily specials offer home-cooked food that is locally sourced wherever possible. There's a good selection of wines and cask beers on tap to quench the fiercest thirst. There is an extensive garden with two bookable heated pods. Closer to hand is the Woodland Café in the Anglers Country Park visitor centre by the car park.

What to look out for
Look out for herons. The tall, grey heron is one of Britain's most easily recognised birds. At one time it was believed the heron's skill at catching fish must be due to magical substances in its legs.

While you're there
Nearby Nostell Priory is a magnificent house built in 1733 on the site of a medieval priory. It is home to art treasures, paintings and tapestries – with a particularly fine collection of Chippendale furniture. There are extensive grounds and gardens, with a scented rose garden and peaceful lakeside walks.

HAREWOOD AND AROUND THE ESTATE

DISTANCE/TIME	7 miles (11.3km) / 2hrs 45min
ASCENT/GRADIENT	693ft (211m) / ▲
PATHS	Good paths and parkland tracks all the way
LANDSCAPE	Arable farmland and parkland
SUGGESTED MAP	OS Explorer 289 Leeds
START/FINISH	Grid reference: SE334450
DOG FRIENDLINESS	Keep on leads in conservation areas, near sheep and deer and on roads
PARKING	From the traffic lights at junction of A61 and A659 (Harewood Ave), take A659 and park in first lay-by on left, some way down the road
PUBLIC TOILETS	None on route

The grand old houses of West Yorkshire tend to be in the form of 'Halifax' houses (such as East Riddlesden Hall). Self-made yeomen and merchant clothiers built their mansions to show the world that they'd made their 'brass'. But Harewood House, on the edge of Leeds, is more ambitious, and is still one of the great treasure houses of England.

The Harewood Estate passed through a number of wealthy hands during the 16th and 17th centuries, eventually being bought by the Lascelles family, who still own the house. Edwin Lascelles left the 12th-century castle in its ruinous state, to overlook the broad valley of the River Wharfe, but demolished the old hall. He wanted to create something special in its place and hired the best architects and designers to turn his vision into grand reality. John Carr of York created a veritable palace, in an imposing neoclassical style, and laid out the estate village of Harewood too. The foundations were laid in 1759 and 12 years later the house was finished. Thomas Chippendale, born in nearby Otley, made furniture for every room, as part of the house's original plans. Inside are paintings by J M W Turner and Thomas Girtin, who both stayed and painted there. Turner was particularly taken with the area, producing pictures of many local landmarks. The sumptuous interior, however, is in sharp contrast to the world of those below stairs, whose life and work is depicted in the Old Kitchen and servants' quarters.

The extensive grounds were preened and groomed to be as magnificent as the house. They were shaped by Lancelot 'Capability' Brown, the most renowned designer of the English landscape. In addition to the formal gardens, he created the lake and the woodland paths you visit on this walk. Like many stately homes, Harewood House has had to earn its keep in recent years. The bird garden was the first commercial venture, but now the house hosts a range of events such as art exhibitions, vintage car rallies and open-air concerts.

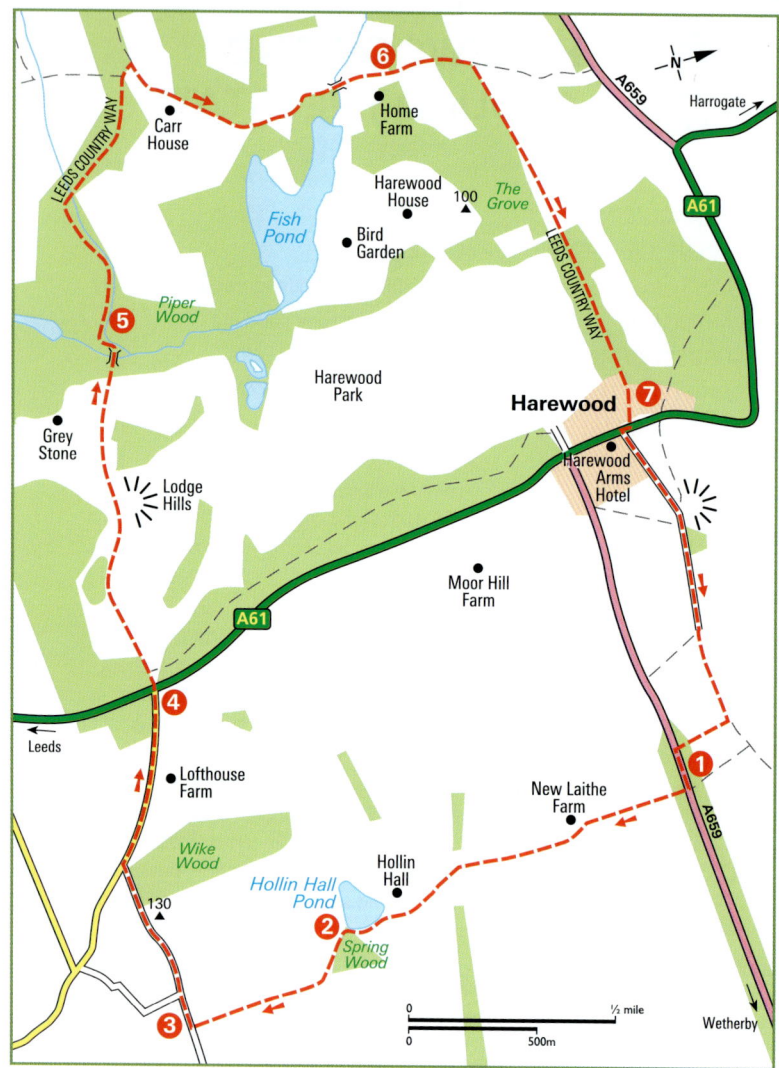

1. From the lay-by, walk 50yds (46m) away from the village of Harewood, cross the road and walk right down the access track to New Laithe Farm. Pass left of the farm buildings to pick up a gravel track heading into the valley bottom. Go through a gate and bear half left up a field, towards Hollin Hall. Keep left of the buildings to pass Hollin Hall Pond.

2. Beyond the pond, swing left around the corner of Spring Wood and follow a track at the field edge to the top corner. Through gates continue up the hill, the track later becoming enclosed and ending at a junction.

3. Go right along the crest of the hill to have easy, level walking on an enclosed sandy track (now following the Leeds Country Way). Keep straight ahead past a junction, through a gate. Skirt woodland to emerge onto a lane. Follow it right to reach the A61.

4. Cross the road to enter the Harewood Estate (via the right-hand gate, between imposing gateposts). Follow the broad track ahead, through landscaped parkland, soon getting views of Harewood House to the right. Enter woodland through a gate, turning immediately left after a stone bridge.

5. After 100yds (91m), bear right at a fork and keep with the main track. It later swings right, dipping across a stream and eventually reaching a crossing. Go right down to another junction and turn right again, the way curving left out of the trees to pass Carr House. Carry on at the edge of the park, then swing left again at the next junction, rising beside a high wall to meet a metalled drive. Bear left to a crossroads and keep ahead over a bridge and another crossing, climbing beside the Home Farm complex.

6. Follow the drive into the deer park, keeping right at the next junction. Continue through woodland until you come to the few houses that comprise the estate village of Harewood.

7. Cross the main A61 road and walk right, for 50yds (46m), to take a metalled drive just before the Harewood Arms Hotel. Beyond Maltkiln House, the way continues as a gated field track, with views over Lower Wharfedale. Carry on through a second gate for a further 350yds (320m) to a junction and go right over a cattle grid along a permissive bridleway, before regaining the A659 beside the lay-by.

Where to eat and drink

Almost opposite the main gates of Harewood House is the Harewood Arms Hotel, a former coaching inn that offers the chance of a drink or meal towards the end of the walk and a beer garden in good weather.

What to see

The red kite, a beautiful fork-tailed bird of prey, is once again becoming a familiar sight. Centuries of persecution had brought the species close to extinction in England, but Harewood has successfully reintroduced them to this part of Yorkshire. As evening falls, look out for other hunting birds, including three of Britain's owl species.

While you're there

As well as the house with its fabulous state rooms and art treasures, there are endless paths among the terraces and gardens. There is much to see in the bird garden, which houses exotic and rare species from around the world. Complete the walk in the morning to work up a healthy appetite for lunch and spend the rest of the day exploring the house and grounds.

RURAL LEEDS AND THE MEANWOOD VALLEY

DISTANCE/TIME	5.25 miles (8.4km) / 2hrs 15min
ASCENT/GRADIENT	729ft (222m) / ▲
PATHS	Urban paths, parkland and woodland paths
LANDSCAPE	Mostly woodland
SUGGESTED MAP	OS Explorer 289 Leeds
START	Grid reference: SE293350
FINISH	Grid reference: SE270402
DOG FRIENDLINESS	Keep on leads near roads
PARKING	Street parking off main road at both ends of the walk; bus services 1 and X84 operate between the two points
PUBLIC TOILETS	In Meanwood Park

This walk is a splendid ramble, surprisingly rural in aspect throughout, even though it begins just a stone's throw from the bustling heart of Leeds. You start among the terraces of redbrick houses that are so typical of the city, and five minutes later you are in delightful woodland.

The walk follows the first 5 miles (8km) of the Dales Way link path from Leeds to Ilkley. This link path begins at Woodhouse Moor Park – where fairs and circuses have long pitched their tents.

The path follows Woodhouse Ridge into Meanwood Park and along the Meanwood Valley, cocooned against creeping suburbia by a slim sliver of woodland. The route is also promoted as the Meanwood Valley Trail, so there are regular waymarkers to keep you on track.

Leeds is fortunate to have so many parks within the city limits, from long established green spaces such as Roundhay Park to newer parks created from brownfield sites, once the site of industry. The first few miles of this walk are through some of this pleasant parkland. Then, after crossing beneath the busy Leeds ring road, you will have the more natural surroundings of Adel Woods to enjoy.

The walk finishes near Adel church, dedicated to St John the Baptist. Though small, it is one of the most perfectly proportioned Norman churches in the country, having been built about 1170. The ornamental stone carving is noteworthy – especially the four arches framing the doorway. From Adel, there's a reliable bus service back to Woodhouse Moor – but check the timetable before you set out.

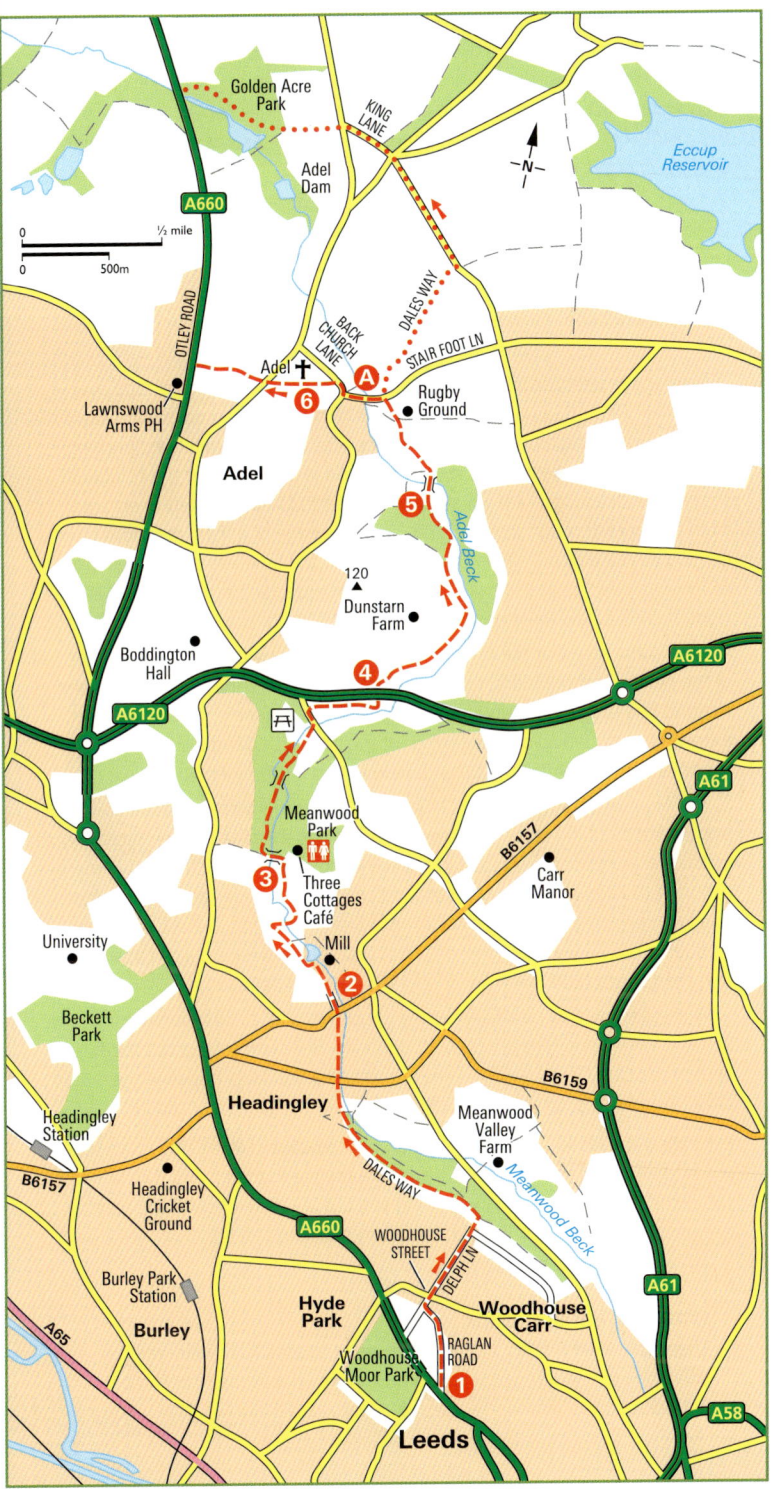

1. Walk down Raglan Road and on along Cathcart Street. At the T-junction, turn right onto Rampart Road, cross Woodhouse Street, and walk ahead up Delph Lane. At the end, go forward through a gap and left onto the higher path along Woodhouse Ridge. Keep with the main trail to a barrier. Where it splits, take the middle option to Grove Lane. There, cross to the path opposite, which shortly emerges at Monk Bridge Road.

2. Cross the road into Highbury Lane, recovering the path beside Meanwood Beck beyond its end. At a junction by a converted mill, go left and then right onto a path between allotments. Keep on to emerge onto a street and walk ahead. After 100yds (91m), by a postbox, turn right into Meanwood Park. Follow the drive to reach a car park. Pass through and swing left onto a lane that leads to a terrace of stone cottages, Hustlers Row.

3. Near the houses, drop left along a stony track to cross a footbridge over Meanwood Beck. Bear right just beyond at a fork and head upstream above the beck, shortly rising along a raised bank beside a disused mill leat. Ignoring side paths, it eventually leads to a pair of bridges. Swing over the bridge on the right above a weir and walk forward to a broad path. Go left to emerge from the trees through a gate. Carry on at the edge of a field into more trees, coming out by a picnic site onto a lane. Follow the lane left but, just before reaching a junction with a main road, turn off along an unmarked track on the right. It runs below the embankment before heading through an underpass.

4. Take some steps, at the far end, onto a path that follows Adel Beck. Keep left of the next pile of boulders, rising to a path along the fringe of the woodland. Keep to this higher path until you eventually reach a major fork. Bear right, following an aqueduct across the dip of the valley. Curving left, the path continues through Adel Woods, in time meeting a prominent junction.

5. The Meanwood Valley Trail is signed left, dropping across a stone slab bridge and climbing steps to a small pond. Cross the small feeder stream and fork right. Occasional waypoints mark the ongoing path, which shortly emerges to run at the edge of more open ground. Joining a broader path keep left, finally emerging through a car park onto Stair Foot Lane. Go left, dropping through a dip and up to a junction. Turn right along Back Church Lane but, as that then bears right, keep ahead along a path to Adel church.

6. Walk past the church and leave the churchyard by a collection of millstones. Cross the road and take a field path opposite. Bear half left across the next field to the Otley Road (A660). Turn left to find a bus stop, opposite the Lawnswood Arms, for the bus back to Woodhouse Moor, in Leeds.

Extending the walk To extend the walk by 1.5 miles (2.4km), don't turn left down Stair Foot Lane (at Point A), but take the track ahead, and turn left when you come to King Lane. This will bring you out at Golden Acre Park, near Bramhope (on the X84 bus route for getting back to Leeds).

> ### Where to eat and drink
> There are several pubs just off the route of this walk, or wait until the finishing point where you will find the Lawnswood Arms. The Three Cottages Café is also worth a visit at Meanwood Park.

GOLDEN ACRE PARK AND BREARY MARSH

DISTANCE/TIME	6 miles (9.7km) / 2hrs 15min
ASCENT/GRADIENT	392ft (119m) / ▲
PATHS	Good paths, tracks and quiet roads, many stiles
LANDSCAPE	Parkland, woods and arable country
SUGGESTED MAP	OS Explorer 297 Lower Wharfedale & Washburn Valley
START/FINISH	Grid reference: SE266417
DOG FRIENDLINESS	Keep on leads at all times
PARKING	Golden Acre Park car park, across road from park itself, on A660 just south of Bramhope
PUBLIC TOILETS	Golden Acre Park, at start of walk

Leeds is fortunate to have so many green spaces. Some, like Roundhay Park, are long established; others, like Kirkstall Valley Nature Reserve, have been created from post-industrial wasteland. However, none have had a more chequered history than Golden Acre Park, which is 6 miles (9.7km) north of the city on the main A660.

The park originally opened in 1932 as an amusement park. The attractions included a miniature railway, nearly 2 miles (3.2km) in length, complete with dining car. The lake was the centre of much activity, with motor launches, dinghies for hire and races by the Yorkshire Hydroplane Racing Squadron. An open-air lido known, somewhat exotically, as the Blue Lagoon, offered unheated swimming. The Winter Gardens Dance Hall boasted that it had 'the largest dance floor in Yorkshire'. Though visitors initially flocked to Golden Acre Park, the novelty soon wore off. By the end of the 1938 season, the amusement park had closed down and was sold to Leeds City Council. The site was subsequently transformed into botanical gardens – a process that's continued ever since. The hillside overlooking the lake has been lovingly planted with trees and unusual plants, including rock gardens and fine displays of rhododendrons. The boats are long gone; the lake is now a haven for wildfowl. Within these 127 acres (51ha) – the 'Golden Acre' name was as fanciful as 'the Blue Lagoon' – is a wide variety of wildlife habitats, from open heathland to an old quarry. Lovers of birds, trees and flowers will find plenty to interest them at every season of the year.

Reflecting the park's increasing popularity with local people, a large car park has been built on the opposite side of the main road, with pedestrian access to the park via a tunnel beneath the road. This intriguing park offers excellent walking, and wheelchair users, too, can make a circuit of the lake on a broad path.

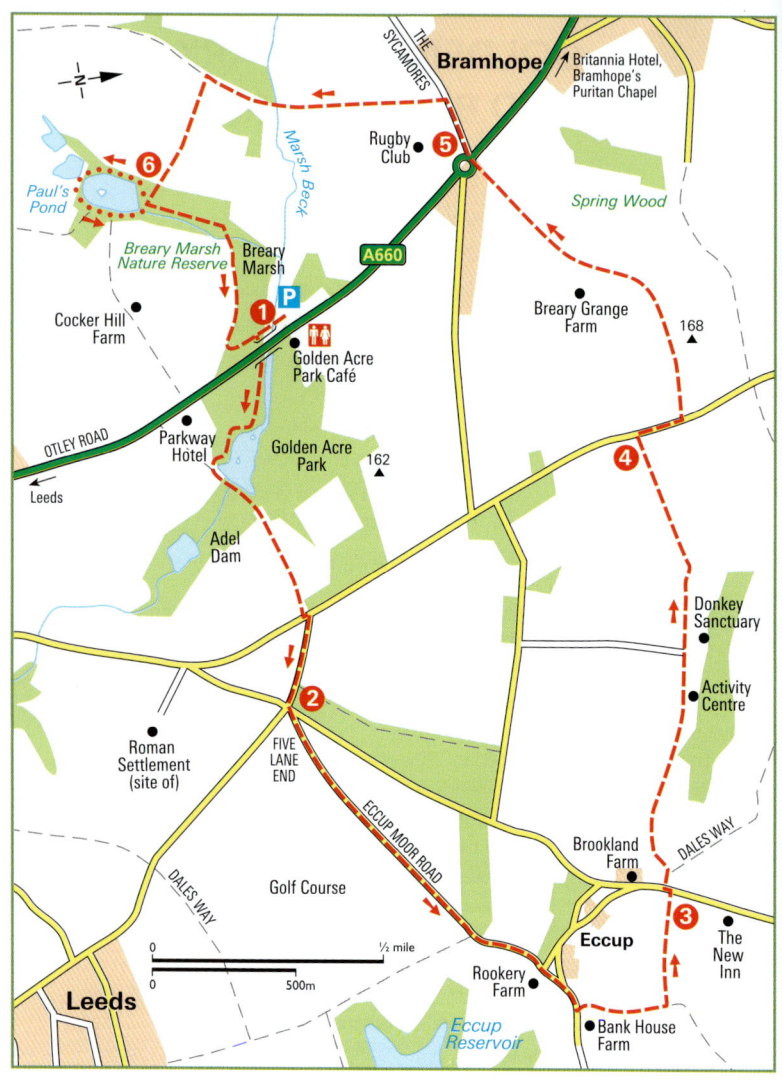

1. From the southern corner of the car park, an underpass leads into Golden Acre Park. Turn right on a path that winds to the far end of the lake. Ignore the path heading off left across the lake dam and walk forward out of the park onto a tree-lined bridlepath. Go left beside the park boundary to emerge at a junction of lanes. Take the one that's ahead, up to the Five Lane End junction.

2. Take the second road on the left (Eccup Moor Road). Stick with it for a mile (1.6km) past junctions until you reach the outbuildings of Bank House Farm, where a waymarked bridleway leaves on the left. It soon narrows to a hedged path. About 50yds (46m) before the footpath later swings right, take a stile in the fence on your left. Follow the field edge away to a wall stile and continue forward across another field to emerge onto a lane (The New Inn is then just along to your right).

3. Go left along the road for just 20yds (18m) to take a stile on your right. Keep ahead over an intersection to join another track, which leads forward to a gate and stile. Carry on for 150yds (137m) by the boundary to a waypost and bear right across the pasture to a stile in the end wall. Walk on towards an activity centre, bypassing it through a couple of kissing gates to meet a track. Go right and immediately left along an enclosed grass track past a donkey sanctuary. When it finishes, maintain your direction walking beside successive fields to reach a road.

4. Go right for 150yds (137m) then take a waymarked kissing gate on the left. Follow the field-edge path by the left fence. Beyond two more kissing gates bear left across another field behind Breary Grange Farm to a ladder stile beyond a large oak. Maintain the same direction to a stile at the far corner and continue across a final field. Leave over a stile next to buildings onto the A660 by a roundabout.

5. Cross the main road and turn into The Sycamores. Walk past the Rugby Club, but some 100yds (91m) further on, leave through a kissing gate on the left. Head away at the edge of successive fields towards a wood. Crossing a beck, carry on beside the trees. Reaching a stile, swing left along a track towards a farmhouse. Continue on the field path beyond to a gate that leads into the Breary Marsh Nature Reserve.

6. The path heading off sharp right makes a circuit around the lake, a pleasant extension if you're not pushed for time. Otherwise, bear slightly right onto a path below the foot of the dam. At a junction, go left with the Leeds Country Way, signed towards the A660. Wind with the bridleway across a bridge but, at the next junction, turn left back to the car park.

Where to eat and drink
It requires the shortest of detours, at about the halfway point of this walk, to visit The New Inn, near Eccup. A sign welcomes walkers – as do the open fires and beer garden – and an extensive menu will whet your appetite. The Golden Acre Park Café, in the park of the same name, offers everything from a snack to a full meal.

What to see
Look for the damp-loving alder trees in Breary Marsh. Their seeds float on the water. During winter, you should see little siskins (a type of finch) feeding on the seeds, of which they are particularly fond. You may also spy the vivid caterpillar of the alder moth.

While you're there
Bramhope's Puritan Chapel, adjacent to the entrance to the Britannia Hotel on the A660, is a small, simple chapel built in 1649, by devout Puritan Robert Dyneley. Although it's generally locked, peering through the windows reveals its original furnishings, including box-pews and a three-deck pulpit.

STOODLEY PIKE AND THE CALDERDALE WAY

DISTANCE/TIME	3.8 miles (6.1km) / 1hr 30min
ASCENT/GRADIENT	500ft (152m) / ▲▲▲
PATHS	Moorland paths and rough pastures – plenty of opportunity for mud, several stiles
LANDSCAPE	Exposed peaty moorland, often wet
SUGGESTED MAP	OS Explorer OL21 South Pennines
START/FINISH	Grid reference: SD986232
DOG FRIENDLINESS	On leads near livestock
PARKING	Withens Clough car park, Rudd Lane, Cragg Vale
PUBLIC TOILETS	None on route

This walk may not be the longest or lengthiest in this book, but it is amongst the steepest, and possibly muddiest. The moorlands here are covered in peat, forming a gigantic reservoir, absorbing and retaining millions of gallons of water like a giant sponge. Peat is a miracle substance. Without it, the rain would simply run off the moors, causing regular, severe flooding in the process. It is formed by partially decayed moorland vegetation, principally sphagnum moss, though it is a slow process.

Britain's peaty uplands, especially the Pennines, are also the equivalent of our own rain forest, as peat is a natural carbon sink, trapping up to 5,000 tonnes of carbon in every hectare (2.47 acres). Take away the peat, and there are even fewer checks on global warming. So important are the moors of West Yorkshire for birdlife that many have been given European protection as part of the South Pennines Special.

That's all hard to appreciate when you're crossing a sodden moor and you suddenly slip knee-deep into a bog. If you do find your boots filling up, just contemplate its importance and take solace in the anticipation of a luxurious bath when you get home.

As for this walk being one of the steepest, you'll be heading up to Stoodley Pike. Stoodley will have been popping up in your views all over the region and is an unmistakeable landmark. The Stoodley Pike monument is 121ft (37m) high and built to commemorate the end of the Crimea war. You can climb up the spiral stairs within the monument to emerge at a viewing platform offering wonderful panoramic views over Calderdale and beyond. However, if you are planning to do this, note that the stairs are unlit stone steps, so it's useful to have a torch for this walk.

You'll pass two other stone marker posts: the Long Stoop and, as the Calderdale Way approaches open moorland, look out for a squat, inscribed stone. Known as the Te Deum Stone, it may have marked an old packhorse route between Cragg Vale and Mankinholes, and is believed to have been used to rest coffins being carried over the moors for burial in Mankinholes. The full inscription reads 'Te Deum Laudamus', or 'We Praise Thee, O Lord'.

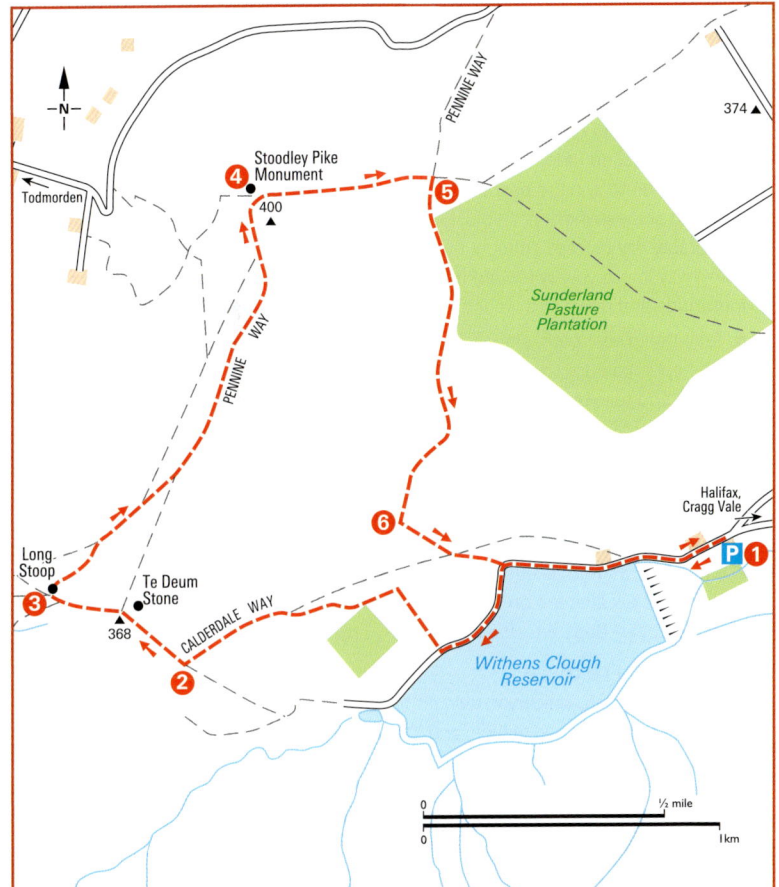

1. Turn left out of the car park, through two gates and along the track beyond, past the embankment of Withens Clough Reservoir and a farmhouse. Ignore the first path to the right and take the track 600yds (549m) beyond the farmhouse, signed 'Calderdale Way'. Leave this track and the Way after just 240yds (219m), bearing left on a permissive bridleway to pass through an open gate, winding along the top side of a small plantation. Beyond another field gate, the Calderdale Way soon rejoins from the right and the fence-side track continues a further 340yds (310m) to a crossroads.

2. Bear right here, ignoring a walled lane ahead to stay with the Calderdale Way to a gate by the inscribed Te Deum Stone. The track continues across open country beyond the gate; keep right when it forks, to follow causey stones, to a crossroads of paths by a 7ft (2.1m) tall obelisk, Long Stoop.

3. The stoop marks the point at which you turn right on the Pennine Way along the edge of Langfield Common, which brings you to Stoodley Pike.

4. The Pennine Way bears right here. Stay with it for a further 550yds (503m), past a spring, the Slake Trough, to pass through a stone gap stile. Just beyond, the Pennine Way bears left over a wall. You, however, turn right, across the field, and pass through a stone stile in the wall opposite.

5. Follow the wall on your left. The path briefly becomes a narrowing walled track before passing through a gate and dropping across open country by a fence towards Withens Clough Reservoir. Yellow-topped poles guide you through a wet, reedy area and over a tiny wooden footbridge. You should then bear immediately right, over to a pair of stone gate posts and through a new gate into a walled lane. This is sometimes so wet as to be impassable. Instead, walk parallel to it in the pasture to its right and left, using the toppled wall as stepping stones where possible. Enter the lane at a point at which it looks acceptably dry (accept, though, that your boots will get wet!). When the walls fade away, more yellow topped markers guide you over a second rotted small footbridge and down to a walled enclosure, from which several paths depart.

6. Take the lowest path, signed 'To Withens Clough', cutting a diagonal line across open pasture toward another fingerpost by the wall below. Go through the wall and turn left along your outward track to the car park.

Where to eat and drink
The Robin Hood freehouse, in Cragg Vale, offers home-cooked food Thursday to Sunday, and specialises in lamb from landlord Roger Wood's own farm, as well as other locally reared meats. Several Yorkshire-brewed cask ales are on offer in the bar and are looked after admirably in the cellar. Dogs are also welcome.

While you're there
The B6138 road, which you turn off to reach the start of this walk, offers Britain's longest road incline, and formed one of the most challenging stages of the Tour de France's Yorkshire Grand Départ in 2014. The unrelenting climb starts in busy Mytholmroyd, and ends 5.5 miles (8.8km) later on the moors beside Blackstone Edge Reservoir, 1,270ft (387m) above sea level.

AROUND NEWMILLERDAM

DISTANCE/TIME	4.5 miles (7.2km) / 1hr 45min
ASCENT/GRADIENT	328ft (100m) / ▲
PATHS	Good paths by lake and through woodland, several stiles
LANDSCAPE	Reservoir, heath and woodland
SUGGESTED MAP	OS Explorer 278 Sheffield & Barnsley
START/FINISH	Grid reference: SE330157
DOG FRIENDLINESS	Keep on lead beside roads
PARKING	Pay-and-display car park at western end of dam, on A61 opposite Fox and Hounds pub
PUBLIC TOILETS	Near start of walk

Called Thurstonhaugh by Norse settlers, this area subsequently became part of a large medieval estate held by the Neviles until the 18th century. The lake is actually a mill pond and the place gained its present name in the 13th century with the construction of a new corn mill. The original mill is thought to have stood near the boathouse, but has seen several reincarnations before ending up in its present location in the 17th century after the lake had been extended to increase the head of water to drive the machinery. The mill continued to operate until 1960 and, although subsequently partly destroyed by a fire, still stands.

The Pilkingtons bought the estate in 1765 as a hunting preserve, and at one time nine keepers were employed to manage the game and prevent poaching. Each was housed in a separate lodge, two of still stand by the main entrance to the park (one housing an Italian restaurant).

The Pilkingtons also built the impressive lakeshore boathouse in 1820 to serve as a pavilion where the ladies could relax while watching their menfolk shoot wildfowl from punts. A Grade II listed building, it has been restored and is now hired out as a meeting venue with a difference.

Wakefield Council bought the park in 1954 and opened it to the public. Today, the park is a popular haunt for local people who come to walk, fish, watch birds or feed the ducks. The lake is surrounded by three woods containing a mixture of larch and pine as well as oak, beech, birch and sycamore. The beech are from the Pilkingtons' time as are clumps of rhododendron, which were planted as game cover. The majority of trees, however, date from the 1950s, planted as a commercial crop to provide timber for pit props. The softwoods and rhododendrons are now gradually being removed to allow a more diverse woodland that will benefit flowers and wildlife. Bluebells and wood anemone are beginning to carpet the understorey and birds such as tree creepers, long-tailed tits, coot and heron can be spotted amongst the branches or around the shore. Great crested grebe breed on the lake and several species of bat can be spotted on summer evenings.

Nearby Seckar Wood, which you'll visit on this walk, was part of a separate estate. It was bought by local photographer Warner Gothard, who left it for the enjoyment of local people on his death in 1940. Encompassing heath, wood and wetland, it is now a Site of Special Scientific Interest (SSSI), rich in wildlife from woodpeckers to weasels. Go quietly and you might spot roe deer.

1. Turn right out of the car park and follow the main road down across the dam. At the far side, swing right in front of the Dam Inn through the park gates and follow the lakeside path. Ignore a causeway and carry on beyond the head of the lake to find a bridge across Bushcliff Beck.

2. On the far bank, go left and immediately right onto a path climbing into the trees. Keep with the main path to the crest of the hill, continuing ahead to a junction. Swing left on a broadening track, walking for 300yds (274m) to a major junction. Turn right, crossing a bridge over the disused Chevet branch line to follow a rough track out to the main road.

3. Cross and turn right, walking downhill for 350yds (320m) to find a barriered track leading left into Seckar Wood. Stick to the main path rising through the trees, ignoring a crossing and eventually emerging onto the edge of open

heath. Keep going forward across the high ground to a belt of trees that appears on the far side, passing out through them onto a crossing track.

4. Follow it right beside the wood, eventually crossing a stile and footbridge into the next field. Go right, passing through a gap in the corner to then swing left beside the hedge. Approaching houses, turn right within the corner and follow the hedge down to a broad gap. Turn left on a field track that soon leads out onto the road at Chapelthorpe.

5. Walk right, passing the former Bay Horse and then a junction to a mini-roundabout. There go right along Wood Lane for almost 0.25 miles (400m). After passing the Pennine Camphill Community, turn off left along a field path that leads through to the bend of a lane. Follow it ahead down to the A61 and turn left back to the car park.

Where to eat and drink
The Fox and Hounds, opposite the car park offers a varied menu including snacks and has a good reputation for its food. The Dam Inn serves a daily carvery and is situated, appropriately, by the lake's dam. The Boathouse on the edge of Newmiller Dam serves coffee, delicious homemade food and fantastic sweet treats. It is also dog friendly. The Pledwick public house lies a little further along the main road towards Barnsley and it too has a welcoming restaurant.

What to look out for
Ducks, geese and swans are all to be found at Newmillerdam. The most common of the ducks you'll see is the mallard. The females are brown and make the satisfying 'quack quack' sounds which delight children. The males have distinctive green heads, yellow bills and grey bodies. Their tone is more nasal and much weaker sounding. Mallards pair off in the late autumn but the males leave egg incubation and rearing of the young to the females.

While you're there
Immediately to the north of Newmillerdam is Pugneys Country Park, a popular place of recreation with people from Wakefield. A large lake is overlooked by what remains of Sandal Castle. The original motte-and-bailey building dates from the 12th century, the later stone castle from the days of Richard III. He had planned to make Sandal Castle his permanent stronghold in the north of England before he was killed at the Battle of Bosworth in 1485.

TONG AND FULNECK VALLEY

DISTANCE/TIME	5 miles (8km) / 2hrs
ASCENT/GRADIENT	607ft (185m) / ▲
PATHS	Ancient causeways, hollow ways and field paths, many stiles
LANDSCAPE	Mostly wooded valleys
SUGGESTED MAP	OS Explorer 288 Bradford & Huddersfield
START/FINISH	Grid reference: SE222306
DOG FRIENDLINESS	Keep on lead across golf course and by livestock
PARKING	Lay-by in Tong village, near village hall, or on edge of village
PUBLIC TOILETS	None on route

This walk takes you through two delightful valleys: Fulneck Valley and Cockers Dale. In these wooded dells, criss-crossed by ancient packhorse tracks and hollow ways, you feel a long way from the surrounding cities. On an attractive ridge between these valleys is the village of Tong (the name means 'a spit of land'), which has kept its traditional shape and character, and managed to avoid being absorbed by creeping suburbia. You'll also pay a visit to the Fulneck Moravian Settlement.

The Pennine areas of Yorkshire have long been strongholds for non-conformist faiths. The harsh conditions and uncertain livelihoods produced people who were both independent of mind and receptive to radical ideas. Some travelling preachers could fill churches, with congregations overflowing into the churchyard. The Revd William Grimshaw of Haworth, for example, was one such tireless orator. He was always prepared to ride many moorland miles to preach the gospel and – if necessary – to chase drinkers out of the pubs and into church. In the 18th-century, John Wesley found converts here, and imposingly austere Methodist chapels sprang up in the smallest village.

Just to the south of Pudsey is Fulneck, where another non-conformist church found a home. Pre-Reformation dissenters from the Roman Catholic Church, the Moravians, originated in Bohemia in the 15th century, and soon spread to Moravia. During the 18th-century, a group of Moravian missionaries arrived in England and a meeting with Benjamin Ingham, a Church of England clergyman, encouraged them to settle here. The Moravians constructed a street on the ridge, and built a collection of handsome buildings along it. Soon there was a chapel, family houses, a shop, inn, bakery and workshops forming a close-knit, self-sufficient settlement. Two schools were built (one for boys, one for girls), originally just for the children of Moravian Brethren, but they are now a fee-paying school.

Take the time to explore this evocative place and perhaps visit the museum (open Wednesday and Saturday afternoons), which explains the history of the Moravian Church and this unique Yorkshire outpost.

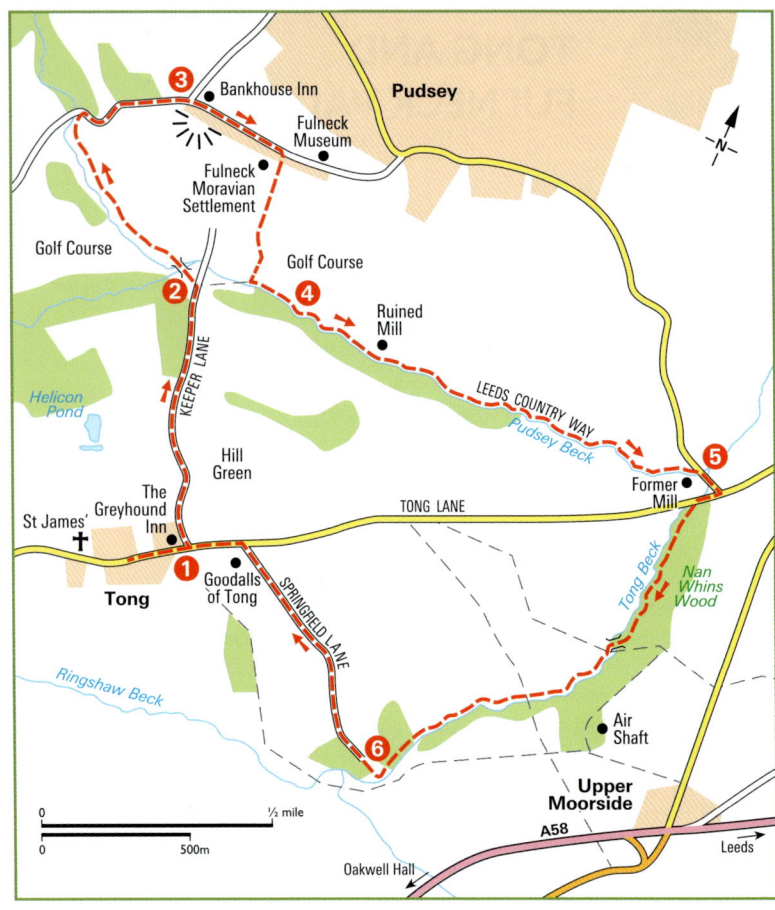

1. From the village hall, walk down past The Greyhound pub and turn left into Keeper Lane. Becoming a track beyond a gate, it wends downhill to a footbridge below a confluence of streams.

2. Cross and, ignoring the track ahead, swing left on the Leeds Country Way with the main beck on your left. Exiting a wood, keep ahead across a field. Leaving over a stile, turn sharp right up a path away from a bridge. Meeting a track, follow it right and later on, right again to come out on the bend of a lane opposite the Bankhouse Inn.

3. Follow the road right past 20th-century housing into the Fulneck Moravian settlement, where the fine Georgian buildings command superb views across the valley. Just past No 54 Tearooms and Antiques turn right beside the main school building, following a sign to Fulneck Golf Course. Keep right again but, passing the corner of the Robinson Building, watch for a stepped path leaving on the left. It heralds a delightful sunken lane that drops steeply within a dense line of trees across the golf course. Emerging at the bottom, cross a fairway to rejoin Pudsey Beck. Follow it left.

4. Leaving the golf course, keep going over stiles to a ruined mill. Dog-legging

right and left, the path continues through a succession of fields and scrubland, straightening the course set by the accompanying squiggling beck. Finally, a walled path brings you out on to a lane.

5. Go right, past a converted mill, to a T-junction. Cross the main road and take a waymarked footpath between gateposts into Sykes' Wood. Immediately bear right, through a gap (signed 'Leeds Country Way'). Follow the path downhill, soon with Tong Beck. After walking about 0.5 miles (800m) through woodland, take a footbridge over the beck and bear left by the boundary up to a kissing gate. Follow a path along the edge of a field, then through woodland. Keep left, when the path eventually forks to a gate. Ignoring side paths, remain on this bank of the stream until you reach a kissing gate.

6. Through that, turn away from the river along a rising track, Springfield Lane. When you meet a road, go left past Goodalls of Tong to arrive back in Tong village.

Where to eat and drink
The Greyhound Inn, in Tong, is a comfortable village inn with its own cricket pitch. The 17th-century building has beamed ceilings and a fine collection of antique toby jugs. Alternatively, stop at the Bankhouse, on the approach to the Moravian Settlement at Fulneck. It's a traditional country pub serving classic homemade food daily. They are a dog-friendly venue and have a large garden with stunning views.

What to look out for
Many of the footpaths in the area follow old packhorse routes: some are secluded sunken lanes, others still have their lines of causeway stones (paving slabs) intact. They offer good walking, even in wet weather.

While you're there
Immediately over the M62, you will find Oakwell Hall, dating from 1583. It is a splendid merchant clothier's house, built in the 'Halifax' style reminiscent of East Riddlesden Hall. Remarkably, the interior of the house has undergone only minor changes, and retains many of its original Elizabethan features – not least the heavy oak panelling.

BURLEY IN WHARFEDALE

DISTANCE/TIME	5 miles (8km) / 2hrs 15min
ASCENT/GRADIENT	966ft (294m) / ▲▲
PATHS	Good tracks and moorland paths, several stiles
LANDSCAPE	Moor and arable farmland
SUGGESTED MAP	OS Explorer 297 Lower Wharfedale & Washburn Valley
START/FINISH	Grid reference: SE163458
DOG FRIENDLINESS	On leads around grazing sheep
PARKING	Roadside parking near station
PUBLIC TOILETS	None on route

According to the legend, a giant called Rombald used to live in these parts. While striding across the moor that now bears his name he dislodged a stone from a gritstone outcrop, and created the Calf, of the Cow and Calf Rocks on Ilkley Moor. Giants such as Rombald and Wade – and even the Devil himself – were apparently busy all over Yorkshire, dropping stones or creating big holes in the ground. It was perhaps an appealing way to explain the more unusual features of the landscape. Rombalds Moor is pitted with old quarries, from which good quality stone was won.

At Burley Woodhead, a pub called The Hermit commemorates the life of Job Senior, born in 1780. Job worked as a farm labourer, before succumbing to the demon drink. He met an elderly widow of independent means, who lived in a cottage at Coldstone Beck, on the edge of Rombalds Moor. Thinking he might get his hands on her money and home, Job married her. Though she died soon after, Job took no profit. The family of her first husband pulled the cottage down, in Job's absence, leaving him homeless and penniless once more. Enraged, he built himself a tiny hovel from the ruins of the house. He must have cut a strange figure, with a coat of multicoloured patches and trousers held up with twine. He had long, lank hair, a matted beard and his legs were bandaged with straw. He made slow, rheumatic progress around Rombalds Moor with the aid of two crooked sticks.

His eccentric lifestyle soon had people flocking to see him. He offered weather predictions, and even advised visitors about their love lives. The possessor of a remarkable voice, he 'sang for his supper' as he lay on his bed of dried bracken and heather. These impromptu performances encouraged Job to sing in nearby villages, and even in the theatres of Leeds and Bradford. His speciality was sacred songs, which he would deliver with great feeling. Nevertheless, accommodation was never forthcoming, forcing him to bed down in barns or outhouses. It was while staying in a barn that he was struck down with cholera. He was taken to Carlton Workhouse, where he died in 1857, aged 77. He is buried in the churchyard of Burley in Wharfedale.

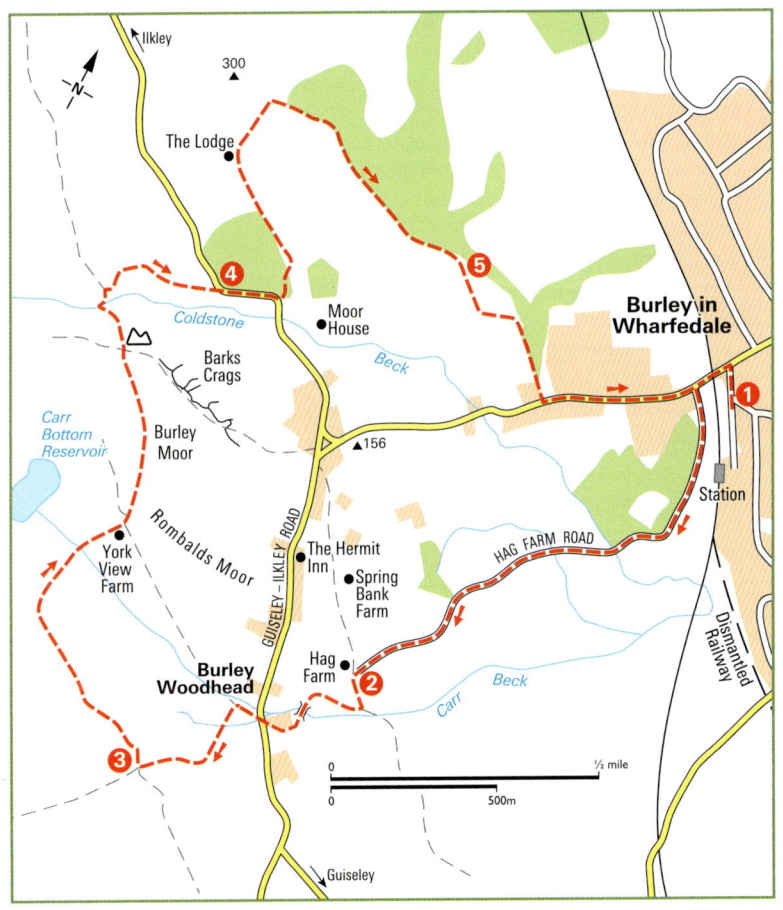

1. From the station, walk back to Station Road, turn left to cross underneath the line and go left along a quiet lane. Follow the lane past houses and between fields up to Hag Farm.

2. When the track wheels right, into the farmyard, keep left on a track to a stile and a gate. Follow a wall downhill for 100yds (91m) to a gap stile in the wall. Don't pass through, but turn right, climbing beside a stream up to a stile. Carry on uphill, crossing two more stiles and then a footbridge across the stream. Continue up to cottages, winding out between them to meet the Guiseley–Ilkley road. (To visit The Hermit Inn, go right here for 0.25 miles/400m.) Cross the road and continue on a stony track opposite. After 50yds (46m), leave left to ford a stream. Follow a path uphill through trees and then between walls to a gate. Turn right beside the wall, which soon curves away, leaving you heading upwards on a rough footpath.

3. Meet a stony track and follow it to the right, along the moorland edge. Follow a wall to a stile by a gate. Immediately after, keep right when the track forks. Keep to the right again as you approach a small brick building. Route-finding is now easy, as the track wheels around a farm. At the next farm (called York View because on a clear day, you can see York Minster from here), branch left off the main track, gradually descending by a wall on your right. As you approach a third farm, look out for two barns and a gate, on the right. They stand opposite an indistinct path to the left, which curves around a small quarry. Now enjoy some level walking through bracken with great views over Lower Wharfedale. After 0.25 miles (400m), drop into a narrow ravine to cross Coldstone Beck. As you climb away, bear right and follow a path downhill to meet a road by a sharp bend.

4. Walk 100yds (91m) down the road to another sharp bend. Turn off along Stead Lane, a stony track that leads past several houses, to continue between the fields beyond. After passing a wooden chalet, leave the track as it swings left towards a farm, dropping through a kissing gate to the right. Walk away beside the wood on your left. Beyond another kissing gate, keep by the right-hand boundary, leaving at the far side to follow a fenced path ahead.

5. Reaching a track, go right, but after 200yds (183m), bear off left along a path which leads to a second track within trees. Follow it right to the road and turn left back to the station.

Where to eat and drink
The Hermit Inn is a welcoming stone-built pub in Burley Woodhead. During the walk it is easy to make a short detour to the inn, with its views of Wharfedale. Alternatively, the village of Burley boasts a number of places to get a bite to eat.

What to see
Rombalds Moor is home to red grouse. Grouse take off from their heather hiding places with heart-stopping suddenness, with their unmistakable and evocative cry of 'go back, go back, go back'. The moorland habitat is carefully managed to maintain a supply of young heather for the grouse to nest and feed in as grouse shooting is a lucrative business.

While you're there
Ilkley's parish church, which can trace its origins to the 7th century, contains three beautiful Anglo-Saxon crosses. It occupies the site of a Roman fort overlooking the River Wharfe and, although only a short stretch of wall remains visible, many of the artefacts discovered during excavations can be seen in the nearby Ilkley Manor House. Other exhibits describe the prehistoric art scattered across the surrounding hillsides and explore Ilkley's growth as a spa town.

AROUND FARNLEY TYAS

DISTANCE/TIME	5.4 miles (8.7km) / 2hrs
ASCENT/GRADIENT	804ft (245m) / ▲▲
PATHS	Field paths, a little road walking on quiet lanes, many stiles
LANDSCAPE	Arable, rolling countryside and woodland
SUGGESTED MAP	OS Explorer 288 Bradford & Huddersfield
START/FINISH	Grid reference: SE162125
DOG FRIENDLINESS	Keep on lead near roads
PARKING	Roadside parking in Farnley Tyas by recreation ground
PUBLIC TOILETS	None on route

Despite its proximity to Huddersfield, the area to the south of the town is surprisingly rural. Farnley Tyas and the fortification of Castle Hill face each other across the valley, and across the centuries. The village was mentioned in the Domesday Book, as 'Fereleia', but the history of Castle Hill extends at least 4,000 years.

The site was inhabited by neolithic settlers who defended it with earth ramparts. Axe heads and other flint tools dating from this era are now displayed in Huddersfield's Tolson Museum. They were just the first of many peoples who saw the hill's defensive potential. Its position, with uninterrupted views on all sides, made it an ideal place for a fortification. The de Lacy family built a motte-and-bailey castle here, having been given land as a reward for their part in the Norman Conquest. Though the structure was demolished in the 14th century, the site has been known ever since as Castle Hill. In the 16th century, it was used as a beacon site, one of a chain to warn of the Spanish Armada. During the 18th and 19th centuries, the Hill was used for cock fighting, bull baiting, bare-knuckle fighting, political rallies and religious meetings. The building that can be seen today is a Jubilee Tower built in 1898 to commemorate 60 years of Queen Victoria's reign. The tower rises 106ft (32m) above the hill's plateau, and dominates the skyline. It is open during summer weekends and school holidays, when you can climb the 165 steps inside and enjoy the panoramic views from the top.

The village of Farnley Tyas gained its double-barrelled moniker to differentiate it from other Farnleys – one near Leeds, the other near Otley. The 'Tyas' suffix is the name of the area's most prominent family, who owned land here from the 13th century onwards.

Originally a farm, the Golden Cock pub has been here since the 17th century. During the 19th-century, a group called the Royal Corkers used to ride over from Huddersfield to enjoy supper here. Corks were placed on the dining table, with the last person to pick up a cork having to pay for supper for the whole party.

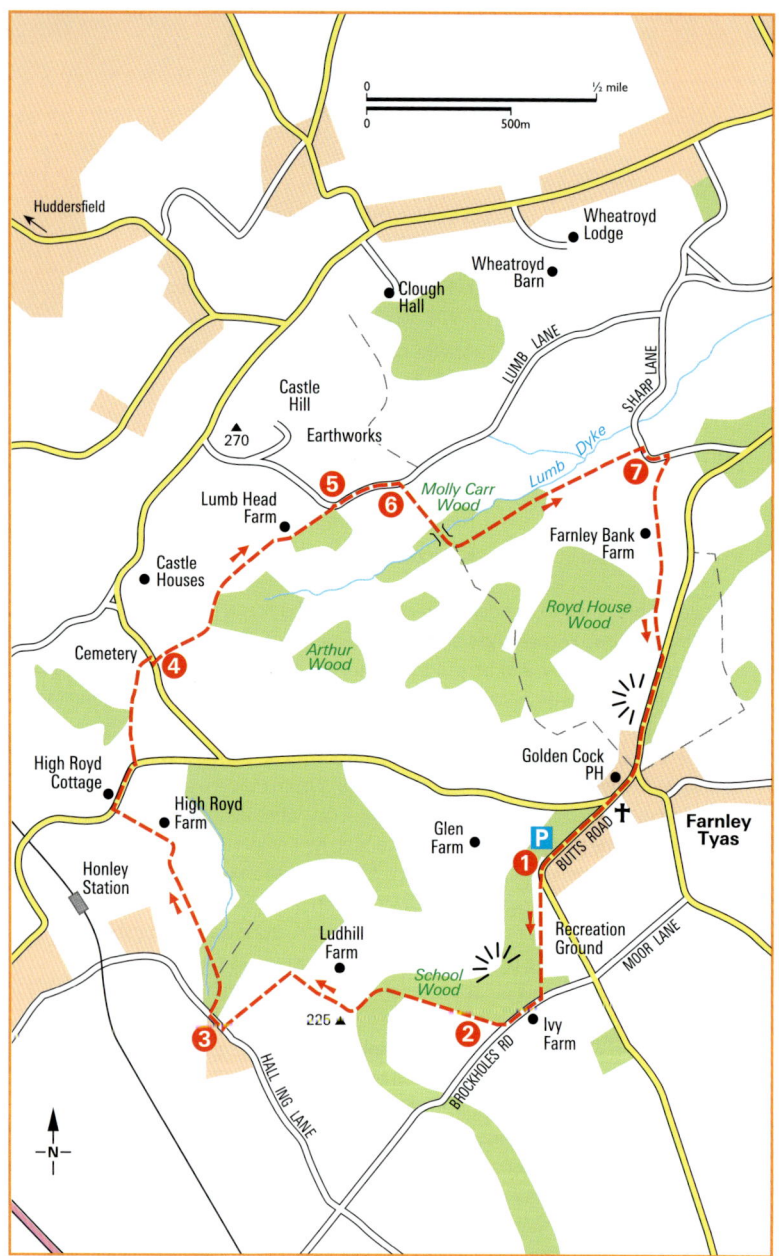

1. Enter the recreation ground and walk away past a play area by the right wall. Beyond a second field, follow a walled track out to meet a road. Go right along Brockholes Road.

2. After 100yds (91m), turn right down a walled track, with School Wood to your right. Leaving the trees, there is a view of Castle Hill ahead and beyond to Huddersfield. When the track bends right for the second time, towards Ludhill

Farm, go straight on along a walled path. Walk downhill to cross a stile next to a metal gate, turn left across a field to another stile, and bear right, descending more steeply through scrub. The way then bends left down to meet Hall Ing Road.

3. Go right, then just after the terrace of cottages, turn right on a track into woodland. Some 50yds (46m) beyond a gate, bear left onto a narrow path that descends to a stile. Continue across a field, aiming towards a house on the opposite hillside. Cross a stream on stepping stones and walk up through a spur of woodland. Climb another field into the top corner, just left of a house. A path leads to a drive, which climbs left to meet a road opposite High Royd Cottage. Turn right for 100yds (91m), then take a gap stile by a gate in the left wall, a path leads to a gate. Passing through, bear right uphill along the edge of a small plantation. Beyond a squeeze stile in the corner, head diagonally across another small field. Keep beside the left hedge of the next field, until you meet a road by the cemetery.

4. Go right here for just 20yds (18m), turning left by a broken gate. Go along the field-edge path, later through a waymarked gap to continue, with the wall on your right, towards a wood. Over a stile, keep to the edge of the next field, with a little wooded valley on your right. Leaving the wood behind, head onwards to Lumb Head Farm. Wind through the farmyard and join the access track to meet a road.

5. Walk left for 300m (330yds) then turn sharp right, signed to a car park, and go up to the top of Castle Hill. Follow a path around the ramparts, then at the far northwest end drop down to the left. After 50yds (46m), fork right. Continue along a track towards Clough Hall, after the woods take the path on the right and follow it around to the right. At a junction of paths turn left, then right on Lumb Lane, then left over a stile towards Molly Carr Wood.

6. Walk down into the valley, following the wall on your right. Cross a stile and cross a meandering stream, Lumb Dike, on a plank bridge. Climb away to a redundant stile and then turn left to follow the stream, but at a higher level, through Molly Carr Wood. Descend to where two streams meet and follow the combined watercourse along the valley bottom. After crossing a side beck walk on, rising to join a grass track that leads to a gate. However, bypass the gate and continue to a stone stile just beyond. Over that, bear left on a rough track passing behind a farmhouse. It leads around to the far end of the yard, from which a track takes you out to the road.

7. Go right, uphill. After 75yds (69m), take a waymarked track sharply to the right, signed to Farnley Bank. Pass a house and when the track drops right to Farnley Bank Farm, take a stile ahead, and follow a field path uphill. Meet a road, and walk right, back into Farnley Tyas. At a T-junction, by the Golden Cock pub, turn right, then fork left by the church on to Butts Road to return to your car.

Where to eat and drink
With three real ales on tap, an interesting selection of dishes offered on the menu and an ever-changing specials board, the Golden Cock in Farnley Tyas makes a perfect spot at which to finish the day.

HOLME AND THE RESERVOIRS

DISTANCE/TIME	3.25 miles (5.3km) / 1hr 20min
ASCENT/GRADIENT	550ft (168m) / ▲▲
PATHS	Mostly good reservoir tracks with one short muddy section, several stiles
LANDSCAPE	Wooded valley sides, open pasture and reservoirs
SUGGESTED MAP	OS Explorers 288 Bradford & Huddersfield or OL1 The Peak District (Dark Peak area)
START/FINISH	Grid reference: SE115056
DOG FRIENDLINESS	Dogs can be off-lead much of the way but should be on lead around livestock
PARKING	Car park at end of Brownhill Lane, south of Holmbridge
PUBLIC TOILETS	In Holme village, opposite the Fleece Inn

You don't have to drive all the way to Cumbria to enjoy a landscape of large water features. At the head of the Holme Valley, Kirklees has its own Lake District in miniature. To the south of Holmbridge, four reservoirs occupy an area of less than 1.5 square miles (4sq km). They were built over a period of 54 years: Yateholme was the first, in 1878, while Brownhill, closest to the village, was completed in 1932. The other two, Riding Wood and Ramsden, were completed in 1883 and 1892 respectively.

The dams lie across several streams, the names of some of which – Gusset Dike and Boggery Dike – give a clue to the nature of the ground. Fortunately, most of the walk follows a good track and only on one section are you likely to encounter boggy terrain. Those streams drain the highest ground in West Yorkshire. The imposing moorland slopes that rise ahead of you as you pass Yateholme Reservoir are those of Holme Moss, the flanks of Black Hill, the notoriously boggy summit of which is 1,909ft (582m) above sea level. Its peat hags and mires were long feared by Pennine Way walkers until the worst sections of Britain's first National Trail were improved by the laying of stone flags, imported from demolished cotton mills, across the peat.

The reservoirs' waters flow out towards Holmbridge, where they join with those of Marsden Clough to become the River Holme, which flows through the valley to meet the Colne near Huddersfield town centre.

Although not technically on the route, you can't miss the radio transmitter on Holme Moss, standing at 750ft (228m). Coupled with its altitude of 1,719ft (524m) above sea level, that makes it one of the highest in the country – so high that the television signal it used to transmit could be received on the Isle of Man and in Dublin. Today, it broadcasts signals for a number of digital and analogue BBC radio stations, as its TV duties having been adopted by the Emley Moor transmitter.

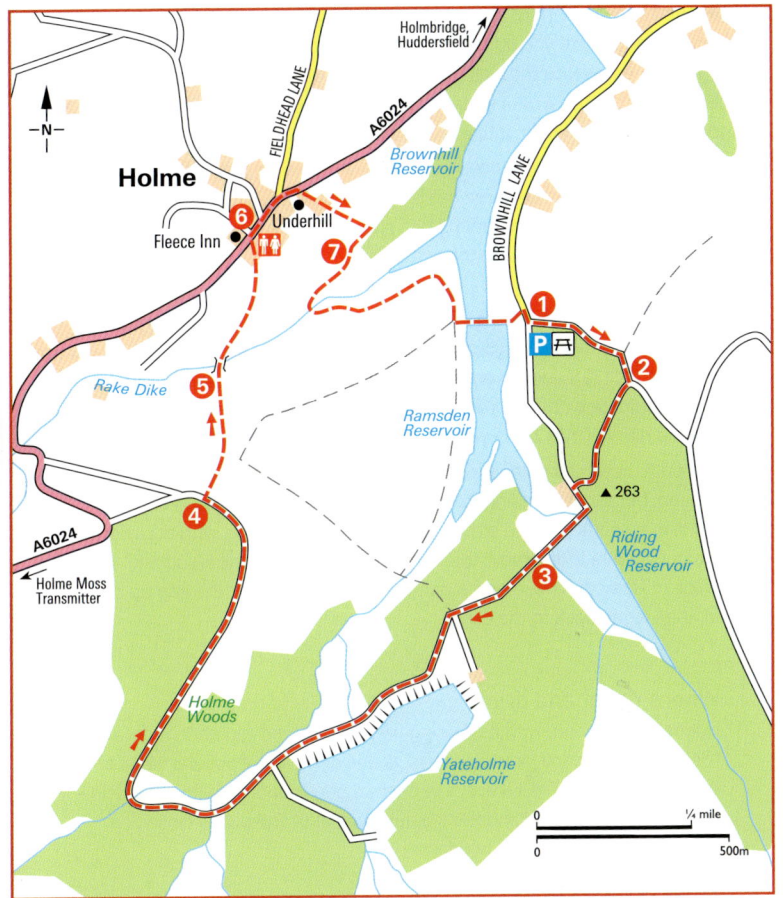

1. Walk through the picnic area next to the car park and cross the stile into a lane. After climbing for 80yds (73m), pass between stone gate posts and swing right, on a grassy track and over a stream, past a conifer plantation. Continue uphill on a wide track, which re-crosses the stream, to a junction. Waymarked trails continue ahead and left here; your way, however, turns right, between wooden posts. After 90yds (82m), you come to a junction with a well-defined rough track.

2. Turn right, downhill, into the conifers, occasionally glimpsing Ramsden Reservoir through the trees. After 300yds (274m), the track reaches a junction, by an isolated house. Turn left to cross the dam wall of Riding Wood Reservoir, high above Ramsden Reservoir on your right, with views across to the village of Holme.

3. Continue along the track beyond the dam, past the huge retaining walls of Yateholme Reservoir. Although this track is very quiet and rarely used, be aware that timber-hauling lorries and machinery might occasionally come this way. After crossing several streams the track crosses to the opposite side of the clough, gently climbing to offer fine views down the Holme Valley.

4. About 1.3 miles (2.1km) after crossing Riding Wood Reservoir, a public footpath sign directs you off the track right, over a wooden step stile down a boggy field, parallel to the wall 20yds (18m) to the right: scout around for the driest ground. Cross a dilapidated wall after 140yds (128m) and turn left along it to cross a wooden stile, into oak and birch woodland and down stone steps.

5. Cross Rake Dike on a wooden footbridge. An obvious path slants right, up the opposite bank, climbs three fields and passes through a gate into a garden, and out the other side through a gated stile. Ascend a driveway to emerge on a road opposite Holme's Fleece Inn.

6. Turn right, past the public toilets and an old phone box, now an information booth. Just 65yds (60m) past Holme Sunday School, turn right on a public footpath, past Underhill to your right. Beyond a narrow metal gate, the path drops along the left edge of a field, passing through a wooden gate half-way down to continue within an enclosed path. Beyond a stone step stile, turn right through a narrow gap in the wall to drop diagonally down the next field.

7. The path, beyond a stile at the bottom, follows the wall on the right, above woodland, before descending to cross Rake Dike above a small waterfall. Beyond, it ascends a rough stone path back to the treeline, with occasional views of Brownhill Reservoir, then drops again through the woodland. Cross the face of Ramsden Reservoir's dam wall and bear left at the end up to the road, then right, back to the car park.

Where to eat and drink

Holme's Fleece Inn, with its roaring fire, real ale and reputation for family-friendly lunches and evening meals, is one of the most popular pubs in the Holme Valley. The Fleece now offers a dog-friendly dining area inside the pub and a covered and heated outdoor patio. The pub is closed on Mondays, except for bank holidays.

What to look out for

Underhill in Holme, passed as you leave the village, was Britain's first underground house. Architect Arthur Quarmby, who also designed the underground Rheged Visitor Centre, near Penrith in Cumbria, built it for his family in the 1970s. Behind its Hobbit-like circular wooden door is a spacious home, complete with music room and swimming pool. The earth-sheltered building is insulated by the soil and plants above.

YORKSHIRE SCULPTURE PARK AND BRETTON HALL

DISTANCE/TIME	3 miles (4.8km) / 1hr 15min
ASCENT/GRADIENT	279ft (85m) / ▲
PATHS	Good paths and tracks all the way
LANDSCAPE	Pasture, fields and parkland
SUGGESTED MAP	OS Explorer 278 Sheffield & Barnsley
START/FINISH	Grid reference: SE294125
DOG FRIENDLINESS	Dogs can enter the YSP but must be on leads and stick to dog-walking routes. Dogs not allowed in the galleries spaces, Menagerie Wood or around Upper Lake
PARKING	The Weston entrance car park, beside A637 near M1 junction 38
PUBLIC TOILETS	At car park and at the Sculpture Park
NOTES	An entrance fee must be paid to enter the YSP to walk this route

The Yorkshire Sculpture Park (YSP) was established back in 1977, which makes it the first such venture in the UK. Exhibitions of contemporary art are displayed in 500 acres (202ha) of Bretton Estate and four galleries, providing a changing programme of exhibitions, displays and projects.

This extraordinary 'art gallery without walls' is home to works by Dame Barbara Hepworth, who was from Wakefield, and sculptures by Henry Moore. Born in Castleford, Moore began his artistic career at Leeds School of Art and remained close to his Yorkshire roots, whilst his reputation was international. He was a pioneer of outdoor sculpture, often creating works with particular landscape locations in mind, where they would be encountered by people who might not otherwise visit a gallery. So it seems fitting that a dozen of Moore's monumental bronze figures have found a permanent home here.

For more than half a millennium, the Bretton estate had been held by just three families, the Dronsfields, Wentworths and Beaumonts, passing from one to the next by marriage. It was Sir William Wentworth who demolished the medieval hall and chapel in 1720 to make way for a fine new mansion in the grand Palladian style, a design inspired by memories of the classical cities of Europe visited during his Grand Tour. He sited his house on the hillside to take advantage of the views across the valley of the River Dearne and his son Sir Thomas continued his vision by landscaping the park and creating the lakes, which remain outstanding features of the estate. The long line of tenure finally came to an end when it was sold to West Riding County Council after the war in 1947. The hall then became Bretton Hall College for a time, but is now being converted into a hotel.

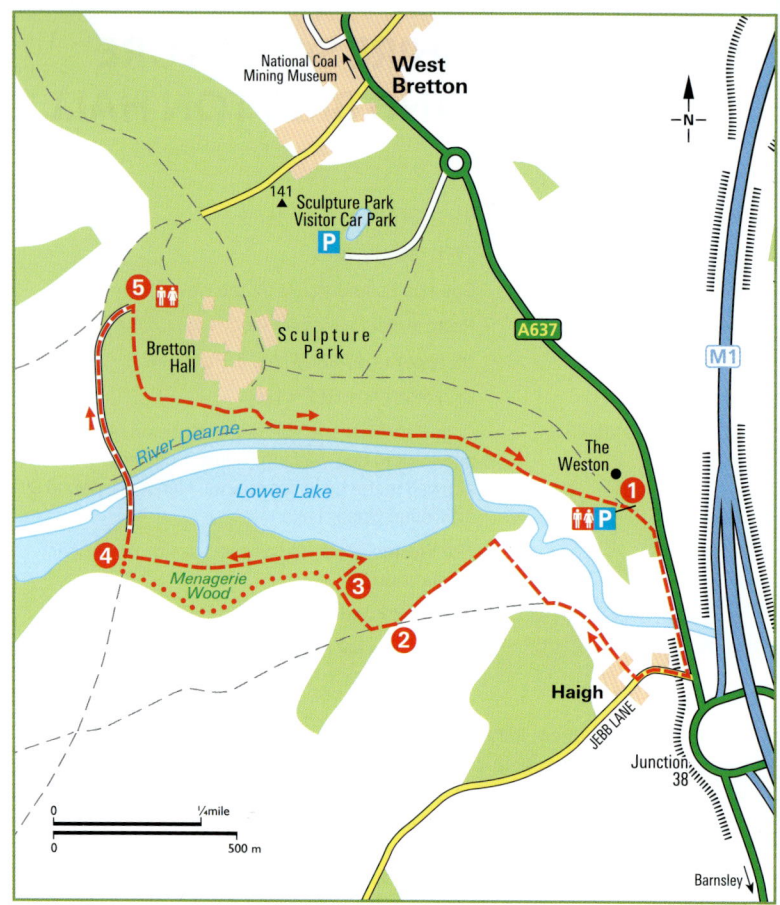

1. Be sure to have paid the entrance fees to YSP and then from the car park, rejoin the main road and walk right along the footpath for 200yds (182m) before going right again into Jebb Lane. Follow it past some cottages and around a bend, shortly turning off just before a barn on the right onto a track. Through a kissing gate at the end, head out across a field, closing with a wood on the left. Beyond the trees, cross a stile by a gate and continue right, along the other flank of the fence towards more trees. Swing left at the field corner and climb beside the boundary to reach an opening into the estate.

2. Bear right through a gap in the wall to a fork in the path. Take the right branch, signed as a footpath, which descends gently into woodland. Breaking cover, fork right and continue down to a second junction. Ignore the path off left, but at a fork a few paces further on, keep right into more trees and another junction.

3. Those with dogs must go left on a path skirting the perimeter of Menagerie Wood. At the far end, pass through a field gate and walk forward to a track. Turn right through wrought iron gates into the park. Without a dog, you can take the right path, which, after crossing a sunken fence, winds through trees to a junction by the lake. Turn left through a gate and continue through the woods, where highland cattle freely roam. There are occasional views across the lake to Bretton Hall. The track runs beyond the lake, leaving through a gate. Turn right along the main drive away from the wrought iron gates.

4. Follow the drive over two bridges to more wrought iron gates, passing through to continue gently uphill alongside the perimeter fence. Keep ahead as a path joins from the left, but at a fork just beyond, bear right beside a field gate and continue up to emerge at the edge of a car park. The café at YSP Learning is just ahead, but the main complex lies a little further on.

5. There are any number of routes you might take through the Sculpture Park to explore the art, one being a bowered path that drops from the bottom of the car park, near the point at which you first entered. Meeting a crossing path, go left towards the hall. At the next junction, swing right towards the river and lake. However, just before reaching a bridge turn left through a gate to parallel the river at the edge of the open park. Through another gate, keep ahead past the foot of the lake and through more parkland. Eventually joining a drive, follow it right back to the Weston car park.

Where to eat and drink
There are several choices within the YSP, including The Kitchen at YSP Centre, The Restaurant at The Weston (at the start of the walk) and the Café at YSP.

What to look out for
Be sure to pick up a map of the YSP, which locates all the outdoor works and those within the galleries. There are also two great shops to visit.

While you're there
Take a trip to the National Coal Mining Museum for England, on the A642 halfway between Wakefield and Huddersfield. When the coal seams at the Caphouse Colliery were exhausted, during the mid-1980s, the site was converted into a museum. Visitors can explore the oldest coal mine shaft still in everyday use in Britain today, and learn about an industry which already seems to belong to our nation's past. Local miners are now guides through the workings, taking you 450ft (137m) below ground. There are also pit ponies, rides on the miners' train and a licensed café and shop.

HOLMFIRTH AND THE HOLME VALLEY

DISTANCE/TIME	4.5 miles (7.2km) / 2hrs 30min
ASCENT/GRADIENT	800ft (244m) / ▲
PATHS	Good paths and tracks, several stiles
LANDSCAPE	Upland pasture
SUGGESTED MAP	OS Explorer 288 Bradford & Huddersfield
START/FINISH	Grid reference: SE143084
DOG FRIENDLINESS	On lead in fields with livestock, off on lanes
PARKING	Crown Bottom car park on Market Street or Sands Lane long stay car park
PUBLIC TOILETS	At Sands Lane long stay car park

Holmfirth and the Holme Valley have been popularised as 'Summer Wine Country', forever linked to the whimsical TV series *Last of the Summer Wine*, written by Roy Clarke and starring a trio of incorrigible old buffers, Compo, Foggy and Clegg. The cast were familiar faces in the town until the series ended in 2010 after running for 37 years. When Londoner Bill Owen (lovable rogue Compo) died in 1999 at the age of 85, he was laid to rest overlooking the little town he had grown to call home. Visitors come to Holmfirth in their droves, in search of film locations such as Sid's Café and Nora Batty's house. But Holmfirth takes its TV fame in its stride, for this isn't the first time that the town has starred in front of the cameras. In fact, Holmfirth very nearly became another Hollywood. Bamforths, better known for its naughty seaside postcards, began to make short films here in the early years of the last century. They were exported around the world to popular demand. Local people were drafted in as extras in Bamforths' overwrought dramas. Film production came to an end at the outbreak of World War I and was never resumed.

Holmfirth town, much more than just a film set, is the real star along with the fine South Pennine scenery that surrounds it. By the time you have completed half of this walk, you are a mile (1.6km) from the Peaks National Park. The town grew rapidly with the textile trades, creating a tight-knit community in the valley bottom: a maze of ginnels, alleyways and narrow lanes. The River Holme, which runs through its middle, has flooded on many occasions, but the most devastating flood occurred back in 1852, when, after heavy rain, Bilberry Reservoir burst its banks. The resulting torrent of water destroyed the centre of Holmfirth and claimed 81 lives.

In more recent times, Holmfirth has become something of a hub for road cyclists. The Tour de France Grand Départ passed through here in 2014 on its way up the infamous Holme Moss. Subsequent Tour de Yorkshire routes (a legacy of the Grand Départ) have passed through the town, drawing huge crowds to cheer on the cyclists.

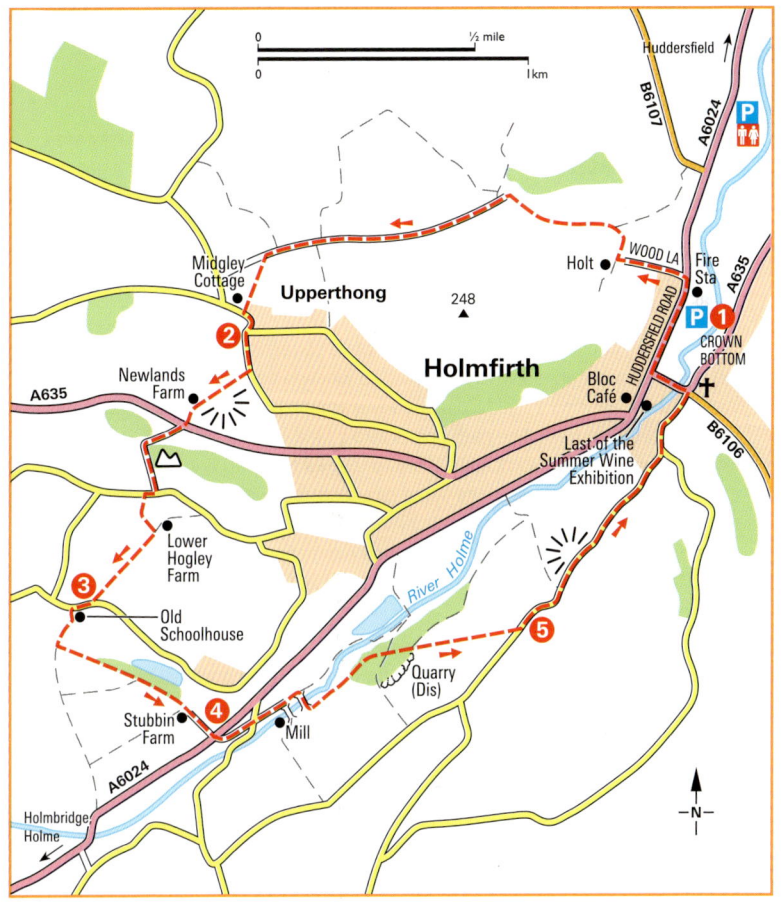

1. From Crown Bottom car park, walk to the right along Huddersfield Road for only 100yds (91m) before bearing left just after the fire station, up Wood Lane. The road soon narrows to a steep track. Keep left of a house and through a gate, to continue on a walled path. At the top of the hill, by a bench, follow the road to the right, leading to a track. Follow this track, soon enclosed, as it wheels left, down into a valley. Soon after you approach woodland, you have a choice of tracks: keep left on the walled path, uphill. When it eventually joins a stone farm track, turn left and after about 50yds (46m), climb steps on the left to cross a stile. Immediately afterwards, go through a swing gate and across a field path to another gate. Walk on an enclosed path to a track. Turn left to join another enclosed path before emerging on a road by Midgley Cottage. Turn left and follow the road as it bends through the top of the village.

2. Continue along the road, which wheels round to the right. Walk downhill, with great views opening up of the Holme Valley. After 150yds (137m) on the road, take a cinder track on the right. Walk down to meet a road. Cross over and take the tarmac lane ahead, steeply down into a little valley and up the other side. When this minor road forks at the top, go right, uphill. Immediately after the first house, go left on a gravel track. Follow this track to Lower

Hogley Farm, where you keep right, past a knot of houses, to a gate and stile. Cross this on to a field path, with a wall to your left. Go through four fields, aiming for the mast on the horizon, and descend to the road.

3. Go right for just 50yds (46m) to bear left around a path. Follow the walled footpath downhill, through a gate; as the footpath opens out into a grassy area, bear left on a grass track down into the valley. Go over a stile next to a gate, following an enclosed path above woodland. On approaching houses, cross a stile and join a metalled track at a fork. Bear right here, then immediately left, on a narrow footpath between houses. Follow a field path, keeping right at a fork to go through a gate; pass houses and continue downhill past Stubbin Farm to meet the main A6024 road.

4. Cross the road, then, by a row of diminutive cottages, take Old Road to the left. Keep straight ahead when you reach a junction between houses, down Water Street. Beyond a mill, cross the River Holme on a metal footbridge and follow a riverside path. The path opens into a field; approximately 20yds (18m) later, fork right over duckboards. Keep to the right (uphill) and cross a stile to enter woodland. Continue in the same direction, following the uphill fork to the right until you reach some steps to the right. Go down the steps and turn right and immediately left, continuing in the same direction (uphill) to emerge at a field. Cross two fields and join a track by a house. Pass some more cottages to meet a road.

5. Go left, along the road. Enjoy fine views down into the Holme Valley as you descend to a junction. Turn left and continue on the long downhill road back into Holmfirth.

Where to eat and drink
With so many visitors, Holmfirth is well supplied with pubs and tea shops, where you can stop for refreshments. Bloc Café serves a brunch-style menu of toasty treats and is located opposite the gallery of famous Yorkshire artist Ashley Jackson.

What to see
Holmfirth seems to have grown without much help from town planners. It is an intriguing maze of ginnels, stone steps and small cobbled alleyways, rising up between gritstone houses. After a few minutes' climb you will be rewarded with a view over the roofscape of the town. A *Last of the Summer Wine* exhibition is located on Scarfold, near the River Holme.

While you're there
If you drive through Holmfirth on the A6024, you pass Holmbridge, then Holme, before the Holme Valley comes to a dramatic end, surrounded by a huge sweep of rugged moorland and splendid views. As you climb steeply to the height of Holme Moss, topped with a television mast, you enter the Peak District National Park. The area also boasts a vineyard, situated on the hills above Holmbridge.

A CIRCUIT OF ADDINGHAM AND ILKLEY

DISTANCE/TIME	5.5 miles (8.8km) / 2hrs
ASCENT/GRADIENT	527ft (160m) / ▲
PATHS	Riverside path and field paths, some road walking, several stiles
LANDSCAPE	Rolling country and the River Wharfe
SUGGESTED MAP	OS Explorer 297 Lower Wharfedale & Washburn Valley
START/FINISH	Grid reference: SE083498
DOG FRIENDLINESS	On lead near livestock and farms
PARKING	Lay-by at eastern end of Addingham, on bend where North Street becomes Bark Lane by information panel
PUBLIC TOILETS	On riverside near footbridge in Ilkley

Addingham's houses extend for a mile (1.6km) on either side of the main street, with St Peter's Church at the eastern end of the village. So it's no surprise that the village used to be known as 'Long Addingham', and that it combines three separate communities that grew as the textile trades expanded at the end of the 17th century. Within 50 years, Addingham's population quadrupled, from 500 to 2,000. At the height of the boom, there were six woollen mills in the village. Low Mill, built in 1787, was the scene of a riot by a band of Luddites – weavers and shearers who objected to their jobs being done by machines. Though the mill itself was demolished in 1972, more houses were added to the mill-hands' cottages to create Low Mill Village, a pleasant riverside community.

Ilkley is a town that seems to have more in common with Harrogate than with the textile towns of West Yorkshire. The Romans established an important fort here – believed to be Olicana –on a site close to where the parish church is today. Two Roman altars were incorporated into the base of the church tower, and taken into the church for safekeeping are three Anglo-Saxon crosses from the 8th or 9th centuries. One of the few tangible remains of the Roman settlement is a short stretch of wall near the handsome Manor House, which is now a museum.

Like nearby Harrogate, Ilkley's commercial fortunes changed with the discovery of medicinal springs. During the reign of Queen Victoria, the great and the good would come here to 'take the waters' and socialise at the town's hydros and hotels. Visitor numbers increased with the coming of the railway, and, with its open-air swimming pool and riverside promenades, Ilkley was almost an inland resort. Ilkley remains a prosperous town, unashamedly dedicated to the good things of life.

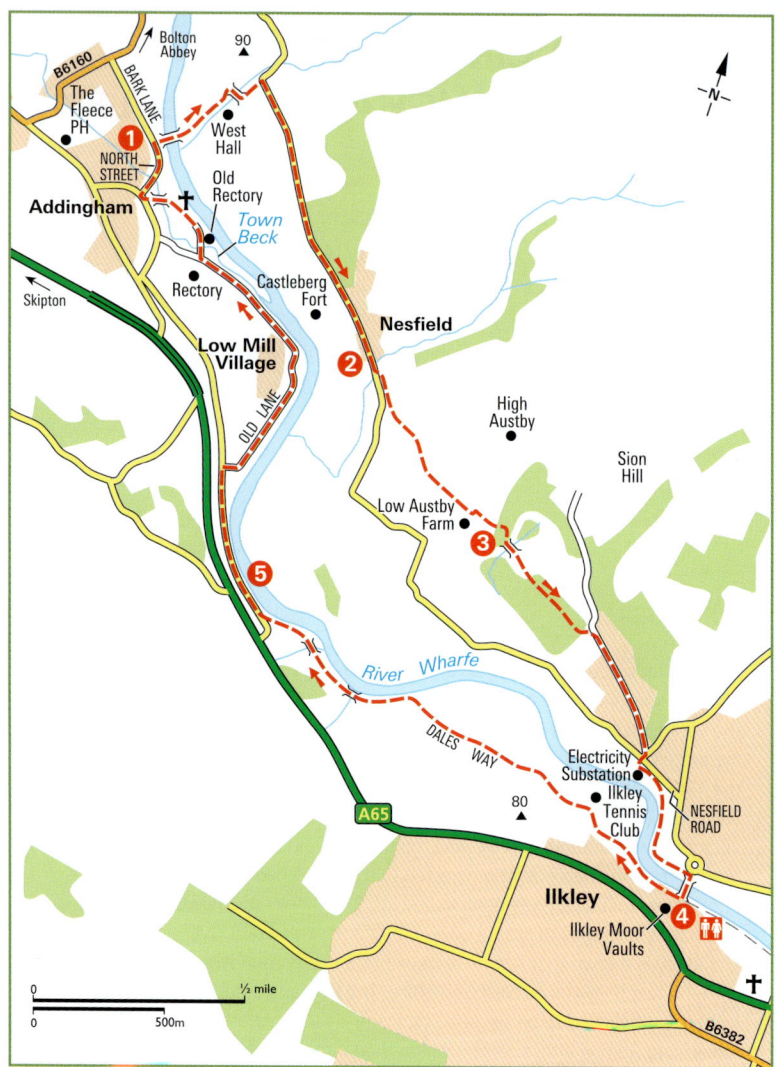

1. Walk 50yds (46m) up the road, and take stone steps down to the right, (signed 'Dales Way'). Turn immediately right again, dropping to cross the River Wharfe on a suspension bridge. Follow a metalled path along a field edge. Turn over a stream at the end and follow a farm track left to emerge on the bend of a minor road. Go right here; after about 0.5 miles (800m) of road walking, you reach the little community of Nesfield.

2. About 100yds (91m) beyond the last house and, immediately after the road crosses a stream, bear left up a stony track (signed as a footpath to High Austby). Immediately take a stile between two gates. Cross to the gate in the far-right corner. Through it there is no obvious path, but follow the boundary on your right, heading in the direction of Low Austby Farm. Carry on in the final field past the farm, bearing slightly left beneath a gnarled oak towards the wood ahead.

3. Cross a footbridge over a stream; beyond a stile you enter woodland. Follow a path downhill, leaving the wood by another step stile. Bear right across the slope of a field to a stile at the far end, to enter more woodland. Follow an obvious path through the trees, before reaching a road via a wall stile. Go right, downhill, until you reach a road junction. Go right again, cross Nesfield Road, and take a path to the left of an electricity substation. Leading to the river, it accompanies the wooded bank to Ilkley's old stone bridge. Cross to the south side.

4. To explore the town, go left by the river through the park. Swing right towards its far end to come out by the ancient church. Otherwise, follow the Dales Way back to Addingham by turning right on a riverside path. At its end, keep ahead along the drive to Ilkley Tennis Club. Reaching the clubhouse, bear off left through a kissing gate across pasture. Partway along the second field, take a kissing gate on the left and walk beside two more fields back to the river. Over a stream, continue through trees. Beyond a second stream, a stony path drops back down to the Wharfe. Carry on at the edge of grazing, emerging at the far end onto a now-quiet lane, once the main Skipton road.

5. Walk right for just over a quarter of a mile (400m) before turning off along Old Lane. Reaching Low Mill village, bear right to follow the street between cottages. At the end, keep ahead on a path that quickly reverts to a lane. After another 0.25 miles (400m), beyond the old Rectory set back within spacious grounds, look for a gate on the right from which steps drop to a tiny arched bridge over Town Beck. Swing left across a pasture in front of the church to join a drive at the far side. Go left but immediately bear off right through a gate over another bridge. Wind between cottages to emerge onto North Road and turn right back to the parking spot.

Where to eat and drink

In Addingham, try The Fleece for traditional pub food. Ilkley has a huge range of places to eat and drink. At the bottom end of Ilkley you are close to the 'The Taps' or the Ilkley Moor Vaults pub as it is officially called, and the Riverside Hotel, which is particularly child-friendly.

While you're there

Addingham lies at the northwestern edge of the county. Just a mile (1.6km) to the north you enter the Yorkshire Dales National Park. By following the B6160 you soon come to Bolton Abbey, with its priory ruins in an idyllic setting by a bend in the River Wharfe.

SHIPLEY GLEN TRAMWAY AND BAILDON MOOR

DISTANCE/TIME	4 miles (6.4km) / 1hr 45min
ASCENT/GRADIENT	964ft (294m) / ▲▲
PATHS	Moor and field paths
LANDSCAPE	Moorland, fields and gritstone rocks
SUGGESTED MAP	OS Explorer 288 Bradford & Huddersfield
START/FINISH	Grid reference: SE131389
DOG FRIENDLINESS	Keep on leads by roads or near livestock
PARKING	Lay-bys on Glen Road, between Bracken Hall Countryside Centre and Old Glen House pub
PUBLIC TOILETS	In Saltaire, near railway station

For the people of Shipley and Saltaire, Baildon Moor has long represented a taste of the countryside on their doorsteps. Mill-hands could leave the mills and cramped terraced streets behind, and breathe clean Pennine air. They could listen to the song of the skylark and the cry of the curlew. There were heather moors to tramp across, gritstone rocks to scramble up and, at Shipley Glen, springy sheep-grazed turf on which to spread out a picnic blanket.

There was also once a funfair to visit – in fact, a veritable theme park. Towards the end of the 19th-century, Shipley Glen was owned by a Colonel Maude, who created a number of attractions, including the Switchback Railway, Marsden's Menagerie, the Horse Tramway and the Aerial Runway. More sedate pleasures could be found at the Camera Obscura, the boating lake in the Japanese garden, and the Temperance Tea Room and Coffee House.

Sam Wilson, a local entrepreneur, created the Shipley Glen Tramway in 1895. Saltaire people could now stroll through Roberts Park, past the steely gazed statue of Sir Titus Salt, and enjoy the tram ride to the top of the glen. Thousands of people would clamber, each weekend, onto the little cable-hauled 'toastrack' cars.

The heyday of Shipley Glen was during the Edwardian era when as many as 17,000 people would take the tramway up to the pleasure gardens. Losing out to more sophisticated entertainments, however, Shipley Glen went into a slow decline. Sadly, all the attractions are now gone, but you can still take the ride on the tramway – which runs on Sunday afternoons throughout the year (weather permitting). There is an attractive souvenir shop at the top, while the bottom station houses a small museum and replica Edwardian shop. The Old Glen House is still a popular pub, though the former Temperance Tea Room and Coffee House is now the Bracken Hall Countryside Centre.

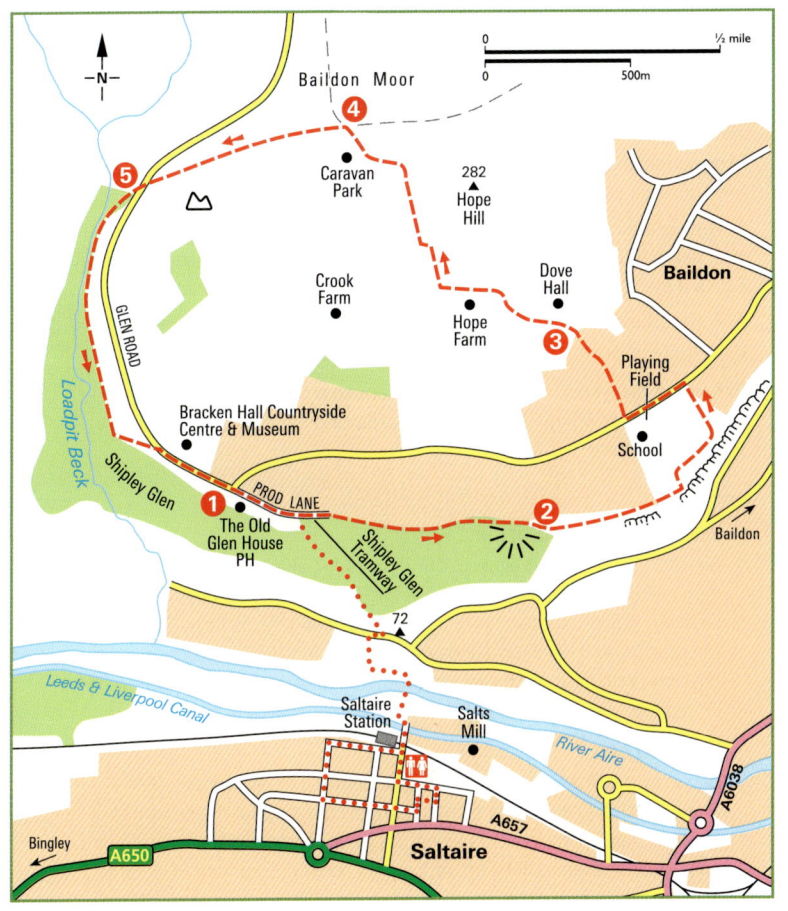

1. Walk down Glen Road, passing The Old Glen House pub. Continue as the road becomes Prod Lane, signed as a cul-de-sac. Where the road ends at the entrance to the Shipley Glen Tramway, keep straight ahead to locate an enclosed path to the right of a house. Follow this path, with houses on your left, and woodland to your right. As you come to a metal barrier, ignore a path to the left. Keep straight on downhill. About 100yds (91m) beyond the barrier, there is a choice of paths; bear left here, contouring the steep hillside and soon getting good views over Saltaire, Shipley and the Aire Valley.

2. Keep going as a path later joins from the right, undulating through scrub and more open heath beneath the old quarried face of a sandstone cliff. After a further 0.25 miles (400m), watch for a stepped path and handrail climbing to the left. At the top, turn right on a fenced path that skirts two sides of a school playing field. Emerging onto a road, cross and go left for 150yds (137m). Drawing level with the entrance to the primary school, turn off onto a narrow, enclosed path that climbs between the houses on the right. Meeting a street higher up, cross to the ongoing path. Continue up to a gate, which opens onto the bottom of a sloping pasture.

3. Go half left uphill to a kissing gate at the far corner of the field. Head out to join an access track along the field top to Hope Farm. Walk past the buildings on a cinder track, leaving just before its end onto a bridleway through a gate on the right. Emerging onto Baildon Moor, the onward path runs alongside the wall on the left. Keep straight on beyond the corner towards a caravan park. Cross a metalled track leading to the campsite and keep ahead to the corner of the boundary wall. Swing left to walk on beside it.

4. Walk gradually downhill towards the distant suburbs of Bingley. When the wall bears left, keep straight ahead, through bracken, more steeply downhill. Cross a metalled track and carry on down to meet Glen Road again.

5. Follow the path along the rocky edge of wooded Shipley Glen, leading you back to the Bracken Hall Countryside Centre and Museum and your car.

Extending the walk The walk can be extended by taking the tramway or adjacent path down into the valley and exploring Salts Mill and the lovely village of Saltaire.

Where to eat and drink

Sir Titus Salt wouldn't allow public houses in Saltaire, but that prohibition didn't extend to Shipley Glen, where The Old Glen House, near the upper tramway station, is open for lunches and evening meals from Tuesday to Saturday and lunch on Sunday. The food is locally sourced wherever possible, with fresh herbs coming from the garden. You'll find local beers on tap too, such as Saltaire Blonde and Timothy Taylor's Landlord.

What to see

Call in at the Bracken Hall Countryside Centre and Museum on Glen Road, which has a number of interesting displays about the history of Shipley Glen, its flora and its fauna. There are also temporary exhibitions on particular themes, interactive features and a programme of children's activities throughout the year. The gift shop sells maps, guides, natural history books and ice creams.

While you're there

Be sure to visit Salts Mill, a giant of a building on a truly epic scale. At the height of production, 3,000 people worked here. There were 1,200 looms clattering away, weaving as much as 30,000yds (27,500m) of cloth every working day. The mill is a little quieter these days – with a permanent exhibition of artworks by David Hockney, another of Bradford's most famous sons.

DIGLEY RESERVOIR AND BILBERRY DAM

DISTANCE/TIME	2.5 miles (4.4km) / 1hr 5min
ASCENT/GRADIENT	465ft (142m) / ▲▲
PATHS	Good farm tracks and field paths, many stiles
LANDSCAPE	Pastures, intakes and reservoir sides
SUGGESTED MAP	OS Explorer 288 Bradford & Huddersfield
START/FINISH	Grid reference: SE110072
DOG FRIENDLINESS	Dogs should be on lead near livestock
PARKING	Car park off Digley Royd Lane, near Holmbridge
PUBLIC TOILETS	None on route

Digley Reservoir, which drains an area of some 14,000 acres (5,665ha) of moorland, is a relative newcomer as Pennine dams go, having been built in 1952. The reservoir it was built to supersede, however, earned a dark place in the history books, a century earlier. Bilberry Dam, which lies upstream of Digley Reservoir, burst its embankment on 5 February 1852, causing one of the worst ever losses of life from a flood.

Plans for Bilberry Dam were prepared in 1838 by engineer George Leather. Against his advice, the commissioners employed Messrs Sharp and Sons, of Dewsbury, who had submitted the lowest tender – £9,324 – to construct the dam. Leather wasn't present when the embankment's foundations were built but had misgivings about the work's integrity. He frequently revisited the dam at his own expense after its completion in 1843, and was proven right: it leaked. His advice on repairs was, however, shrugged aside by the commissioners, on grounds of cost.

In early February 1852, torrential rain saw water levels reach record heights. More than two inches (5cm) fell on the moors over 24 hours, and the reservoir had to cope with 633 million gallons (2,880 million litres) of water on top of its existing capacity. With one overspill channel blocked and the other overwhelmed, it became obvious to anxious observers that the dam was going to go, and alarms were raised. Shortly after midnight, a wall of water burst down Digley Clough and onwards into the towns and villages of the Holme Valley, wreaking destruction and terror: entire mills, dye houses, rows of cottages and bridges were swept away.

Many people fled to higher ground but 81 people lost their lives, the UK's fourth highest flood toll. In the Digley and Holme valleys, 7,000 people were put out of work. The disaster led to new laws dictating that only experienced and qualified engineers would be permitted to design dams. George Leather's reputation was in tatters and his career ended. The commissioners, who had ignored his advice and allowed the mill to go into operation escaped prosecution, as they were effectively a government body. The inquest into the disaster however, noted they were 'guilty of great and culpable negligence'.

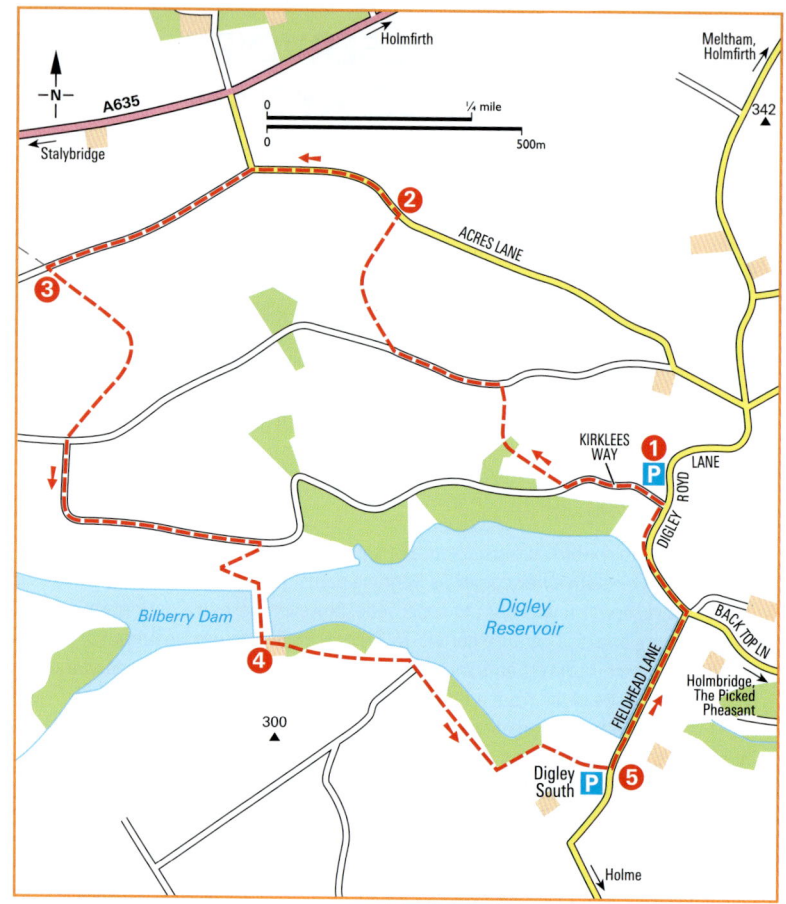

1. Take the ascending track to the side of the car park entrance. After 150yds (137m) take a path right, into an old quarried area. At a fork bear left, away from the quarry edge, soon swinging right up to a wooden stile by a bench. Ascend an enclosed path beyond to another stile. Cross that and continue for 20yds (18m), then turn left into a walled lane. The track forks after 250yds (229m); bear right, to a stile by a gate and into another walled lane. By an old quarry, 140yds (128m) later, the track becomes reedy but remains obvious and soon crosses a step stile into Acres Lane.

2. Turn left for 350yds (320m). When the road bends abruptly right, keep ahead over a stile by a metal gate and follow the lane beyond for 550yds (503m), down to a crossroads of tracks.

3. Turn left, into another walled lane, winding down to a wooden stile and into a staggered crossroads of tracks. Keep ahead, descending to a bench where a sharp turn right, off this track, has you zig-zagging down, passing through a metal gate, to cross the rebuilt wall of Bilberry Dam.

4. Bear left up a path that's initially steep and bouldery, then sandy and well-defined. Pass through a redundant gate and swathes of bilberry and heather. Turn left through the next gate, onto a purpose-built path. Through a second gate, turn left beyond a small stream, off the waymarked path, and on to Yorkshire Water's reservoir path. This contours easily across fields above the wooded reservoir edge. Beyond a third gate the path, now enclosed, heads through Digley South car park.

5. Turn left out of the car park, down Fieldhead Lane and across Digley Reservoir's wall to turn left along Back Top Lane, past the eight-arched flow chamber of Digley Reservoir. About 150yds (137m) beyond that, step off the road through a wooden gate on your left, to return to the car park via a short flight of steps, away from traffic.

Where to eat and drink
The Pickled Pheasant in Holmbridge is a family-run 18th-century coaching house set in the heart of the town. The pub offers morning coffee, lunch and afternoon teas.

What to look out for
You won't see any sign of the disaster on the walk, but in Holmfirth there's a memorial plaque to the dead on rebuilt Victoria Bridge, which had been demolished by the torrent. Elsewhere in the town, a memorial pillar for the 1801 Peace of Amiens also bears a plaque, at a height of about 7ft (2m), marking the level reached by the floodwaters.

While you're there
After reflecting on the 1852 tragedy, you could do with something to make you smile. Nearby Holmfirth was the birthplace of saucy seaside postcard company Bamforth & Company. James Bamforth, portrait photographer and silent movie pioneer, began selling the cheeky cartoon cards, famous for buxom wives and hapless hubbies, in 1910. Holmfirth Library has a few examples, and the business's former home in Station Road can still be seen.

SURPRISE VIEW AND OTLEY CHEVIN

DISTANCE/TIME	3.5 miles (5.6km) / 1hr 30min
ASCENT/GRADIENT	525ft (160m) / ▲
PATHS	Easy walking on good paths and forestry tracks
LANDSCAPE	Heath and woodland
SUGGESTED MAP	OS Explorer 297 Lower Wharfedale
START/FINISH	Grid reference: SE204441
DOG FRIENDLINESS	Dogs can run free all over the Chevin
PARKING	Surprise View car park on York Gate, opposite The Royalty Inn
PUBLIC TOILETS	None on route

This walk begins at Surprise View and, if this is your first visit, you will have a surprise indeed. By strolling just a few paces from your car you can enjoy a breathtaking panorama across Lower Wharfedale. Almscliffe Crag is a prominent landmark in the valley and, on a clear day, you may be able to see Simon's Seat and even the famous White Horse carved into the hillside at Kilburn, some 30 miles (48km) away. With so much to see, it is easy to forget that you are only a mile (1.6km) away from the bustle of the Leeds–Bradford International Airport.

The Chevin has traditionally been a popular destination for walkers and picnickers. In 1944 Major Fawkes of Farnley Hall gave a piece of land on the Chevin to the people of Otley. By 1989, when it was designated a local nature reserve, the Chevin Forest Park had grown to 700 acres (283ha) of woodland, heath and gritstone crags. Local people come here to walk their dogs and the broad forest tracks are ideal for horse riders and mountain bikers. The park is criss-crossed by any number of good waymarked paths and the walk featured here is merely one possibility.

To while away the rest of the day, you might wander down the hill to the market town of Otley, which straddles the River Wharfe and is well worth visiting in its own right. Thomas Chippendale, the famous furniture maker, was born in Otley in 1710 and it was here that the Wharfedale Printing Machine was developed, the first major breakthrough since the invention of the printing press in the 15th century.

Otley was granted its market charter by Henry III back in 1222, and the cobbled market square still occupies the centre of town. On market days (Tuesdays, Fridays and Saturdays) the stalls overflow along the main street of Kirkgate. There is a monthly farmer's market and the Otley Show is a big draw each spring. The Otley Folk Festival attracts music lovers every autumn. Otley was famous – or perhaps infamous – for having more pubs per head of population than anywhere else in Yorkshire (the jury's still out). For outdoor relaxation, Wharfemeadows Park offers riverside strolls, gardens and a children's play area.

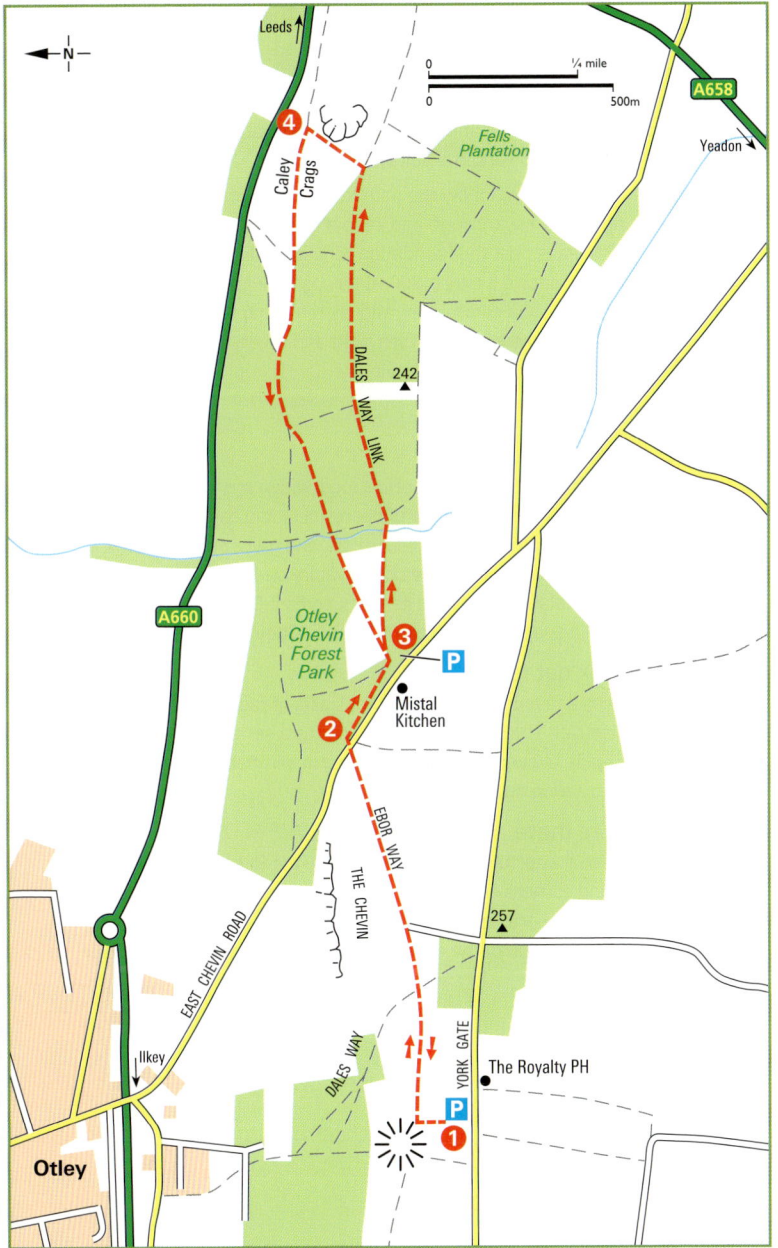

1. Walk through the car park to find a path running along the ridge overlooking the valley. Follow it right and keep to the higher branch at a fork. Beyond a gate, ignore the trail off right and continue ahead on the descending track that leads to the main road.

2. Cross to a signed footpath into the trees opposite, which runs parallel to the road to a junction of paths below a small car park.

3. There, turn left along the middle path, a broad, tree-lined avenue signed as the Dales Way Link. Keep ahead, shortly crossing a bridge. Climb away, still keeping to the main trail. Eventually, at a junction of paths at the far end of the plantation, go through a kissing gate on the left. Take the rightmost of the two paths leading away, keeping ahead to meet another path running along the rim of the rocky edge overlooking the valley.

4. After admiring the view, follow the path left, joining with other paths to reach a kissing gate. Pass through and keep ahead on a broader track, the Ebor Way, which leads past the foundation remains of Keeper's Cottage. The undulating path runs for 0.5 miles (800m) through the forest to reach a bridge. Wind left and right as you climb away, shortly returning to the junction of paths at the corner of the car park. Turn right and reverse your outward route back to the car park on top of The Chevin.

Where to eat and drink
The Royalty on top of the Chevin serves food, with a menu that changes with the seasons. There is a range of beers, including cask ales. The Royalty is popular with walkers and cyclists, and there are panoramic views across Wharfedale from the conservatory and the outdoor beer garden. The Mistal Kitchen by the car park on East Chevin Road and the many pubs, chip shops and tea rooms down in Otley offer alternatives.

What to look out for
Otley Chevin is a favourite place for enthusiasts of radio-controlled gliders to fly their aircraft. The shape of the hill creates a series of thermals which give uplift, allowing the fliers to perform aerobatic manoeuvres without the irritating buzz of little motors.

While you're there
Visit Otley, a characterful little market town by the River Wharfe. The little nooks and corners are well worth investigating. In the churchyard, you will find an elaborate memorial to the 23 workers who were killed during the construction of the nearby Bramhope railway tunnel between 1845–49.

HALIFAX AND THE SHIBDEN VALLEY

DISTANCE/TIME	5 miles (8km) / 2hrs 30min
ASCENT/GRADIENT	1,541ft (470m) / ▲▲
PATHS	Old packhorse tracks and field paths
LANDSCAPE	Surprisingly rural, considering the proximity to Halifax
SUGGESTED MAP	OS Explorer 288 Bradford & Huddersfield
START/FINISH	Grid reference: SE096251
DOG FRIENDLINESS	Keep on leads crossing busy roads
PARKING	Choice of pay-and-display car parks in Halifax
PUBLIC TOILETS	At Shibden Park

Set among the Pennine hills, Halifax was a town in the vanguard of the Industrial Revolution. Its splendid civic buildings and huge mills are an indication of the town's prosperity, earned through the woollen trade. Ironically, the most splendid building of all came close to being demolished. The Piece Hall, built in 1779, predates the industrial era. Here, in a total of 315 rooms on three colonnaded floors, the hand-weavers of the district would offer their wares (known as 'pieces') for sale to cloth merchants. The colonnades surround a massive square. The mechanisation of the weaving process left the Piece Hall largely redundant. In the intervening years, it has served a variety of purposes, including as a venue for political oration and as a wholesale market. During the 1970s, having narrowly escaped the wrecking ball, it was spruced up and given a new lease of life. It now houses a visitor centre, art gallery and speciality shops and hosts a programme of events throughout the year.

The cobbled thoroughfare up Beacon Hill is known as the Magna Via. Until 1741, when a turnpike road was built, this was the only possible approach to Halifax from the east, for both foot and packhorse traffic. Also known as Wakefield Gate, the Magna Via linked up with the Long Causeway, the old high level road to Burnley. That intrepid 18th-century traveller, Daniel Defoe, was one of those who struggled up this hill. 'We quitted Halifax not without some astonishment at its situation, being so surrounded with hills, and those so high as makes the coming in and going out of it exceedingly troublesome'. The route was superseded in the 1820s by the turnpike constructed through Godley Cutting. Today the Magna Via, too steep for modern motor vehicles, remains a fascinating relic of the past.

Situated on a hill above Halifax, Shibden Hall is magnificent half-timbered house is set in 90 acres (36ha) of beautiful, rolling parkland. Dating from 1420, the hall has been owned by prominent local families – the Oates, Saviles, Waterhouses and, latterly, the Listers. All these families left their mark, but the core of the original house remains intact. The rooms are furnished in period style, to show how they might have looked over almost six centuries. The oak furniture and panelling have that patina of age that antique forgers try in vain to emulate. Barns and other outbuildings have been converted into a folk museum, with displays of old vehicles, tools and farm machinery. Shiden Hall was home to landowner and diarist Anne Lister, whose life is explored in the BBC drama *Gentleman Jack*.

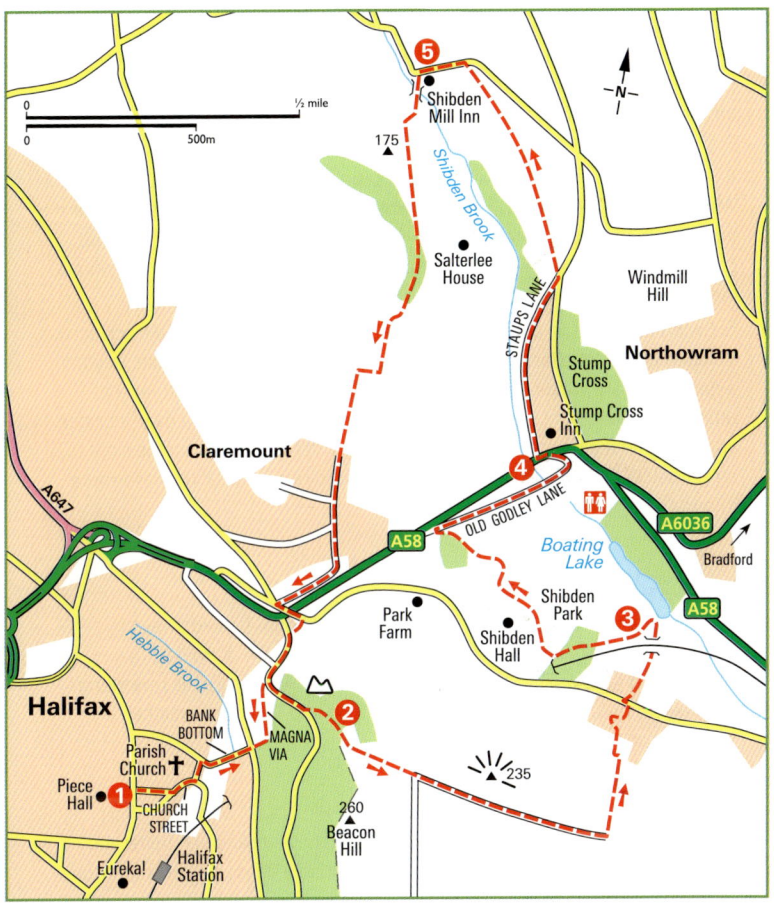

1. Begin opposite the tall spire that once belonged to Square Church, walking down Alfred Street East and left along Church Street, passing the smoke-blackened parish church. Bear left again into Lower Kirkgate, then right along Bank Bottom. Cross Hebble Brook and walk uphill; where the road bears sharp left, keep straight ahead up a steep cobbled lane, the Magna Via. Meeting a road at the top, go right for about 200yds (183m). Just after the entrance to a warehouse, take a cobbled path on the left that makes a steep ascent up Beacon Hill.

2. Keep with the main trail, which, higher up, curves left over the shoulder of the hill and runs beneath a high buttress wall to a kissing gate and barrier. Walk forward along a broad cinder track, taking the left fork a little further on where views open across the surprisingly rural Shibden Valley. After a further 100yds (91m), take a walled path on the left. Drop steeply to a small housing

estate and turn right out to the main road. Almost opposite, beside a farm entrance, a path continues downhill, passing beneath the railway line into Shibden Park.

3. Walk forward to the lake and bear left past the boathouse up to a junction with the main drive. Go left and then left again in front of a pool onto a track that climbs beside the railway embankment. Reaching another pool, the house and gardens are to the left, otherwise, branch right towards the car park. At the next junction, drop right past a display of traditional walling, descending through trees to a drive. Climb left to the park entrance and turn right down Old Godley Lane. It finally swings left up to the main road at Stump Cross.

4. Cross over the road and take Staups Lane, to the left of Stump Cross Inn. Walk along the lane, which soon becomes cobbled, to meet another road at the top. Go left and immediately left again down a drive, which, through a gate, continues across the fields into Shibden Dale. Emerging at the far end onto a lane, turn left down to the Shibden Mill Inn.

5. Swing left past the pub, leaving the far end of the car park on a track across Shibden Brook. At a fork, bear right, later passing an isolated house. Beyond, a narrower path winds up to Claremount. Keep ahead along a street that ultimately bends right above Godley Cutting. At the end, go left over a bridge spanning the main road and then immediately descend steps on the right to a street below. Go left to its end and then right to retrace your outward route into Halifax.

Where to eat and drink
At the halfway point of this walk is Shibden Mill Inn. Tucked away in a leafy corner of Shibden Dale, yet close to the centre of Halifax, this picturesque inn enjoys the best of both worlds. A sympathetic reworking of an old mill, this is the place for good food and, when the weather is kind, a drink in the beer garden.

What to see
The bird's-eye view of Halifax from Beacon Hill is well worth the effort of climbing it. A century ago this view would have looked very different: mills were here in unhealthy profusion, casting a dense pall of sulphurous smoke over the valley.

While you're there
As well as the Piece Hall, which houses an art gallery and craft shops, children will enjoy a visit to visit Eureka!, a hands-on discovery museum. It is designed for children up to the age of 12, with more than 400 interactive exhibits exploring science, nature and the world.

A CIRCUIT OF NORLAND MOOR

DISTANCE/TIME	5 miles (8km) / 2hrs
ASCENT/GRADIENT	722ft (220m) / ▲
PATHS	Good moorland paths and tracks
LANDSCAPE	Heather moor and woodland
SUGGESTED MAP	OS Explorer OL21 South Pennines
START/FINISH	Grid reference: SE055218
DOG FRIENDLINESS	Dogs can roam off lead, though watch for grazing sheep
PARKING	Small public car park on Moor Bottom Lane, opposite the former Moorcock Inn, south of Sowerby Bridge
PUBLIC TOILETS	None on route

Norland Moor and North Dean Woods are close to the start of the Calderdale Way, a 50-mile (80km) circuit of the borough of Calderdale. There are panoramic views straight away, as the waymarked walk accompanies the edge of Norland Moor. The route was inaugurated during the 1970s to link some of the best Pennine landscapes and historical sites – moors, mills, gritstone outcrops, wooded cloughs, hand weaving hamlets and industrial towns – into an invigorating walk.

Norland Moor is a 253-acre (102ha) tract of heather moorland overlooking Sowerby Bridge and both the Calder and Ryburn valleys. Criss-crossed by paths, it is popular with local walkers; driven by old quarry workings, it is a reminder that here in West Yorkshire you are seldom far from a site of industry. Originally a part of the Savile estates, the moor was bought for £250 after a public appeal in 1932. It still has the status of a common. Part of its attraction is to find such splendid walking country so close to the busy towns in the valley.

Ladstone Rock is a gritstone outcrop with a distinctive profile that stares out over the Ryburn Valley from the edge of Norland Moor. If you believe the stories, human sacrifices were carried out on Ladstone Rock by blood-thirsty druids, and convicted witches were thrown off it. The name may derive from Celtic roots, meaning to cut or to kill. There is a tradition in the South Pennines of carving inspirational quotations into such rocks. And here on Ladstone Rock, amongst the names, dates and expressions of undying love, is a small metal plaque inscribed with a short psalm from the Bible.

As you leave the nature reserve of North Dean Woods behind, you get good views across the valley to Sowerby Bridge and the outskirts of Halifax. Dominating the view is a curious edifice known as Wainhouse Tower (and also tellingly, as Wainhouse Folly). It was built by John Wainhouse, who had inherited his uncle's dyeworks. His first plan was to build a tall chimney that would help to disperse the noxious fumes from the dyeworks. But then he decided to add a spiral staircase, inside the chimney, leading up to an ornate viewing platform at the top. By the time the tower was actually built, in the 1870s, the original purpose seems to have been forgotten. To climb to the full height of the tower, 253ft (77m), you need to tackle more than 400 steps. The tower is opened up to the public, but on just a few occasions each year – generally on bank holidays. If Wainhouse failed to make a chimney, then he succeeded in creating a distinctive landmark.

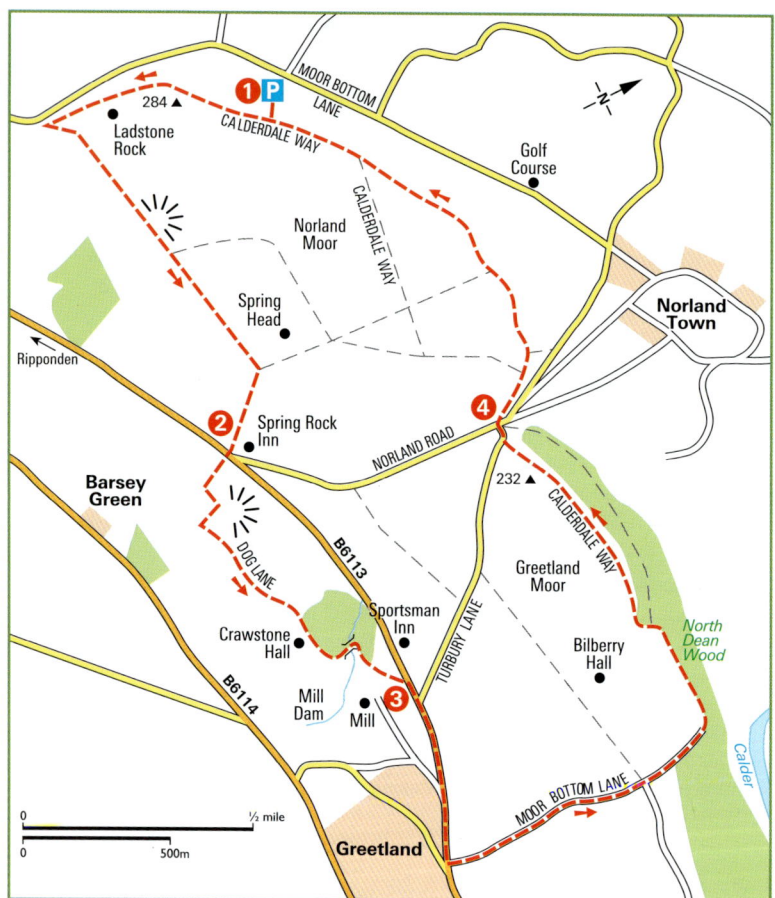

1. Walk uphill from the car park, bearing successively right near the top to follow a clear path along the edge of Norland Moor. Enjoy expansive views across the Calder Valley as you pass the gritstone outcrop known as Ladstone Rock. Keep straight ahead, now on a more substantial track which descends to run beside the road. Reaching the corner of a residential park, turn left beside the wall. Ignore a waymarked gate and bear left with the path, climbing across the slope of the heath to meet another wall corner higher up. Continue by the wall for 0.5 miles (800m), ignoring a junction and ultimately meeting a farm track. Follow it right to emerge beside the Spring Rock Inn.

2. Cross the road and continue on the narrowest of walled paths opposite. Extensive views open up as the path later goes right, down stone steps. Where the walled path ends, go left on a track. Keep ahead past cottages and again further on, as a lane joins from the right. After 200yds (183m), bear right at a fork, branching off left just before the gates of a house along a waymarked path into a small wood. The path soon descends to cross a stream on a stone-slab bridge, then bears right uphill to meet a walled track. Cross to the ongoing path, which follows a wall behind houses before turning out between them to meet the B6113.

3. Walk right, along the road to the outskirts of Greetland and turn left into Moor Bottom Lane. Continue ahead along this straight track for 0.5 miles (800m). Entering North Dean Wood, the track curves left to a fork. Take a marked path between the two branches and follow a wall along the upper edge of the woodland. Over a stile, keep right at the edge of a large field above the wood. Eventually, a developing track leads out through a gate onto a lane. Go right, past its junction with Norland Road to a sharp right-hand bend.

4. Turn left on a stony track across Norland Moor. At a junction beside a pylon, bear left on a path following the line of overhead cables. Ignoring side paths, keep ahead, eventually joining a prominent path from the right along the edge. Shortly after passing a railed enclosure, bear off right by a marker post, to drop to the path by which you first ascended from the car park.

Where to eat and drink
There are two pubs near the route, both near Greetland. Look out for The Sportsman Inn and the Spring Rock Inn both serving food and stocking a range of beers and wines.

What to look out for
The plateau of Norland Moor, overlooking Sowerby Bridge and the Calder Valley, is a particular delight in late summer, when the heather is in purple flower. Although we now consider heather to be the natural plant to grow on these moors, its introduction is relatively recent. Heather will not grow in the shade, and so it was not until all the trees had been cleared off these hills by early settlers that it really took a hold. You should also look for the bittersweet tasting bilberry, which is a favourite with grazing sheep around the end of June, and the less palatable (and mildly poisonous) crowberries, which cluster on rockier ground.

While you're there
Eclipsing the original hillside Norse settlement, Sowerby Bridge developed as the junction between two important waterways, the Rochdale Canal and the Calder and Hebble Navigation. Warehouses and mills grew around the basin, which, now restored as a marina, provides an attractive focus to the town. Immediately upstream on the Rochdale Canal is Tuel Lane Lock, which, with a fall of almost 20ft (6m) is the deepest in the country.

BINGLEY AND THE ST IVES ESTATE

DISTANCE/TIME	6.25 miles (10.1km) / 2hrs 45min
ASCENT/GRADIENT	1,247ft (380m) / ▲▲
PATHS	Good paths and tracks throughout, several stiles
LANDSCAPE	Woodland, park and river
SUGGESTED MAP	OS Explorer 288 Bradford & Huddersfield
START/FINISH	Grid reference: SE107391
DOG FRIENDLINESS	Can be off leads on St Ives Estate
PARKING	Car parks in Bingley
PUBLIC TOILETS	In Myrtle Place by the park

Sitting astride both the River Aire and the Leeds and Liverpool Canal, in a steep-sided valley, Bingley is a typical West Yorkshire town. With its locks, wharves and plethora of mills, the town grew in size and importance during the 19th century as the textile trades expanded. But Bingley's pre-eminence did not begin with the Industrial Revolution; it is, in fact, one of the county's oldest settlements, with its market charter being granted by King John as far back as 1212. Bingley has a number of splendid old buildings, such as the town hall, parish church, butter cross, the old market hall and the Old White Horse, a venerable coaching inn, where King John is reputed to have stayed. However, Bingley has more than its fair share of modern buildings around the town centre.

The River Aire rises close to the village of Malham, in the limestone dales of North Yorkshire, and flows past Bingley. By the time it joins the Ouse and decants into the Humber Estuary, it has been one of the hardest worked watercourses in Yorkshire. When the textile trades were at their height, the Aire was both a source of power for the woollen mills and a convenient dumping ground for industrial waste. But, like so many other West Yorkshire rivers, the water quality is now greatly improved.

For part of this walk, you will be exploring the St Ives Estate, which from 1636 was owned by one of Bingley's most prominent families, the Ferrands. It was William Ferrand who, during the 1850s, landscaped the estate and created many of the paths and tracks that climb steeply through the woods. The view from the top of the hill is ample reward for your efforts. From the gritstone outcrop known as the Druid's Altar, you have a splendid panorama across Bingley and the Aire Valley. There is an inscription on Lady Blantyre's Rock, passed later on the walk, which commemorates William Ferrand's mother-in-law. Lady Blantyre often used to sit in the shade of this rock and read a book.

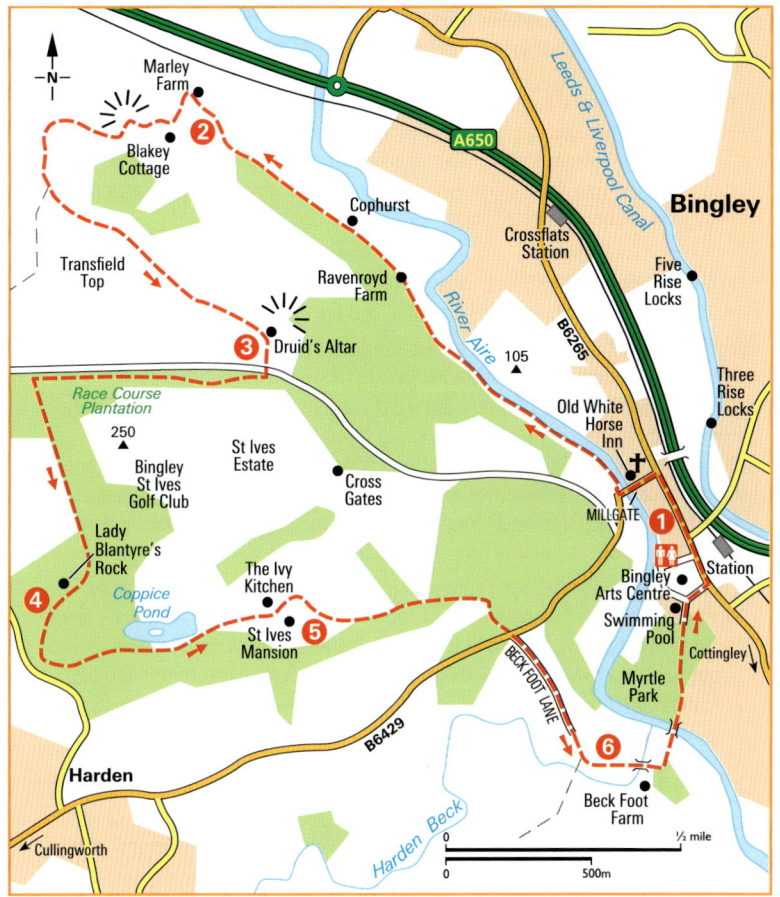

1. Walk northwest from the centre of Bingley towards the church. Go left at the traffic lights beside the Old White Horse pub into Millgate. Cross the River Aire and take the first right, Ireland Street. Swing immediately right again and then left along a riverside track, soon leaving the town behind. Reaching Ravenroyd Farm, bear right and pass between farm buildings to continue on a walled track to Cophurst. Pass left of the cottage and continue beside a wood at the edge of successive pastures.

2. A developing track leaves the third pasture through a gap. Continue to a stile and gate and skirt a hillock, eventually leaving over a stile by Marley Farm. Follow the rough track up left, passing Marley Brow. Where the track subsequently swings into a farm, bear off right on a grass trail across a bracken and scrub slope, ultimately winding up to a small gate. A narrow path rises through more trees. Keep right and then left at successive forks, shortly joining a wall on the right bounding the top of the wood. Eventually, after crossing a broad track, the path leads to a rocky outcrop known as the Druid's Altar, a striking viewpoint.

3. Bear right, after the rocks, to come to a meeting of tracks. Go through a gap in the wall opposite, onto a walled track into the St Ives Estate. Leave immediately through a kissing gate on the right onto a path that runs pleasantly for half a mile (800m) within Race Course Plantation. Ignoring the kissing gate leading out at the end, go left, now descending, initially still within trees through a golf course and then at the edge of open heather moor. When the accompanying wall later turns away, bear right with the main path, dropping through wood once more to come upon Lady Blantyre's Rock.

4. Descend with the main path, past exuberant displays of rhododendrons, and on beside Coppice Pond. Meeting a metalled drive, bear left, soon passing The Ivy Kitchen, the golf clubhouse and then, set back on the right, the house itself, St Ives Mansion.

5. Beyond the house, curve right and left to follow the main drive downhill for 0.5 miles (800m). Just after passing a car park, take a path left into woodland. Keep right where it immediately forks, to reach the B6429, the Bingley–Cullingworth road. Cross it and continue downhill on narrow Beck Foot Lane. After houses the lane becomes an unmade track leading down to a delectable spot: here you will find Beck Foot Farm, in a wooded setting by Harden Beck, with a ford and a packhorse bridge that dates back to 1723.

6. Cross the bridge to Beck Foot Farm and bear left past some allotments. Where they end, take a path left to a footbridge over the River Aire. Walk ahead through Myrtle Park, leaving at its far side between the swimming pool and the supermarket on Myrtle Grove. Turn right and then left to return to the main road running through the town. The Old White Horse, past which the walk began, lies to the left.

Where to eat and drink
With 12th-century origins, the Old White Horse Inn is Bingley's oldest pub and housed the court, police cells and gibbet. Serving food at weekends, it has oodles of character, and claims several resident ghosts. On the St Ives estate, try The Ivy Kitchen.

What to see
Having been removed from the main street, Bingley's ancient stocks, butter cross and old market hall were re-sited in front of the Bingley Arts Centre, near the Market Square Tavern.

While you're there
Next to Bingley is the little town of Cottingley where, in 1917, two young girls took photographs of fairies by Cottingley Beck. Despite the fairies looking like paper cut-outs, the pictures were 'authenticated' by Arthur Conan Doyle, creator of the fiercely logical Sherlock Holmes. Pay a visit to Cottingley Beck, and listen out for the beating of tiny wings.

HONLEY WOOD FROM MELTHAM

DISTANCE/TIME	2.75 miles (4.4km) / 2hrs 45min
ASCENT/GRADIENT	300ft (91m) / ▲▲
PATHS	Woodland paths (some muddy) throughout, few stiles
LANDSCAPE	Peaceful woodland of oak, holly, rowan and more
SUGGESTED MAP	OS Explorer 288 Bradford & Huddersfield
START/FINISH	Grid reference: SE109105
DOG FRIENDLINESS	Plenty of opportunity for dogs to exercise
PARKING	On-street parking around Acre Lane, Meltham
PUBLIC TOILETS	None on route

Meltham's an industrious place. Set in its own small tributary valley of the River Holme, its large late-18th century Meltham Mills complex and neighbouring industrial areas still hum with activity. A few steps away from the mill, however, lies one of the largest areas of semi-natural ancient woodland in West Yorkshire. Honley Wood, beloved by locals for decades, is a 150-acre (60ha) expanse of upland oak and birch that offers immediate respite from and absolute contrast to the busy industries nearby.

The woods were quarried for many years and many of the rock outcrops you pass on this walk are old quarry faces, though nature has done such a good job reclaiming them that they appear completely natural. The woods remain in the ownership of a quarrying company but it has worked with the local authority and Holme Valley communities to improve access. Trails among the woods have been upgraded and the 7-mile (11.3km) Meltham Way – a splendid day's walk in its own right – cuts through the wood on its way round the valley.

The woods form part of the White Rose Forest, an initiative to improve and increase woodland cover and green spaces throughout the county, while educating youngsters about the important relationship between the countryside and human activity. By making the area more attractive to live in, the scheme also hopes to attract investment and contribute to its economic regeneration. As you walk through the wood, you'll occasionally be guided by White Rose Forest symbols.

Meltham's past industrial prosperity was based on Jonas Brook and Brothers' silk mill, established in the town in the late 1800s, which employed 1,000 people in its prime. Their symbol was a goat's head from their coat of arms, and it can still be seen on Meltham Mill's former office building. Like Titus Salt in Saltaire, the Brooks provided their workers with housing and several community buildings. The mills were taken over by David Brown Tractors in 1939 and the company grew to become Britain's largest post-war tractor manufacturer, however, they are no longer in operation.

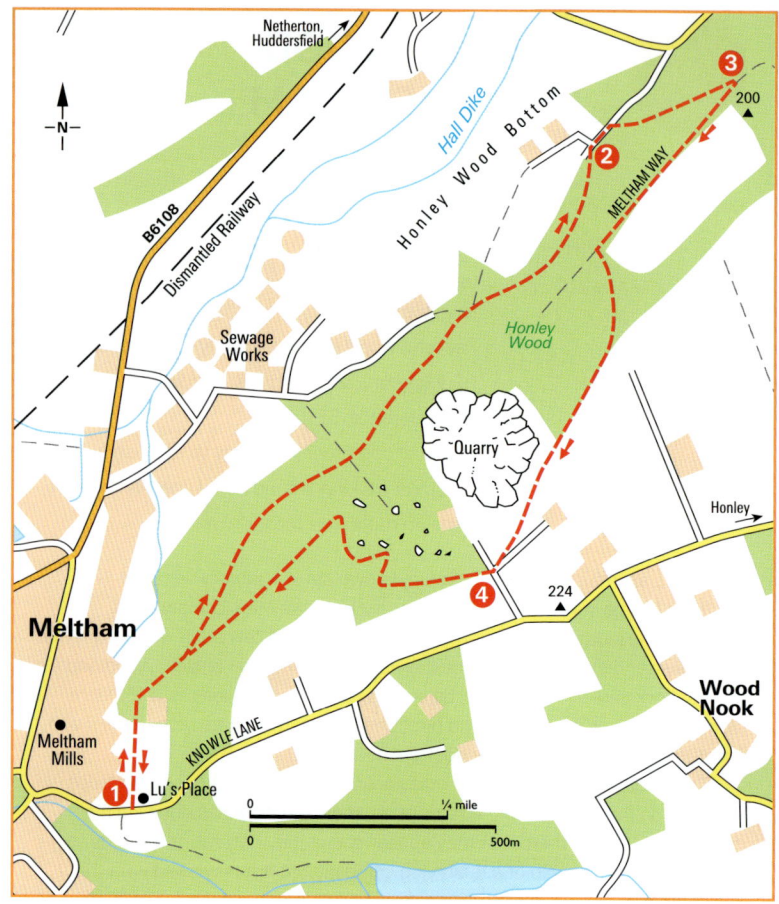

1. Follow the sign for a public bridleway next to the entrance to Lu's Place café, walking between industrial areas to bear right into peaceful woodland. At the first fork bear left. Ignore minor paths to either side to pass springs before rising, after a mile (1.6km), gently away from Meltham's industrial hum. Eventually the path drops to pass through another metal portal, into a track.

2. In 60yds (55m) it meets a better-surfaced lane; continue ahead for 10yds (9m), then pass through a gap stile on your right signed 'Meltham Way'. This carries you back into the woods on a muddy, ascending path, topping out just beyond a large rock outcrop at a T-junction of paths.

3. Turn right, along the level Meltham Way. Breaks in the trees gives you occasional views across the Meltham Valley and beyond to distinctive Pule Hill, above Marsden, as well as Crosland Hall in the Colne Valley below, and the village of Netherton's church tower on the opposite valley side. The braided path flirts between gritstone edge on your right and fence on your left. When the fence bears off left, fork right, along the edge. After 500yds (457m), it crosses a wide track, re-entering woodland. Fork right immediately, on a path

that follows a fence on your right, soon bearing right on another path which joins from the left. It now runs between a wall and a fence for 300yds (274m) to meet a lane, beyond a pair of large boulders.

4. Cross the lane and pass through a metal portal opposite. Take the track ahead-left, which soon winds down into the woods on an engineered trail, past the outcrops of an old stone quarry. It descends to your outward path and back to the start point.

Where to eat and drink
Lu's Place, at the start of the walk, is a modern café serving a great range of food and drink. Sit inside or in The Glasshouse, which is open to the outdoors, or on the terrace, both of which are dog friendly.

What to look out for
Unremarkable, flat earthen plinths, now overgrown and almost indistinguishable among the tress and shrubs on the woodland floor, are all that remain of charcoal hearths that once smouldered among the woods. Charcoal was an important fuel for iron smelting until it was superseded by coke during the Industrial Revolution.

While you're there
Just outside Meltham, on Blackmoorfoot Road towards Huddersfield, stands Wills O' Nats, a dog-friendly pub with a popular restaurant. The pub is named after 1800s tenant William Dyson, son of Nathaniel Dyson. Though then called the Spotted Cow, locals knew it as Wills O'Nats and the name stuck. When new owners renamed it the New House, in the early 1900s, a dray stopped in Meltham to ask directions but no-one had heard of the 'New House'. A quick change to 'Wills O' Nats' ensured the beer didn't go astray again.

RODLEY AND THE LEEDS AND LIVERPOOL CANAL

DISTANCE/TIME	3.5 miles (5.7km) / 1hr 15min
ASCENT/GRADIENT	230ft (70m) / ▲
PATHS	Riverside path and canal tow path
LANDSCAPE	Surprisingly rural, considering you are so close to Leeds
SUGGESTED MAP	OS Explorer 288 Bradford & Huddersfield
START/FINISH	Grid reference: SE222364
DOG FRIENDLINESS	Can be off lead on most of walk
PARKING	On-street parking, close to swing bridge over Leeds and Liverpool Canal in Rodley
PUBLIC TOILETS	None on route

The Leeds and Liverpool Canal was conceived at a meeting in Bradford in 1766, but it was not until 1770 that the first sod was cut near Liverpool. The ambitious scheme followed a convoluted 127-mile (204km) route across the Pennines, linking many of the important textile towns with the coal pits of Wigan and the western port of Liverpool. From Leeds, via the Aire and Calder Navigation and the River Ouse, there was also a continuous waterway to the ports of Hull and Grimsby. There were several major changes of plan along the way and, in the end, the Leeds and Liverpool required the construction of 91 locks and a 1,640-yard (1500m) tunnel to broach the summit at Foulridge.

The canal was finally opened end to end in 1816, although intermediate sections were already in use to great effect. The section from Leeds to Skipton opened to a jubilant fanfare on 8 April 1773, and the arrival of two boatloads of coal halved the previous selling price. The ability to transport raw materials and produce them quickly and cheaply completely changed the face of this part of England and, with the invention of efficient steam engines, the Industrial Revolution became unstoppable.

By 1840, almost 4,500 miles (7,242km) of navigable waterway criss-crossed Britain, opening the hinterland to trade and industry. Some canals, like the Leeds and Liverpool, were highly profitable and returned massive fortunes to their backers. But the writing was already on the wall. In 1825, the Stockton–Darlington railway opened with the Liverpool–Manchester line following five years later. Unaffected by icy winters or summer drought and able to shift far greater loads at speed, the railway age had arrived. By the end of the 19th century the country had 22,000 miles (35,000km) of railway.

Yet, the canals did not suffer an instant death. Many were taken over and operated by the new railway companies, and trade on the major routes, albeit steadily declining, continued well into the 20th century. From the 1950s, recreational use reversed the decline, saving some canals from closure while bringing others back to life. The Leeds and Liverpool remained navigable is today a vibrant corridor linking urban centres to the countryside.

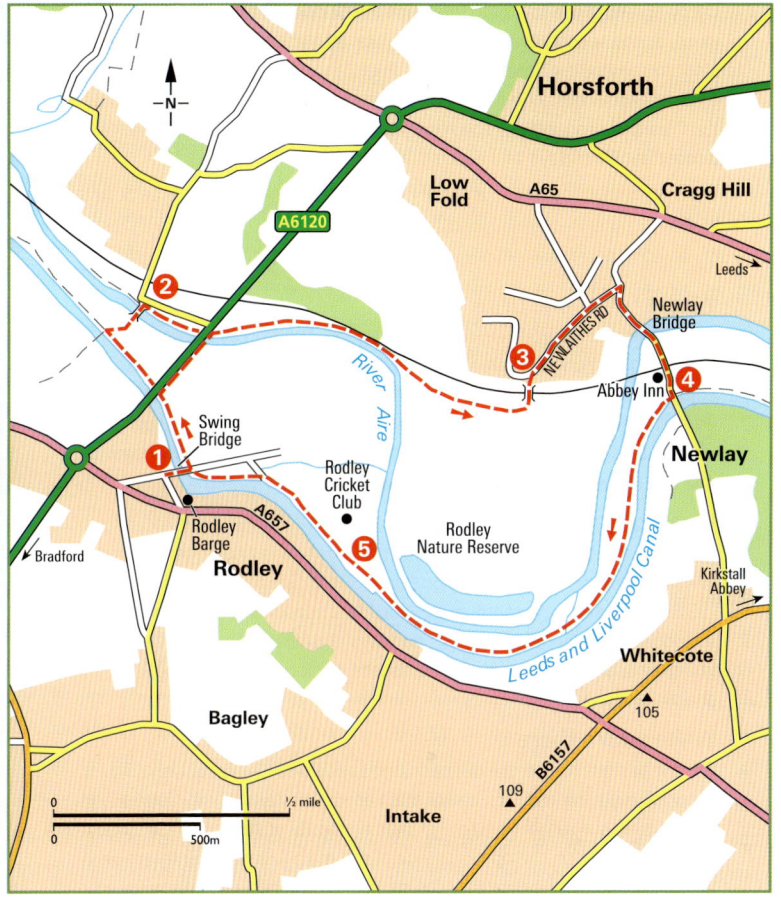

1. Cross the canal swing bridge, and go left along the broad tow path, passing beneath a bridge carrying the ring road. Reaching a second swing bridge, turn right along a paved lane. After only 30yds (27m), drop along a stepped path on the left to a lower track. Follow it over a stone bridge spanning the River Aire.

2. On the far bank, immediately turn off right down steps to a riverside path. Follow it downstream from the bridge, passing back beneath the main road. Carry on for another 0.5 mile (800m) then, as the river swings away to the right, bear off to a kissing gate. Stick with the higher path, signed to New Laithes Road, which rises at the edge of pasture alongside a deepening railway cutting. Eventually reaching another kissing gate, slip through and continue on a contained path that soon swings across a railway bridge and leads out to a street.

3. Turn right and walk along Newlaithes Road for 0.25 miles (400). Approaching its eventual end, watch for a stepped path dropping on the right that cuts the corner onto Newlay Lane. Walk down the hill to Newlay Bridge crossing the river and continue to a second bridge spanning the railway. Walk on past the Abbey Inn to approach a bridge arching over the canal. Drop left to the tow path.

4. Carry on along the tow path, beneath the bridge to the right. After a mile (1.6km), at the second swing bridge, a track off through gates on the right leads into the Rodley Nature Reserve. Pools, marshland, a willow coppice and hay meadow attract wildfowl and many species of small birds as well as butterflies and dragonflies. The reserve is open on Wednesdays, weekends and most bank holidays and admission is free.

5. Walk on beside the canal. It is only just over 0.25 miles (400m) back to the start point.

Where to eat and drink
For refreshments, you have a choice of pubs. The Rodley Barge, at the beginning of the walk, has a small beer garden from which you can enjoy the comings and goings on the canal. Just after Newlay Bridge, an early (1819) example of cast iron bridge building, formerly known as Pollard Bridge, is the Abbey Inn, another characterful hostelry, seemingly marooned between the river and canal.

What to look out for
The canal here, and as far as Armley towards Leeds and Apperley Bridge towards Shipley, has been designated a Site of Special Scientific Interest (SSSI) because of the range of aquatic life it supports. On the surface this includes coots, moorhens, ducks and swans, whilst below the waterline you may spot a pike lurking in the depths. Look out, too, for kingfishers and wagtails.

While you're there
Once it has left the centre of Leeds, the Leeds and Liverpool Canal has a surprisingly rural aspect. Smoke blackened Kirkstall Abbey – founded in 1152 but now a romantic ruin – stands by the River Aire, with the Abbey House Museum on the opposite side of the main A65 road. Both are well worth a visit. It was home to a community of Cistercian monks who led a self-contained life with little contact from the nearby medieval city of Leeds. After its dissolution in 1539, the roofing, windows and much stonework was appropriated for use in local building works. The museum has reconstructions of Victorian street scenes, complete with shops, a Sunday school and even an undertaker's workshop. You can walk to the abbey and museum along the tow path.

STANDEDGE FROM MARSDEN

DISTANCE/TIME	8.25 miles (13.3km) / 4hrs
ASCENT/GRADIENT	1,215ft (370m) / ▲▲
PATHS	Old tracks and byways, canal towpath, several stiles
LANDSCAPE	Heather moorland
SUGGESTED MAP	OS Explorer OL21 South Pennines
START/FINISH	Grid reference: SE047118
DOG FRIENDLINESS	On leads where sheep graze on open moorland
PARKING	Standedge car park by Marsden Station
PUBLIC TOILETS	Peel Street in Marsden town centre

Trans-Pennine travel has, until quite recently, been a hazardous business. Over the centuries, many routes have been driven across the hills to link the industrial centres of West Yorkshire and Lancashire. Some paths were consolidated into paved causeways for packhorse traffic, before being upgraded to take vehicles. This track, linking the Colne Valley to Rochdale and Milnrow in Lancashire, was known as the Rapes Highway.

This was tough terrain for building a canal. When the Huddersfield Narrow Canal was cut, to provide a link between Huddersfield and Ashton-under-Lyne, there was one major obstacle for the canal builders to overcome: the gritstone bulk of Standedge. There was no way round; the canal had to go through.

The Standedge Tunnel, extending 3 miles (4.8km) from Marsden to Diggle, was a monumental feat of engineering. Costly in every sense, it took 17 years to build and many workers lost their lives. The result was the longest, highest and deepest canal tunnel in the country. In an attempt to keep those costs down, the tunnel was cut as narrow as possible, which left no room for a towpath. Towing horses had to be led over the hills to the far end of the tunnel, near Diggle in Lancashire. The bargees had to negotiate Standedge Tunnel using their own muscle power alone. This method, known as 'legging', required them to lie on their backs and push with their feet against the sides and roof of the tunnel. This operation would typically take a back-breaking four hours. Closed to canal traffic for many years, the tunnel is now a tourist attraction, with boat trips and a visitor centre. The Standedge Tunnel Visitor Centre has fascinating films and collections telling the story of the tunnel and people – from its planning and through more than 200 years of history.

In 1812 Marsden became the focus for the Luddite rebellion against mechanisation in the textile industry. A secret group of croppers and weavers banded together to break up the new machinery that was appearing in local mills. Eventually the army was despatched to restore order. Some 60 men were put on trial for their part in the troubles; 17 of them were hanged.

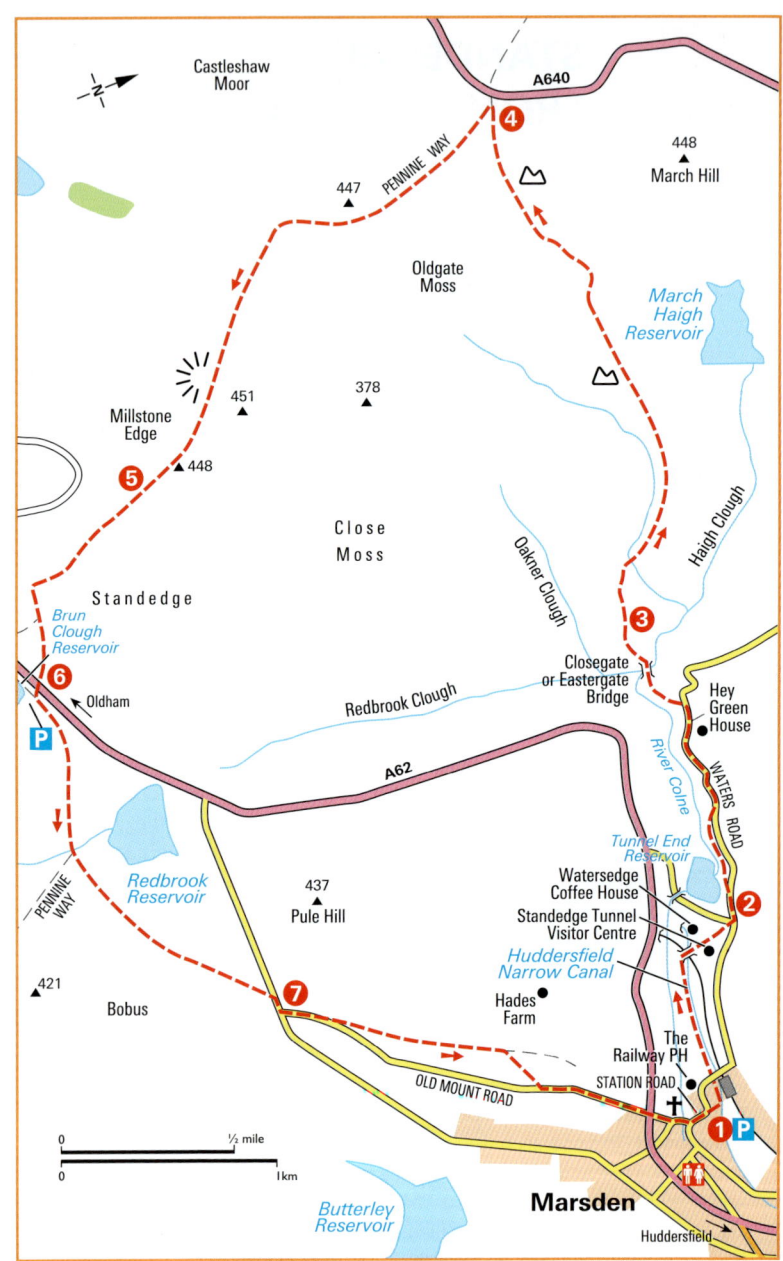

1. From the car park, turn right and then bear right, following the Huddersfield Narrow Canal towpath away from a lock. Approaching Tunnel End, where both canal and railway disappear into tunnels, leave the towpath to cross a footbridge. Bear right uphill past the visitor centre to a T-junction with a house (the old Tunnel End Inn) directly in front.

2. Turn left on to Waters Road. Almost immediately, leave through a gate on the left for a path parallel to the road. After rejoining, keep straight ahead past the entrance to Hey Green House. About 100yds (91m) further on, bear left, just before a cottage, on to a bridleway. The path takes you across Closegate Bridge, known locally as Eastergate Bridge, where two becks meet.

3. Swing right, following the beck for about 100yds (91m), before forking left at a waymarker into a narrow side valley. The path levels higher up, curving towards the rounded prominence of March Hill, now intermittently marked by stone wayposts. After a final push, the path descends towards the A640.

4. Immediately before reaching the road, turn sharp left at a Pennine Way sign over a wooden bridge spanning a little beck. The onward path rises and falls over the moss for just over 0.75 miles (1.2km) to a junction at the abrupt lip of Standedge. Go left along the top of the scarp, enjoying the panoramic view across East Lancashire.

5. Beyond the trig point, the path gently loses height, passing through successive gates and across broken walls to emerge on to a track. Follow it left out to the A62, where a car park overlooks Brun Clough Reservoir.

6. Cross the road and take steps up to the left from the car park. Signed 'Pennine Way', the path is parallel to the deep road cutting before turning away across Marsden Moor. To the left is Redbrook Reservoir, with Pule Hill beyond. Approaching a marker stone, bear left at a footpath sign, dipping across a stream to continue over the moss. Eventually, after 0.75 miles (1.2km), the way narrows and drops steeply to a stream in a gully. Climb beyond to a road.

7. Turn right and then immediately left on to Old Mount Road. After 50yds (46m), bear left again, along a stony track signed to Hades Farm. After 0.5 miles (800m), watch for a discreet sign just off the track for a path that leads to a small gate and descends beside a wall to rejoin Old Mount Road. Continue downhill, crossing the main road into Towngate. Bear left past the church and at the end go left again up Station Road back to the car park.

Where to eat and drink

The Watersedge Coffee House (open Thursday to Sunday) by the entrance to the Standedge Tunnel serves light refreshments, or for more standard pub fare try The Railway by the start of the walk in Marsden, where walkers are very welcome and food is served daily.

What to see

In spring and early summer, listen out for the cuckoo. If an old story is to be believed, the people of Marsden realised that when the cuckoo arrived, so did the sunshine. They tried to keep spring forever, by building a tower around the cuckoo. As the last stones were about to be laid, however, the cuckoo flew away. The people of Marsden celebrate Cuckoo Day in April each year.

HAWORTH AND THE BRONTË WAY

32

DISTANCE/TIME	8.1 miles (13km) / 3hrs 30min
ASCENT/GRADIENT	1,508ft (460m) / ▲▲
PATHS	Well signed and easy to follow
LANDSCAPE	Open moorland
SUGGESTED MAP	OS Explorer OL21 South Pennines
START/FINISH	Grid reference: SE029372
DOG FRIENDLINESS	On leads near sheep on open moorland
PARKING	Pay-and-display car park, near Brontë Parsonage
PUBLIC TOILETS	At entrance to car park

Who could have imagined, when the Revd Patrick Brontë became curate of the Church of St Michael and All Angels in 1820, that the little gritstone town of Haworth would become a literary hot spot to rival Grasmere and Stratford-upon-Avon? But visitors flock here in great numbers: some to gain insights into the works of Charlotte, Emily and Anne, others just to enjoy a day out. If the shy sisters could see the Haworth of today, they would recognise the steep, cobbled main street. But they would no doubt be amazed to see the tourist industry that's built up to exploit their names and literary reputations.

They would recognise the Georgian parsonage too. Now a museum, it has been painstakingly restored to reflect the lives of the Brontës and the rooms are filled with their personal treasures. That three such prodigious talents should be found within a single family is remarkable enough. To have created such towering works as *Jane Eyre* and *Wuthering Heights* while living in a bleakly inhospitable place is incredible. The public were unprepared for this trio of lady novelists, which is why all the books published during their lifetimes bore the androgynous pen names of Currer, Ellis and Acton Bell.

After Patrick Brontë came to Haworth with his wife and six children, tragedy was never far away. His wife died the following year and two daughters did not live to adulthood. His only son, Branwell, succumbed to drink and drugs; Anne and Emily died aged 29 and 30 respectively. Only Charlotte lived long enough to marry but, after just one year of marriage, she, too, fell ill and died in 1855, aged 38. Revd Brontë survived them all, living to the ripe old age of 84.

Tourism is no recent development; by the middle of the 19th century, the first literary pilgrims were visiting Haworth. No matter how crowded this little town becomes, it is always possible to escape to the moors that surround it. You can follow, literally, in the footsteps of the three sisters as they sought freedom and inspiration, away from the confines of the parsonage. As you explore these inhospitable moors, you'll get a greater insight into the literary world of the Brontës than those who stray no further than the souvenir shops and tea rooms of Haworth.

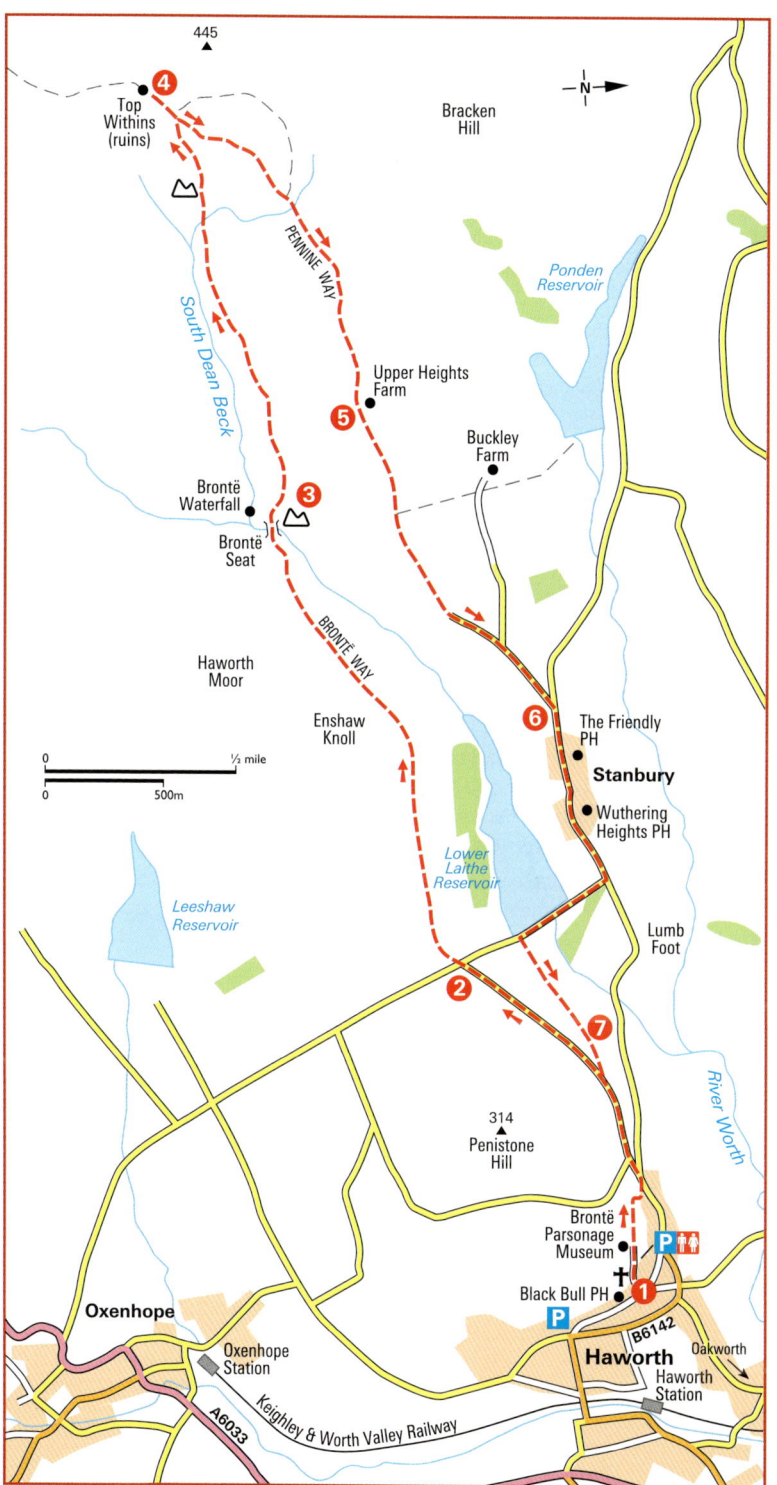

1. Take the cobbled lane beside The King's Arms, signed to the Brontë Parsonage Museum. The lane soon becomes a paved field path that leads to the Haworth–Stanbury road. Walk left along the road and, after just 75yds (69m), take a left fork, signed to Penistone Hill. Continue along this quiet road to a T-junction.

2. Follow the track opposite, signed to the Brontë Waterfall. Becoming a path, it eventually descends to South Dean Beck where, close to the stone bridge, you will find the Brontë Seat (a boulder that resembles a chair) and the Brontë Waterfall. Cross the bridge and climb steeply uphill to a kissing gate and three-way sign.

3. Keep left, uphill, on a paved path signed 'Top Withins'. Beyond another kissing gate, ignore the later left fork. After dipping across a beck the path leads on, eventually climbing to a signpost by a ruined building. Walk a short distance left, uphill, to visit the ruin of Top Withins, which can be imagined as the inspiration for Emily Brontë's Wuthering Heights.

4. Retrace your steps to the signpost, but now keep ahead on a paved path, downhill, signed to Stanbury and Haworth and the Pennine Way. Follow a broad, clear track across the wide expanse of wild Pennine moorland. Carry on for a mile (1.6km) to Upper Heights Farm.

5. At a fork at the farm, bear left with the Pennine Way, shortly passing a second farm. Some 200yds (183m) further on at a junction, the Pennine Way leaves to the left. The route, however, continues with the track ahead signed to Stanbury and Haworth. As other tracks join, the way becomes metalled and leads to the main lane at the edge of Stanbury.

6. Bear right along the road through Stanbury, then take the first road on the right, signed to Oxenhope, and cross the dam of Lower Laithe Reservoir. Immediately beyond the dam, turn left onto a service road and fork right along an uphill track that meets the lane by Haworth Cemetery.

7. From here you retrace your outward route: walk left along the road, soon taking a gap stile on the right, to follow the paved field path back into Haworth.

Where to eat and drink

The Black Bull is Haworth's most famous public house, standing in the little cobbled square at the top of the steep main street. This is where Branwell Brontë came to drown his sorrows. These days you can also have a sandwich, or a snack, or perhaps choose something from the specials board.

While you're there

At the bottom of that famous cobbled street is Haworth Station, on the restored Keighley and Worth Valley Railway. Take a steam train journey on Britain's last remaining complete branch line railway, or browse through the books and railway souvenirs at the station shop.

ILKLEY MOOR AND THE TWELVE APOSTLES

DISTANCE/TIME	4.5 miles (7.2km) / 2hrs
ASCENT/GRADIENT	875ft (266m) / ▲▲
PATHS	Good moorland paths, some steep paths towards end of walk
LANDSCAPE	Mostly open heather moorland and gritstone crags
SUGGESTED MAP	OS Explorer 297 Lower Wharfedale & Washburn Valley
START/FINISH	Grid reference: SE132467
DOG FRIENDLINESS	Under close control at all times
PARKING	Car park below Cow and Calf rocks
PUBLIC TOILETS	At White Wells Spa Cottage

Ilkley Moor is a long ridge of millstone grit, immediately to the south of Ilkley. It's a special place – not just for walkers but for lovers of archaeological relics, too. These extensive heather moors are identified on maps as Rombalds Moor but, thanks to a song, Ilkley Moor is how it will always be known.

The Twelve Apostles is a ring of Bronze Age standing stones sited close to the meeting of two ancient routes across the moor. The 12 slabs of millstone grit (there were probably 20 stones originally, with one at the centre) are arranged in a circle approximately 50ft (15m) in diameter. The tallest stone is little more than 3ft (1m). The circle is the most visible evidence of 7,000 years of occupation of these moors. There are other, smaller circles too, and Ilkley Moor is celebrated for its Bronze Age rock carvings, the most famous of which features a sinuous swastika: traditionally a symbol of good luck, until the Nazis corrupted it. In addition to Pancake and Haystack rocks, seen on this walk, there are dozens of other natural gritstone rock formations. The biggest and best known are the Cow and Calf, close to the start of this walk, where climbers practise their holds and rope work.

Ilkley was a little village until the discovery of mineral springs turned it into a prosperous spa town. Dr William Mcleod arrived here in 1847, and recognised – or perhaps just imagined – the curative properties of cold water. He vigorously promoted what he called the 'Ilkley Cure', a strict regime of exercise and cold baths. Luxurious hotels, known as 'hydros', sprang up around the town to cater for the influx of visitors.

Predating the town's popularity as a spa is White Wells, built in 1700 around one of the original springs. A century later, a pair of plunge baths were added, where visitors could enjoy bathing in cold water and enjoy extensive views over the town.

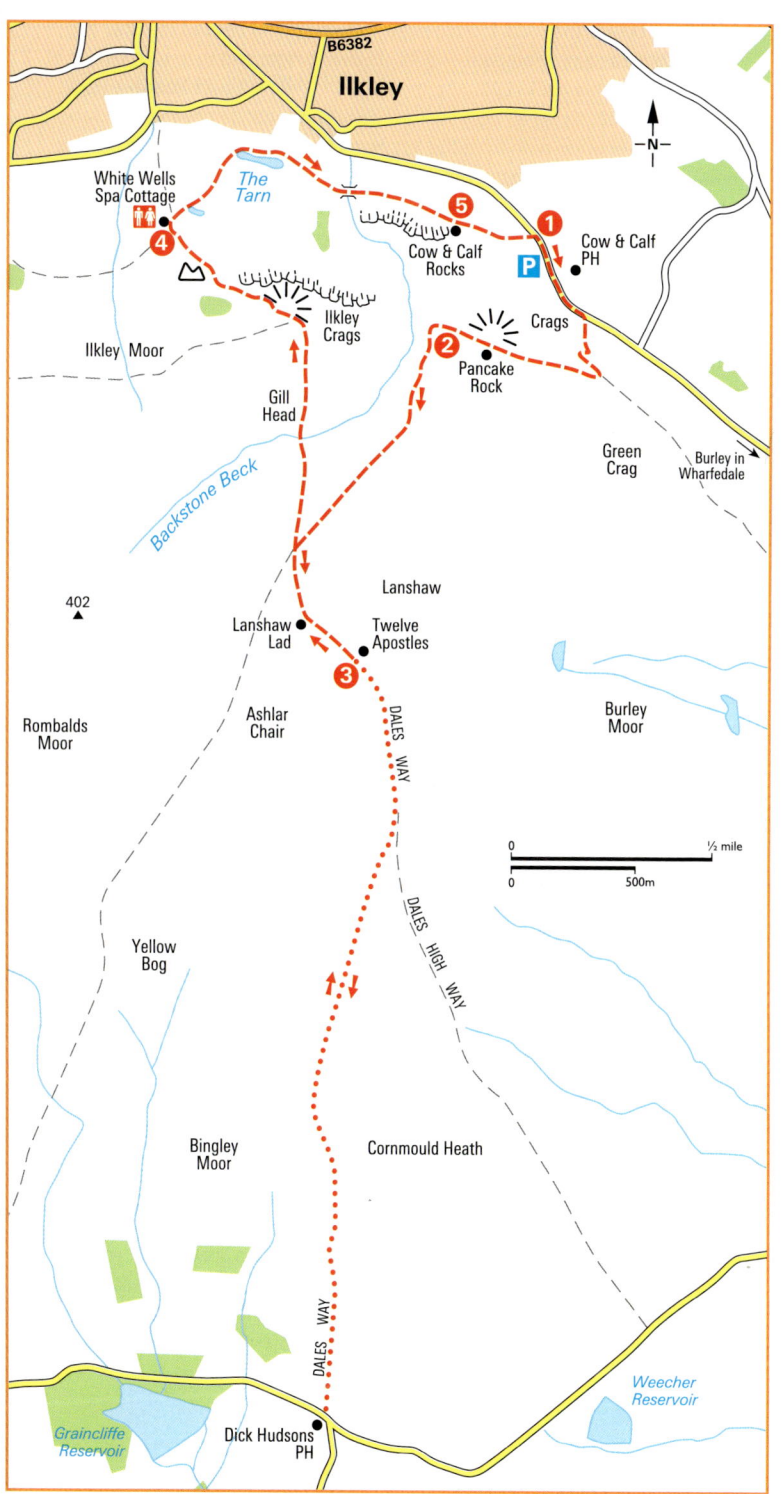

1. Walk up beside the road, forking right 150yds (137m) beyond the Cow and Calf pub onto a signed footpath. Higher up, swing right and then turn left. At a waymarker, double back right onto the edge and follow it past Pancake Rock. Dip across a path rising along a shallow gully and continue beyond Haystack Rock, joining another path from the left. Keep to the left at several successive forks, swinging parallel to the broad fold containing Backstone Beck, over to the right.

2. After gently rising for 0.75 miles (1.2km) across open moor, the path eventually meets the Bradford–Ilkley Dales Way link. Go left along the paved path, cresting the rise by Lanshaw Lad, a prominent boundary stone to reach the Twelve Apostles, lying just beyond.

3. Retrace your steps from the Twelve Apostles, this time staying with the paved Dales Way. Keep ahead beyond the end of the flags, crossing a small stream and then Backstone Beck at Gill Head. Climbing away, take the left fork past a waymarker. After 0.25 miles (400m), keep ahead at a crossing. The path then swings left in a steep descent, eventually leading to White Wells.

4. Swing right in front of the bathhouse, the path passing a small pond and slanting down the rocky hillside to meet a metalled path. Go right, taking either branch around the tarn. Leave up steps at the far end, the ongoing path later dipping to cross Backstone Beck. Over the bridge, bear left and stick with the main trail. Approaching the Cow and Calf Rocks, ignore a crossing path and keep ahead to skirt below the outcrop.

5. It's worth taking a few minutes to investigate the rocks and watch climbers practising their belays and traverses. From here, a paved path leads back to the car park.

Extending the walk A classic 3.5-mile (5.7km) extension of this walk takes you across the moor from the Twelve Apostles (Point 3) to The Dick Hudsons pub, returning by the same route. Follow the waymarkers for the Dales Way.

Where to eat and drink
The Cow and Calf, at the start of the walk, serves seasonal food and cask ales. If you take the extension to the walk, The Dick Hudsons, named after a 19th-century landlord, offers wholesome food and wholesome views.

What to see
Many rocks on Ilkley Moor are decorated with 'cup and ring' patterns – including the Pancake Rock, near the start of this walk. Many more rock carvings can be found if you take the time to search for them.

While you're there
Ilkley Moor is an intriguingly ancient landscape, criss-crossed by old tracks. This walk and its extension offer short and long options, but you could explore for weeks without walking the same path twice. An east–west walk from the Cow and Calf will take you along the moorland ridge, with terrific views of Ilkley and Wharfedale for most of the way.

LUMB FALLS AND LIMERS GATE

DISTANCE/TIME	4.8 miles (7.4km) / 1hr 45min
ASCENT/GRADIENT	335ft (102m) / ▲▲
PATHS	Good tracks and field paths, several stiles
LANDSCAPE	Gritty Pennine valley with wooded sides and extensive views
SUGGESTED MAP	OS Explorer OL21 South Pennines
START/FINISH	Grid reference: SD996324
DOG FRIENDLINESS	On leads around grazing livestock
PARKING	National Trust car park at Midgehole
PUBLIC TOILETS	Near car park at start of walk

Naturally occurring lime, an important mineral for agriculture and building, is in short supply in West Yorkshire and for centuries it has been imported into the county. Pulverised lime is used by farmers to neutralise acidic soils, and in construction as a component of mortar and plaster.

Limers Gate, which crosses Crimsworth Dean near Hebden Bridge, is a centuries-old packhorse route. The word 'gate' is derived from the middle-English term 'geat', for road or path, while 'lime' is a clue as to what cargo was borne along it by packhorse trains.

In the days before turnpike roads and the Industrial Revolution, travellers kept to the higher ground, which allowed easier travel than through the damp valley bottoms. Limers Gate started in limestone country, in Lothersdale, near Skipton, and crossed the high moors above Wycoller and Walshaw Dean before dropping to Lumb Falls in Crimsworth Dean. It then rose again, on to Wadsworth Moor and the heights above Luddenden Dean, towards its final destination in Halifax.

Above Lumb Falls, a delightful packhorse bridge spans Crimsworth Dean Beck above a waterfall which, when frozen in a hard winter, resembles the pipes of a giant church organ. Though its sides are now fenced, the bridge never had parapets as these would have impeded the progress of ponies laden with bulging panniers.

The small dell in which the bridge and Falls sit is classified as a geological Site of Special Scientific Interest (SSSI). The lip of the waterfall is Lower Kinderscout gristone, while the rock beneath is a softer mudstone, hence its slight overhang. Shales beneath the falls have been eroded to form a pool, popular with picnickers and wild swimmers though it's too shallow to allow diving in.

Wildlife thrives here – kestrels hover above surrounding fields, and herons and grey wagtails can be seen around the Falls. The idyllic scene is credited with having inspired the late poet laureate Ted Hughes, born just a few miles away in Mytholmroyd, to put pen to paper.

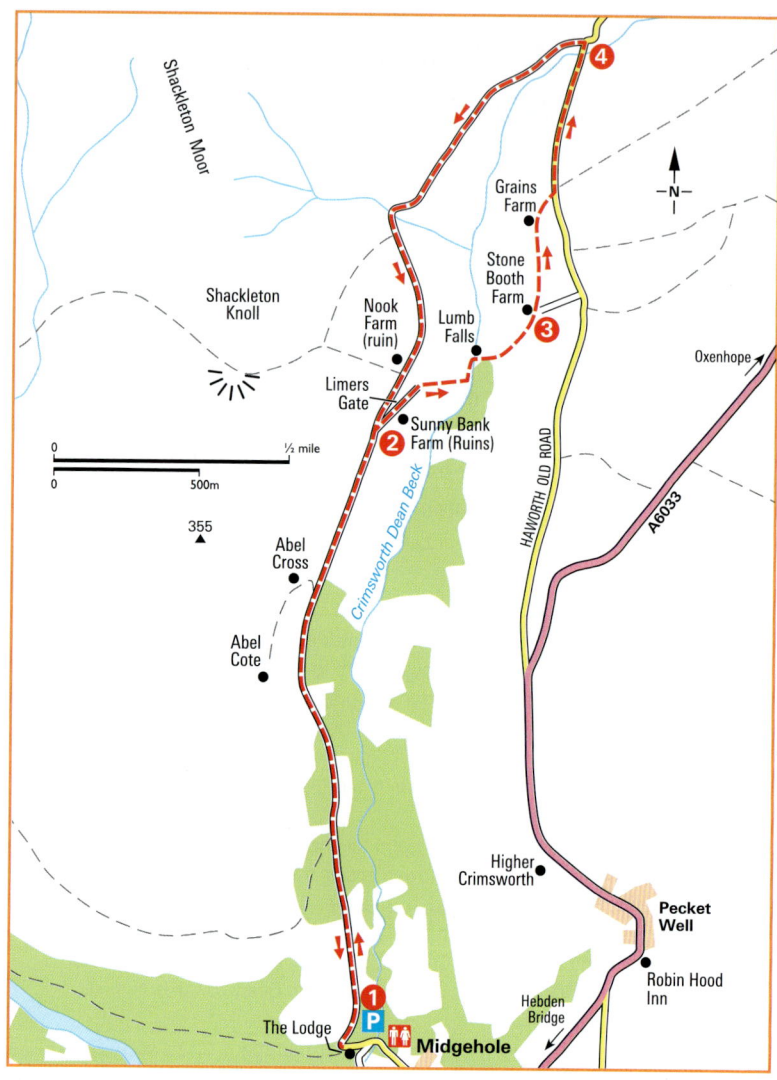

1. From the car park at Midgehole, facing The Lodge, turn right and after 100 yards (90m) turn right and follow the path for a mile (1.6km). Turn off left to visit Abel Cross, actually a pair of old waymarker stones standing beside the track. Return to the main track and continue along the valley passing farm buildings on your right.

2. Bear right and take a walled grassy bridleway signed for Lumb Bridge. This is Limers Gate, the ancient packhorse route, and in places is obstructed by dense reeds and running water but you can easily step off and follow it down on drier ground past the skeletal remains of Sunny Bank Farm. Firmer and clearer ground soon appears in the lane though care should be taken on grass-covered boulders. The lane drops to Lumb Falls, crossing Crimsworth Dean Beck on the ancient packhorse bridge. On the opposite bank, leave Limers Gate by stepping over the stile on your left, then bearing right into an

enclosed flight of stone steps. Emerging into an open field, continue uphill to another stile. Keep ahead beyond, up a pair of steps, then gently bear left to pass through a wooden gate and across a farm courtyard.

3. Take the clearly marked path between barns, scaling a few steps beyond, and bearing right to a latched gate. Cross the field ahead, aiming for the lower of two farmhouses. Beyond the stile through the far wall keep ahead, aiming for the far bottom field corner. Pass through a gated stile here and bear right on a flagged wallside path to a gate into the yard of Grains Farm. Bear right along the surfaced driveway then turn left up the lane.

4. After crossing a stone bridge take the bridleway on the left signed 'Aire Link, Pennine Bridleway', that follows Crimsworth Dean Beck gently downstream, soon passing through a latched wooden gate to cross a second beck near the confluence of the two. For the next 0.6 miles (914m) the track rises gently. The track passes a collapsed farm building and, 550yds (503m) later, crosses the muddy yard of an abandoned farm known as Nook Farm. Follow this path and continue down the valley and at Limers Gate carry on walking south, soon re-entering the woodland of the National Trust estate. Keep left at successive forks, eventually returning to the car park at Midgehole.

Where to eat and drink
'If Robin Hood be not at home, come take a pot with little John.' So says the old sign above the door of the Robin Hood Inn, a former 17th-century coach house that stands at Pecket Well, on the A6033 between Hebden Bridge and Haworth. The pub has a beer garden with views and a log fire inside for chillier days. It offers a full menu at lunchtimes, evenings and all day at weekends. Cask ales are offered and dogs are welcome in the bar area.

What to look out for
Dippers seem to love the waterfalls below Lumb Bridge and can often be seen whirring up and down the beck or stood on the falls' rim, bobbing up and down. This plump, dark bird – it looks black from a distance but its head and underbelly are brown – with a white breast eats insect larvae that it collects by submerging itself and walking underwater.

While you're there
The former mill town of Hebden Bridge escaped the fate of many others when the UK textile industry declined in the later 20th century. Attracted by cheap workers' housing, graduates and creative industries helped the town – already a tourist attraction thanks to its surrounding countryside – reinvent itself. It was the first town in Britain to be awarded Walkers Are Welcome status, and boasts a number of promoted routes.

FELLS OF THE HOLME VALLEY

35

DISTANCE/TIME	4 miles (6.4km) / 2hrs
ASCENT/GRADIENT	886ft (270m) / ▲▲
PATHS	Good tracks most of the way, many stiles
LANDSCAPE	Rolling countryside
SUGGESTED MAP	OS Explorer 288 Bradford & Huddersfield
START/FINISH	Grid reference: SE163067
DOG FRIENDLINESS	Keep on lead near livestock and roads
PARKING	Lay-by at foot of Town Gate in Hepworth
PUBLIC TOILETS	None on route

Presiding over two of the tributary folds that come together in the Holme Valley, Hepworth is one of many villages in this corner of the West Yorkshire Pennines that have retained both charm and communal identity.

The name is of Saxon origin, perhaps identified with a local chief Heppa or merely meaning a settlement occupying the high ground. Handloom weaving and farming were the traditional occupations and determined the style of the houses. Weavers' cottages were usually two or three stories high, with the loom room occupying the whole length of the attic. Rows of narrow, mullioned windows flooded light into the room, which was often reached by an outside staircase and a 'taking in' door.

That the weavers were also farmers and small holders remains evident in the village layout, with long, narrow fields falling behind the old cottages. While staple crops could be grown, the land and climate were generally unsuited to agriculture and farming centred upon dairy cattle and the production of sheep, primarily for wool. But, the local wool was course, and in time, fine wool was imported to produce quality cloths.

Beyond the village, farms were based upon laithe-houses, substantial buildings that combined accommodation, a hay and cattle barn and an upper weaving room under one roof. Examples of these characterful buildings still dot the hillsides around the valley.

Despite relative isolation, Hepworth was not immune to the world's ravages, and has the dubious distinction of being the most northerly place touched by London's Great Plague in 1666. As at Eyam, 20 miles (32km) to the south, the infection arrived in a bolt of cloth. In an effort to stem the contagion, the community threw up a barricade to isolate the afflicted within one half of the village. When normality returned, the dead were remembered in the planting of thirteen trees, one for each departed soul. They still stand (albeit with two replacements) by the village football pitch. The passing of the plague is celebrated to this day in the Hepworth Feast on the last Monday in June, when a band accompanies villagers on a procession to neighbouring Scholes, followed by a fair.

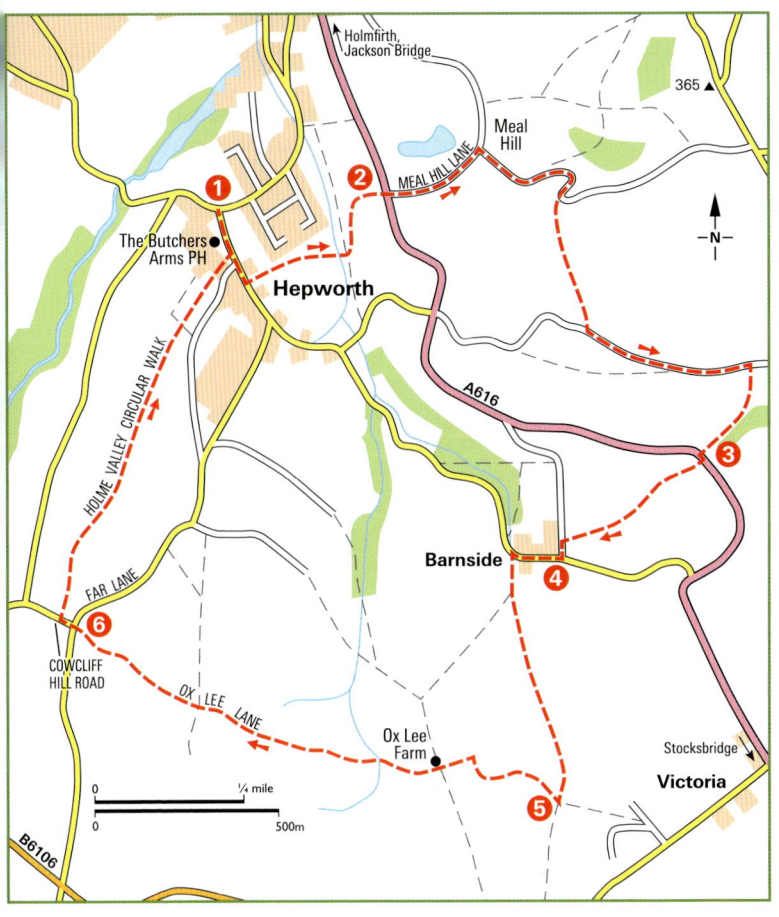

1. Walk south along Town Gate past The Butchers Arms. Some 100yds (91m) beyond, look for steps dropping left beside the end of a terrace from which a path falls steeply along the edge of a narrow field. Towards the bottom, slip over a stile and continue to a bridge spanning the stream at the base of the valley. Walk forward to a crossing path and go left to a fork. Branch right up a stepped path, eventually emerging onto the main road.

2. Cross to Meal Hill Lane opposite, following it beyond houses to a T-junction. Turn right up the hill past the entrance of Bank House Farm. The way climbs on as a rough track, shortly swinging right. Where it subsequently bends sharp left, leave over a stile on the right. A path takes the route more easily across the hillside, in time passing through a gate and stile. Keep ahead as a track joins from the right, walking for another 0.25 miles (400m). Approaching a farmstead, half hidden behind trees, watch for a stile on the right. Drop half right across the steep slope to a gate and continue down by the right boundary. Swinging right towards the bottom, it leads out over a final stile onto the road.

3. Go left 30yds (27m) to a small gate on the right beside a house drive. Cross a paddock to another gate in the far corner and accompany the fence

downhill. Through a squeeze gap beyond the base of the dip, follow the ongoing boundary across the fields to cottages above Barnside. Over a final stile go left past them out to a lane.

4. Turn right through the hamlet. Just beyond cottages at the bottom look for a stile set back from the lane on the left. Walk away, climbing past the indented corner of a wall. Continue beside it to a gate at the top. Cross the next field to a stile and climb the rough hillside beyond to another stile beside a gate in the top boundary. Keep the same line past a redundant stile to meet a crossing track along the top of the hill.

5. Follow it right, through a gate beneath power cables and down to a second gate. The onward path curves right and left above a gully, dropping to a junction of tracks by the abandoned ruin of Ox Lee Farm. Go forward along a walled track. Although occasionally wet and overgrown in places, a parallel path on the right avoids the worst spots. Carry on as the going improves, eventually emerging at a junction of lanes.

6. Cross to Cowcliff Hill Road opposite. After 50yds (46m) leave over a stile on the right. Follow the wall away to another stile and continue across successive fields, part of the Holme Valley Circular Walk, back towards Hepworth, ultimately coming out between buildings by The Butchers Arms.

Where to eat and drink
The Butchers Arms, in the middle of Hepworth village, is the place for a drink and good food. The White Horse Inn at Jackson Bridge – just north of Hepworth, off the A616 – may be familiar even to first-time visitors, since it has featured in many episodes of *Last of the Summer Wine*. Pictures taken from the comedy series are displayed inside.

What to look out for
The little stone village of Hepworth is surrounded by some of the finest countryside in the county; quiet lanes, stone walls and a wide choice of old paths to walk. The proximity of town and country is a striking feature of the area. One minute you are walking on tarmac and cobbles, but within a few minutes you can be out on the moors.

While you're there
Nearby Jackson Bridge is a cramped little community, wedged into a valley around the White Horse Inn. Here you will find rows of distinctive weavers' cottages. To save space, some houses are built on top of each other, providing 'underdwellings' and 'overdwellings', a building solution more familiar in places like Hebden Bridge.

OXENHOPE AND THE WORTH VALLEY RAILWAY

DISTANCE/TIME	6.75 miles (10.9km) / 3hrs
ASCENT/GRADIENT	1,360ft (415m) / ▲▲
PATHS	Good paths and tracks, many stiles
LANDSCAPE	Upland scenery, moor and pasture
SUGGESTED MAP	OS Explorer OL21 South Pennines
START/FINISH	Grid reference: SE032353
DOG FRIENDLINESS	Keep on leads along country lanes and near livestock
PARKING	On-street parking in Oxenhope, near the Keighley and Worth Valley Railway station
PUBLIC TOILETS	None on route

Oxenhope is the terminus of the Keighley and Worth Valley Railway and also the last village in the Worth Valley. To the north are Haworth and Keighley; going south, into Calderdale and Hebden Bridge, requires you to slow down for a scenic drive over the lonely heights of Cock Hill. Apart from the railway, the village is best known for the Oxenhope Straw Race, held each year on the first Sunday in July. Competitors have to carry a bale of straw all around the village, while drinking as much beer as possible. Whoever finishes this assault course first is the winner, but it is the local charities that benefit most.

The Keighley and Worth Valley line, running for 5 miles (8km) from Keighley to Oxenhope, is one of the longest established private railways in the country, and the last remaining complete branch line. It was built in 1867, when the trains were run by the Midland Railway to link to the main Leeds–Skipton line at Keighley. When the line was threatened with closure in 1962, local rail enthusiasts formed a preservation society that bought and restored the line and its stations. Ingrow station, for example, had been so badly vandalised that a complete station was moved to the site stone by stone from Foulridge in Lancashire. Built to the typical Midland style, it now blends in well with the other stations on the line. A regular timetable has continued since 1968. Steam trains run every weekend throughout the year, and daily in summer. But the line doesn't just cater for tourists; locals in the Worth Valley appreciate the diesel services into Keighley, which operate on around 200 days per year.

The line runs through the heart of Brontë country, with stations at Oxenhope, Haworth, Oakworth, Danems, Ingrow and Keighley. The stations are a particular delight: fully restored, gas-lit and redolent of the age of steam. So when Edith Nesbitt's classic children's novel, *The Railway Children*, was being filmed in 1970, the Keighley and Worth Valley Railway was a natural choice of setting. Everyone who has seen the film (it's the one with Jenny Agutter) will enjoy revisiting this much-loved location.

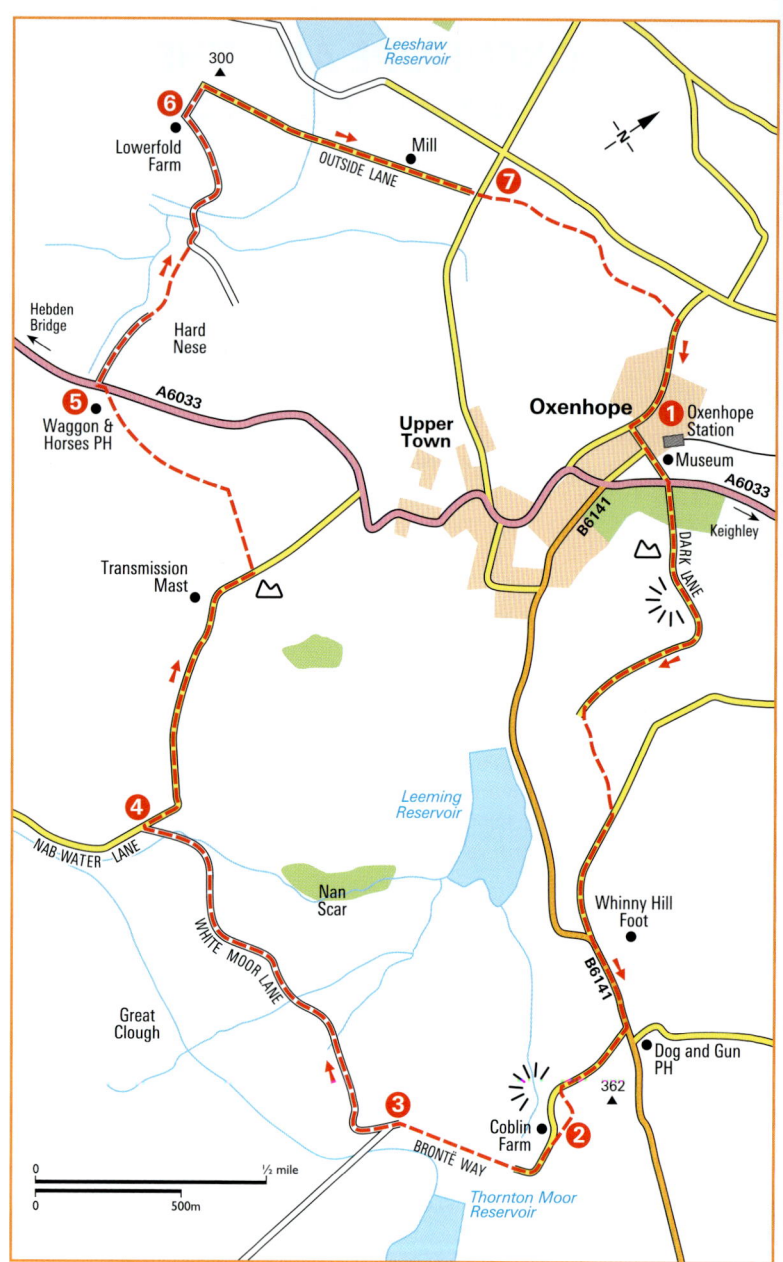

1. Begin along the minor lane beside the entrance of Oxenhope Station, which rises past the overflow car park to the A6033. Cross to Dark Lane opposite and climb steeply away. Later degrading to a track, it eventually ends at a lane. Go right down to the Denholme road (B6141) and follow it left to the Dog and Gun. Turn right opposite the pub into Sawood Lane.

2. At Coblin Farm, your route becomes a rough track. Through a gate at the end, join a metalled track and go right, which is signed 'Brontë Way'. Keep ahead past the entrance to Thornton Moor Reservoir, passing through a field gate along an unmade track. Ignore the Brontë Way, which then shortly drops off to the right.

3. At a fork 50yds (46m) further on, bear right before a gate on a descending track by the wall. It meanders for a mile (1.6km), passing a clump of trees and then crossing a watercourse before eventually meeting a moorland lane.

4. Go right here, eventually passing a cattle grid and a transmission mast. Carry on for another 150yds (137m) but, as the road begins a steep descent, take a wall stile on the left. Later, through another wall stile, head left, uphill, on a broad, walled track that leads to the Waggon and Horses pub.

5. Walk to the left, leaving after 30yds (27m) by a signpost on the right to a steeply descending track. Levelling after 300yds (274m), it swings right. Cross a stile by a gate on the left. Slant right down a couple of fields and continue the line across rough ground, dropping to a walled path at the bottom. Go left across a stream and climb away to Lowerfold Farm.

6. Walk forward past a row of cottages and go right on a metalled track. Follow it away down the hill above the Leeshaw Reservoir for 0.75 miles (1.2km). After passing a converted mill, it finally leads out to a lane.

7. Cross the lane and take the track ahead (signed to Marsh). Pass to the right of the end house, on a narrow-walled path and continue across a small field. Through a courtyard, go left and right past cottages. Emerging, take the kissing gate opposite, from which a path runs through to a walled track. To the right, it leads past houses, across a field and out past more houses to a road. Go right, back down into Oxenhope.

Where to eat and drink
The Waggon and Horses is at the walk's halfway point, on the Hebden Bridge Road out of Oxenhope. It enjoys great views over the valley and has a reputation for good food. If you take the train, there's an excellent café at Oxenhope Station in a stationary British Rail buffet car. It's open whenever trains are running and, additionally, on Wednesday to Sunday.

What to see
Visiting Oxenhope Station is like going back a hundred years. It has been lovingly restored, with enough period detail to make steam buffs dewy eyed with nostalgia. Take a trip to Haworth and back on the Keighley and Worth Valley Railway. You can return on foot along the Worth Way.

MOORLAND AROUND LAYCOCK AND GOOSE EYE

DISTANCE/TIME	8 miles (12.9km) / 3hrs 15min
ASCENT/GRADIENT	1,617ft (492m) / ▲▲
PATHS	Good paths and tracks, though can be muddy, take care with route finding, several stiles
LANDSCAPE	Wooded valley and heather moorland
SUGGESTED MAP	OS Explorer OL21 South Pennines
START/FINISH	Grid reference: SE032410
DOG FRIENDLINESS	On leads where sheep graze on sections of moorland
PARKING	In Laycock; roadside parking at Keighley end of village, close to village hall
PUBLIC TOILETS	None on route

To the west of Keighley, a tranche of moorland sits astride the border between Yorkshire and Lancashire. Here you can walk for miles without seeing another hiker – and perhaps with just curlew and grouse for company.

When we think of textile mills, we tend to associate them with cramped towns full of smoking chimneys. But the earliest mills were sited in surprisingly rural locations, often in the little steep-sided valleys known as cloughs where fast-flowing becks and rivers could be dammed and diverted to turn the waterwheels. There are reminders, in wooded Newsholme Dean, that even a watercourse as small as Dean Beck could be harnessed to provide power to a cotton mill in Goose Eye. Weirs along the beck helped to maintain a good head of water, and continue to be useful to locals – one of the mill dams is now popular with anglers.

The village of Laycock contains a number of handsome old houses in the typical South Pennine style. While Laycock sits on the hillside, with good valley views, neighbouring Goose Eye nestles in a hollow. The village was originally called 'Goose Heights', which the local dialect contracted to 'Goose Ay', and thence to the name we know today. Lovers of real ale will already be familiar with the name, as this was the home of the Goose Eye Brewery, now based in Bingley.

If you head to Keighley, Cliffe Castle Museum is worth a visit. Set in an attractive hillside park on Spring Gardens Lane in Keighley, it was built in the 1880s as a mansion for a wealthy mill owner, and its opulent halls were the scene of many prestigious parties. It is now Keighley's town museum, specialising in natural history and geology.

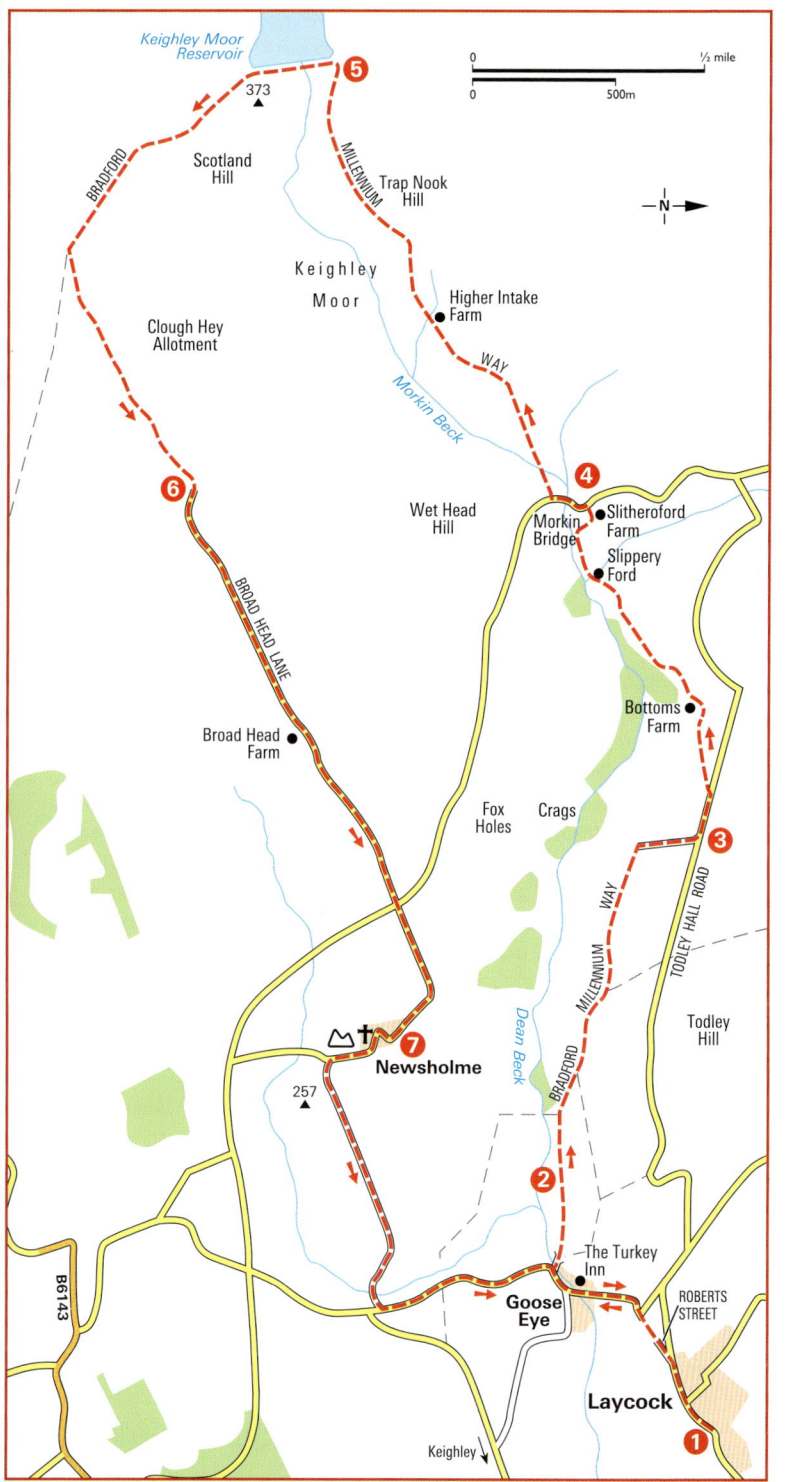

1. Walk through the village of Laycock. Where the road narrows, go left down a paved track, Roberts Street. Beyond terraced houses, descend along a narrow walled path to emerge onto a road, which you follow down into Goose Eye. Pass The Turkey Inn. Just 50yds (46m) after you cross Dean Beck, take the steps on your right and re-cross the beck on a footbridge. Follow the beck upstream and take a footbridge on the right, across the channel of a now-dry mill leat (watercourse).

2. Carry on up the wooded valley, later passing through a gap in a wall. Ignore a path off right and keep ahead, breaking out onto a more open hillside. Before long, the way passes behind a farmhouse to join a farm track. Go left but then branch right on a rough track signed to Slippery Ford. Carry on through a gate, later fording a stream. Just beyond, fork right on a rising hollow path, which later develops as a track. Eventually swinging right it climbs to meet a lane.

3. Walk left along the road for 75yds (69m) before taking an access track on the left to Bottoms Farm. Entering the yard, waymarks indicate a small gate to the right. Skirt beside a barn to a stile from which a path to the left continues across the hillside. Through a gate, carry on over stiles across several fields. At the far side of the fourth field, drop left to find a confluence of two streams. Ford the side beck to a gate and carry on at the edge of another field above the main stream. At the field corner, turn up beside the wall, climbing to a gate near the top of the rise beside Slitheroford Farm. Walk through the yard and out to a lane. Follow the road down to the left to the beck at Morkin Bridge.

4. Reaching Morkin Bridge, turn off right to follow a metalled track through a gate. It rises steadily onto the moors above the fold of Morkin Beck, passing the lonely farm of Higher Intake and eventually leading to Keighley Moor Reservoir, the highest point on the walk.

5. Walk left, across the top of the dam. At the far end, ignore the signed track to the right and instead bear left at a concrete post along a gently descending moorland track. At a boggy section keep ahead, the vague path eventually becoming more distinct as it joins a wall. Follow it for 150yds (137m) to a gateway, turn through and then bear half right to cross a line of grouse butts (shooting stations) on a distinct but narrow path through the heather. Eventually, on meeting a track, follow it right over a cattle grid.

6. Soon leaving the moorland behind, Broad Head Lane runs straight for 0.75 miles (1.2km). Meeting a road by a farm, cross to a track opposite and follow it to cottages at Newsholme.

7. Wind forward between the houses and follow a lane downhill. After 250yds (229m), opposite the entrance to Green End Farm, turn left. Degrading to a track, the way eventually swings across a beck to meet a road. Follow it left down to Goose Eye and The Turkey Inn. Carry on steeply uphill to where the lane swings sharp left, branching off right to reverse your outward route up Roberts Street and back to Laycock.

Where to eat and drink
The Turkey Inn, near the beginning of the walk in Goose Eye, is a splendid village pub with a reputation for good food.

ALONG THE COLNE VALLEY

DISTANCE/TIME	7 miles (11.3km) / 4hrs
ASCENT/GRADIENT	1,000ft (305m) / ▲▲
PATHS	Field paths, good tracks and canal towpath, many stiles
LANDSCAPE	Typical South Pennine rough pastures, canalside
SUGGESTED MAP	OS Explorer OL21 South Pennines
START/FINISH	Grid reference: SE079140
DOG FRIENDLINESS	Towpath is especially good for dogs
PARKING	Plenty of street parking in Slaithwaite; car park next to the library on New Street
PUBLIC TOILETS	Marsden

Transport across the Pennine watershed has always presented problems. The Leeds and Liverpool Canal, built during the 1770s, took a convoluted route across the Pennines, through the Aire Gap at Skipton. Then came the Rochdale Canal. However, its more direct route came at a high price: mile for mile, this canal has more locks than any other inland waterway in the country. With the increase in trade between Yorkshire and Lancashire, a third route across the Pennines was soon needed. The Huddersfield Narrow Canal links Huddersfield with Ashton-under-Lyne in Greater Manchester. Though only 20 miles (32.2km) long, it includes the Standedge Tunnel. Begun in 1794, and dug with pick, shovel and dynamite, the canal was finally opened to traffic in 1811.

The Colne Valley, to the west of Huddersfield, is representative of industrial West Yorkshire. Towns with evocative names – Milnsbridge, Linthwaite, Slaithwaite and Marsden – are threaded along the River Colne like beads on a string. In the 18th century, this was a landscape of scattered farms and hand-loom weavers, mostly situated on the higher ground. As with Calderdale, a few miles to the north, the deep-cut valley of the Colne was transformed by the Industrial Revolution. Once the textile processes began to be mechanised, mills were built in the valley bottom. They specialised in the production of fine worsted cloth. The River Colne provided the power for the first mills, and the canal subsequently improved the transport links.

The mills grew larger as water power gave way to steam, towering over the rows of terraced houses built in their shadows. Throughout this walk you can see the mill chimneys and the sawtooth roof-lines of the weaving sheds, though some mills are in ruins and others are now given over to other trades. Slaithwaite (often pronounced 'Slowitt') is typical of the textile towns in the Colne Valley. It looks to be an unlikely spa town, but that's what it became in the 1820s, albeit briefly, when its mineral springs were compared favourably with those of Harrogate. Now, with the canal restored, Slaithwaite is finding another new lease of life and you'll find a range of independent shops and cafés when you visit.

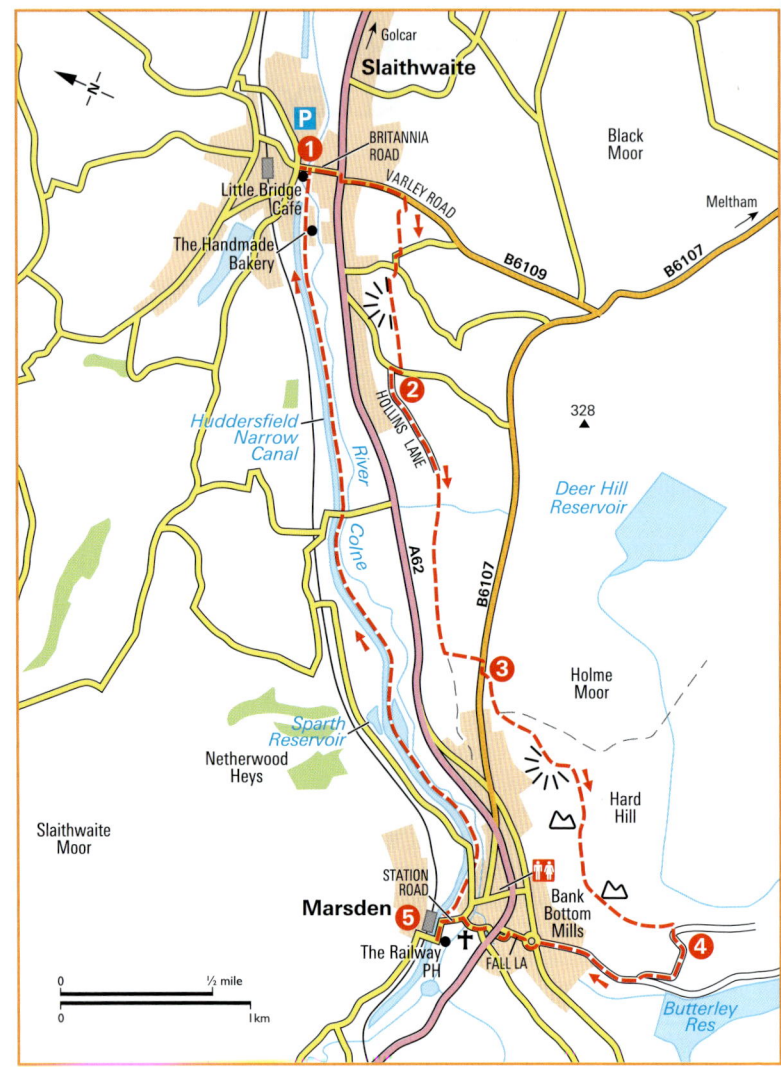

1. Begin along Britannia Road, turning right on to the A62 and crossing to continue up Varley Road. Beyond the last house, go through a squeeze gap on the right and climb to a field. Swinging right and left, follow an indistinct path to a stile on the opposite side. Carry on beside the right-hand wall, crossing through a gate to a tarmac lane. Follow it right and left to a crossroads. Take the track opposite, bearing left after 20yds (18m) on to another track between houses. Go over a stile at the end, keep ahead at the edge of successive fields, crossing more stiles and eventually leaving beside a house on to a tarmac lane.

2. Go briefly right before turning left along a track that ultimately leads to a farm. Walk forwards past the front of a cottage (through the garden), passing through a dilapidated gate into a field corner. Carry on ahead, negotiating

gates either side of a beck at the far side and passing an abandoned farmstead to a walled path. Where the path shortly veers right, take the gate ahead into a field. Follow the right wall, bearing slightly left beyond its end to slant up across rough pastures. Go over a stile and keep forwards, continuing on to reach a walled path. Climb left to another stile, then turn right down to a bend. Scaling a wall stile on the left, walk away at the bottom edge of fields to a kissing gate. Continue through a plantation, swinging left at the far side along a path up to the B6107.

3. Walk right for 75yds (69m), then take a track off to the left. Continue past a house and through a gate, shortly reaching a fork. Keep ahead on the right branch. Cross a beck and fork left uphill; the way narrows to a path. At a junction turn right to pass below old quarries on the shoulder of Hard Hill. Climb to a kissing gate, then drop to a bridge beside a stone aqueduct. After rising to a memorial bench, the way levels and Butterley Reservoir comes into view. Beyond another kissing gate by a small stone building, climb left to a stile, carrying on over a second stile and out on to a metalled track. Follow it down to a tarmac lane.

4. Continue downhill, eventually passing terraced houses dwarfed by Bank Bottom Mills. Keep straight ahead at a roundabout along Fall Lane, bearing left before the end to pass beneath the main road. Keep left over a bridge and then right past the church. At the end go left up Station Road.

5. Join the Huddersfield Narrow Canal towpath opposite The Railway pub. Follow it right, dropping past the first of many locks, for a pleasant 3-mile (4.8km) walk back to Slaithwaite.

Where to eat and drink
The Railway, close to the rail station and canal in Marsden, comes at the halfway point of the walk. Slaithwaite itself has a great selection of cafés and pubs. The café at The Handmade Bakery and the Little Bridge Café Wine Bar are both on the canal towpath.

What to see
Sparth Reservoir, located next to the towpath between Marsden and Slaithwaite, is used to top up water in the canal. It has been a local wild swimming spot since the 1950s and has seen community swimming events held there in the past. Near Slaithwaite, is the country's only working guillotine gate on a narrow canal.

While you're there
Slaithwaite has a number of independent arts and crafts and antiques shops selling work from local artists. The Colne Valley Museum in Golcar (open Saturday, Sunday and Bank Holiday Mondays, noon till 4pm) is based in an old weaver's cottage and has information about the local area. You can either drive there or reach it by walking a further 1.5 miles (2.4km) along the canal towpath.

TEMPLE NEWSAM COUNTRY PARK

39

DISTANCE/TIME	1.5 miles (2.4km) / 30min
ASCENT/GRADIENT	151ft (46m) / ▲
PATHS	Good tracks and paths throughout
LANDSCAPE	Parkland, gardens, lakes and woodland
SUGGESTED MAP	OS Explorer 289 Leeds
START/FINISH	Grid reference: SE357321
DOG FRIENDLINESS	Dogs should be under control
PARKING	Pay-and-display at the House Car Park, off Temple Newsam Road, Leeds
PUBLIC TOILETS	In the tea rooms at Stable Courtyard at start and at the Rose Garden

Temple Newsam is one of England's finest historic houses. The impressive surrounding parklands were laid out by the famous landscape architect Lancelot 'Capability' Brown in the late 1760s for Charles Ingram and today its lakes, woodlands and formal gardens, in the care of Leeds City Council, are available for all to explore.

The earliest record of the property is a mention in the Domesday Book as 'Neuhusam', meaning 'new house'. The preface 'Temple' comes from the fact that it was owned by the Knights Templar between 1155 and 1307, when the order was quashed following Papal decree and the property seized by the state.

Subsequent owners faired little better: Sir Philip Darcy was executed in 1537 for his part in the Yorkshire uprising known as the Pilgrimage of Grace, and the property was seized again in 1565 when Temple Newsam owner Lord Henry Darnley married Mary, Queen of Scots and was later suspected of attempting to murder her to win her throne. He survived a huge explosion at his residence in Kirk o'Field, fleeing in his nightshirt only to be strangled by assailants waiting outside. It was Sir Arthur Ingram, who bought the Temple Newsham estate in 1622, who built the basis of the mansion we see today, incorporating part of the existing brick-built house in the new west wing. A native of Rothwell, Ingram made his fortune during the struggle to make James I and Charles I financially independent of parliament. He was knighted in 1613 and became one of the most powerful men in the county of Yorkshire.

His descendants remodelled various wings over subsequent decades and in the 1760s Charles Ingram, the ninth Viscount of Irvine, commissioned Capability Brown to remodel the estate.

Much of Capability Brown's overall design survives today. He opted for a natural design, breaking up the symmetry imposed by the house and opening up fresh vistas to the west and south. Functional buildings, such as stables, were screened by trees and a new approach along a long driveway, which passed between gates guarded by sphinxes, was created.

It was during this period that the Prince of Wales, later to become George IV, presented Ingram's daughter, Lady Hertford, his mistress, with a pair of 18th-century Brussels tapestries depicting the biblical stories of the discovery of Moses, and the battle of the Israelites and the Amalekites as Moses led his people towards the Promised Land. These, and many other great works of art, including furniture masterpieces by Thomas Chippendale, silver and Leeds pottery, are on display within the house.

Today the estate offers even more to the people of Leeds, with classical and pop concerts, cycling, riding, golf, a farm open to the public and walking.

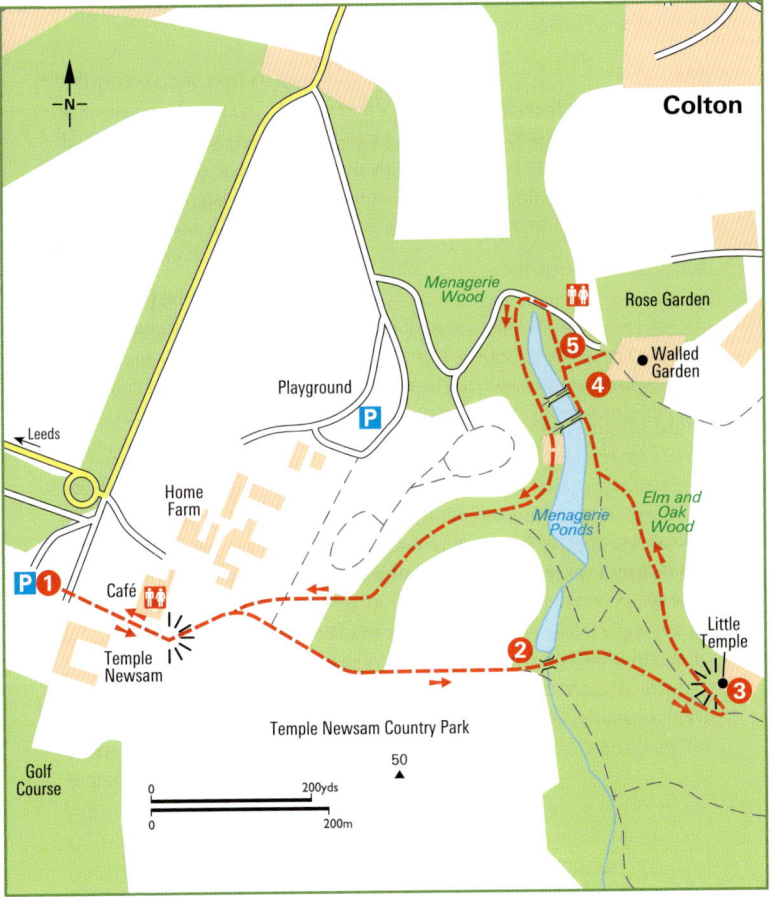

1. Leave the car park and pass by the left side of the main house. Follow the main track that sweeps left downhill below the Stable Courtyard. Fork right beyond the estate buildings, down to a junction by a pond.

2. Leave the hard-surfaced track here and take the narrow path ahead, signed for the Little Temple, across a patch of grass and over the pond's outflow into woodland. The obvious path rises to follow the right edge of a clearing, and to a junction.

3. Turn left here, past the Little Temple on the path signed 'Easy going route to lakes'. This gently descends through rhododendron, zig-zagging at the bottom to a junction with the lakeside path. Bear right, then left down the brick-surfaced track met at a crossroads, to the water's edge.

4. Turn right past two footbridges to a fork. Here, your route continues ahead left but a diversion to the right, to explore the Rose Garden and Georgian Walled Garden, will more than repay the minimal effort involved.

5. Returning to the junction, resume your earlier direction. Bear hard left at the next opportunity to double back down the opposite side of the lakes, past the two footbridges. The trail sweeps up to a junction and bears right to wind its way back to the house, stables and car park beyond.

Where to eat and drink
The Temple Newsam Tea Room in the Stable Courtyard serves snacks, afternoon teas and hot meals, and focuses on local produce including its own sausages and burgers. It is closed on Mondays, except during school summer holidays.

What to look out for
On a hillside gazing across to Temple Newsam House, you'll find the Little Temple, created in the 18th century to enhance the already splendid view from the house. Supported by four classical columns it, in turn, offers an excellent view back across the valley to the house.

While you're there
Temple Newsam's Home Farm was the maintenance base for the grand estate in years gone-by. Today, visitors are welcome to explore its cobbled yards, admire its 17th-century Great Barn and delight in Europe's largest rare breeds farm, which has more than 400 animals including sheep, poultry (don't miss the Transylvanian naked neck hen), cattle, goats and pigs.

A STROLL THROUGH JUDY WOODS

DISTANCE/TIME	3.5 miles (5.7km) / 1hr 15min
ASCENT/GRADIENT	394ft (120m) / ▲
PATHS	Good tracks and woodland paths, several stiles
LANDSCAPE	Arable land and beech woods
SUGGESTED MAP	OS Explorer 288 Bradford & Huddersfield
START/FINISH	Grid reference: SE147268
DOG FRIENDLINESS	Can be off lead in woods
PARKING	Along Station Road (off the A641 at Wyke) near information panel and kissing gate leading into Judy Woods
PUBLIC TOILETS	None on route

Set within the deep fold of Royd Hall Beck, Judy Woods is a fragment of a once extensive forest that stretched to the Midlands. Despite it now being flanked by the conurbations of Bradford and Halifax, it survives as one of the finest semi-natural woodlands in the county and is a haven for all manner of wildlife.

The valley's steep sides saved it from historical clearance for agriculture, but the underlying geology attracted a different sort of activity – mining for coal and later iron ore. Initially, from the medieval period, it was undertaken on a small scale in the form of shallow bell pits, whose remains can still be found amongst the trees in the crater-like hollows of collapsed workings. But mechanisation towards the end of the 18th century enabled deeper mines and the area was taken over to supply raw material for the Low Moor Iron Company, which manufactured a whole range of products including some of the cannons used at the Battle of Waterloo. Over 25 miles (40km) of wagonway were laid through the woods to transport coal and ore to the nearby factory and many of the embankments and inclines are still visible today.

One of the delightful features of the woodland is the large number of massive beech trees, which produce a magnificent spectacle of colour each autumn. Planted during the 18th century, these too were intended for profit – to provide wood for the manufacture of bobbins and spindles for the local textile industry. Despite their majestic appearance, their dense foliage shades the ground to the detriment of other species and they are gradually being replaced by the native birch and oak that would have formed the original woodland cover.

Some time after the beech were planted, the area was opened as a pleasure garden. It acquired the name Judy Woods after Judy North, who lived in a cottage by Horse Close Bridge, a packhorse bridge across the stream and now known as Judy Bridge. Her husband had been employed as gardener on the estate and, after his death Judy and her son continued in his stead. Augmenting their income, Judy sold refreshments to the visitors.

The woods are now managed for the benefit of wildlife and attract a rich variety of birds. In summer, migrant warblers such as blackcap, chiffchaff and willow warbler arrive from Africa, while in winter, fieldfare and redwing come from the north. Owls, woodpeckers, nuthatches and many garden birds can be spotted all year round. Look out too for roe deer and bats. Spring is particularly beautiful for the bluebells that carpet the glades. Autumn is the time, not only for the turning leaves, but also fungi, which can be found in profusion through the valley.

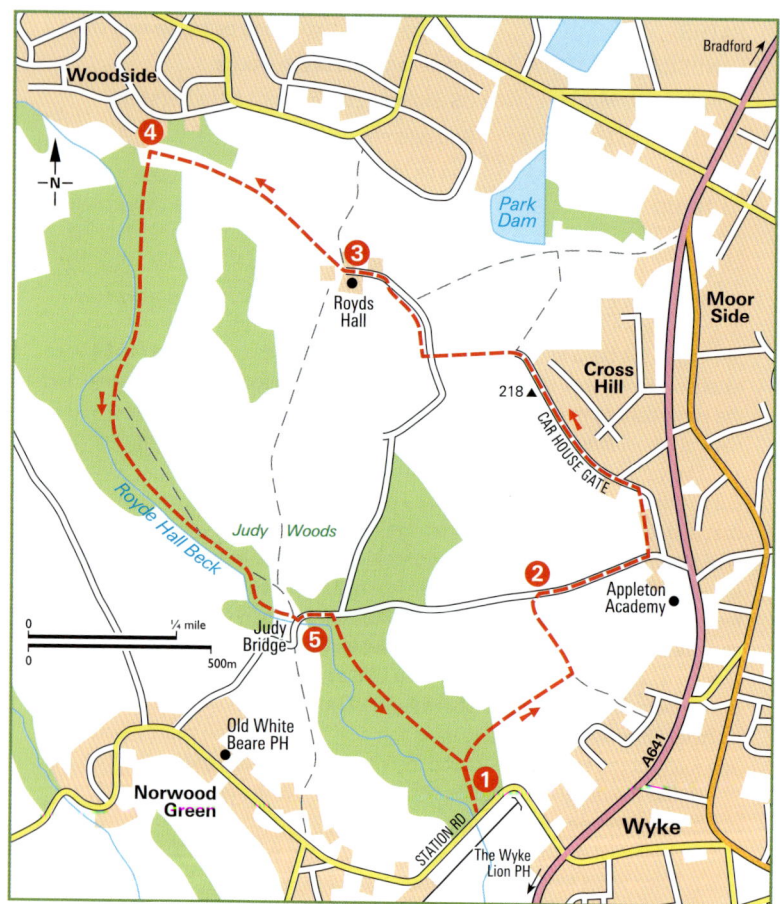

1. From the upper entrance to the woods on Station Road, where there is a notice board and kissing gate, follow a path into the trees signed to Woodside. Where it subsequently swings left, turn off right, walking to a stile at the edge of the trees. Head away across open ground, following an old incline that rises towards a high fence surrounding the perimeter of Appleton Academy. Go left, passing through a gate and continuing out to a lane.

2. Turn right up the hill, walking as far as the entrance to the school. There, turn left onto an unadopted street, Carr House Gate. Follow it past houses to its very end by a breaker's yard. Keep ahead to pick up a path that passes

behind more houses. Swinging beneath the foot of communication masts it continues between open fields. Meeting a track, go right to Royds Hall.

3. Follow the track between cottages and an old stable block. Immediately after it swings right past the entrance to the farm, leave over a wall stile on the left. Walk away on a shallow angle to find another stile set left of the far corner. Carry on beside a wall on the right, continuing forward beyond its end within a fringe of beech trees. Keep ahead until you reach a kissing gate that leads out to houses.

4. However, instead of passing through, swing left on a path towards Judy Woods. Go through the kissing gate there and follow a good path into the trees. Eventually the gravel way peters out, but keep ahead, now gently descending on a rougher path. Later becoming stepped, it drops to a plank bridge across a stream. Cross and follow Royd Hall Beck to Judy Bridge, a short distance downstream.

5. Climb to the track above and follow it left uphill. However, a short distance along slip through a gap in the right wall to continue on a parallel path. At the top, swing right and walk away, again on a gravel path that wends along the broad crest of the wood. Eventually reaching the junction passed at the start of the walk, go right back to Station Road.

Where to eat and drink
At the junction of the A58 with the A641 near the start of the walk, you'll find Ego at the Wyke Lion, which serves freshly cooked food from across the Mediterranean region. Closer to Norwood Green is the Old White Beare. Originally a farmhouse in 1533, it was rebuilt after a fire 60 years later with timbers from an Elizabethan galleon called the White Beare. It's a warm and friendly, family pub, offering food and drink.

What to look out for
In the spring, these beech woods are carpeted with bluebells. For most of the year these riotous flowers survive as tiny bulbs below the woodland floor. From late April until early June, the succulent green stems rise up and the soft blue flowers can be seen everywhere.

While you're there
This walk is close to the centre of Bradford, offering a good opportunity to explore this bustling metropolis, granted city status in 1897 to acknowledge its importance as 'wool capital of the world'. The city centre has some fine architecture reflecting the heyday of the worsted trade that brought it wealth. Particularly impressive is the Italianate town hall and the quarter known as Little Germany. Another magnificent building is Cartwright Hall in Lister Park, which houses a superb collection of 19th- and 20th-century British art, as well as reflecting the city's multicultural heritage in exhibits from the Indian continent and South Asia.

EXPLORING RISHWORTH MOOR

DISTANCE/TIME	7.5 miles (12.1km) / 3hrs
ASCENT/GRADIENT	1,115ft (340m) / ▲▲▲
PATHS	Moorland paths, may be boggy after rain
LANDSCAPE	Open moorland
SUGGESTED MAP	OS Explorer OL21 South Pennines
START/FINISH	Grid reference: SE011190
DOG FRIENDLINESS	Keep on lead near livestock
PARKING	Car park beside A58 at Baitings Reservoir
PUBLIC TOILETS	None on route

Beginning in the upper reaches of the Ryburn Valley, this walk sets out across the dam of Baitings Reservoir, built in 1956 to supply Wakefield. Climbing Rishworth Moor onto Blackwood Edge, the view opens across the neighbouring valley to the M62 motorway as it rises from Scammonden across the flank of Moss Moor to cross the Pennine watershed beneath Windy Hill just south of Blackstone Edge. As you stride out across Rishworth Moor, you're unlikely to sight many other walkers. On the second half of the walk, you get excellent views of the Ryburn Valley and beyond, including Blackstone Edge, Pendle Hill and distant windfarms.

    The South Pennine hills have long been a great obstacle to travel. A fascinating paved road climbs steeply up Blackstone Edge; opinions are divided as to whether it is Roman or a medieval packhorse track. But no one was in any doubt that this was difficult terrain. The redoubtable traveller, Celia Fiennes, coming this way in 1698, described this route as '...a dismal high precipice, steep in ascent'. Daniel Defoe came the same way in August 1724, during a blizzard that was unseasonal even for the Pennines.

    A succession of turnpike roads were built in the 18th and early 19th centuries. Yet it was as recently as the 1970s, with the building of the M62, that trans-Pennine travel became routine. Surveyors did some of their initial work using ponies – the easiest mode of transport in this inhospitable landscape. At an altitude of 1,220ft (372m), the M62 is the highest motorway in the country, and this Pennine section offers some dramatic features.

    One of the most talked-about features of the motorway is the division of east- and west-bound carriageways around Stott Hall Farm. Urban myths tell that this was because of the then farmer's stubbornness to sell out in the face of development. As always, the truth is less sensational, the hillside geology is just too unstable to support adjacent carriageways.

    When built, Scammonden Bridge was the largest single-span bridge in Europe and carries the B6114 across the motorway. Less obvious to motorway users is the Scammonden Dam just to the east. It is the only reservoir embankment in Britain to carry a motorway and the lake it created flooded a dozen farms in the Deanhead Valley.

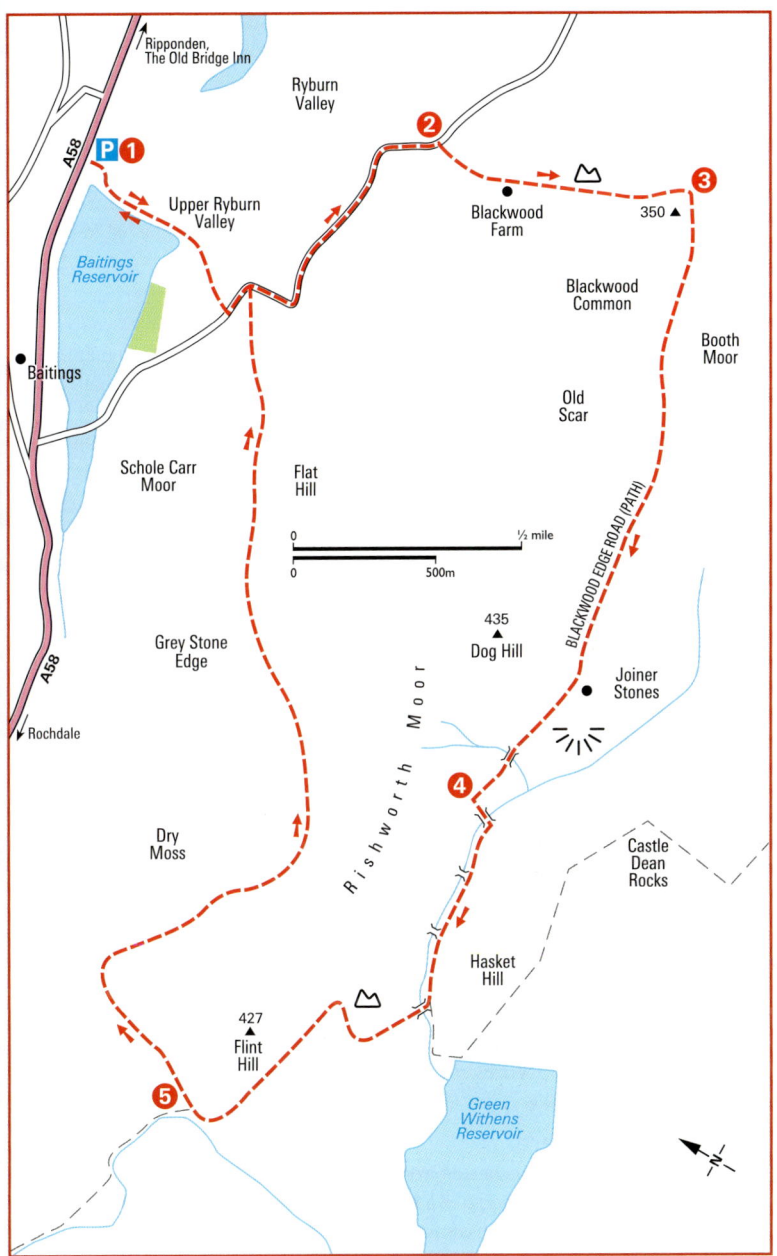

1. Take the path across the dam, a track beyond climbing past a farm to a lane. Turn left and walk for 0.5 miles (800m). Some 50yds (46m) after swinging over a bridge, leave through a waymarked gate in the right-hand wall.

2. Follow a tumbledown wall uphill towards Blackwood Farm. Entering between outbuildings, walk beyond the farmhouse to a gate at the top of the yard. Walk up the next field to a gate and continue steeply uphill, following the

wall on your left. Look for views of the Ryburn Valley as you approach the crest of the hill. You will come to a ladder stile, next to a gate in the wall.

3. Don't cross, but strike off right over rough moorland; the path is distinct but narrow. Occasional yellow-topped markers confirm the route, which runs roughly parallel to the M62, aiming to the right of a tall mast on the far side of the motorway. After a mile (1.6km), the path begins a gentle descent, giving good views down to Green Withens Reservoir ahead. Keep forward above the head of a gully then over a plank bridge as the path falls across the hill to a bridge spanning a reservoir catchment channel.

4. Cross and walk right, following this watercourse towards the reservoir. Ignore the next two bridges across, but at the third, which is about 300yds (274m) before the reservoir embankment and waymarked 'Blackstone Edge and Baitings', revert to the northern bank. Bear slightly left to follow a path uphill – soon quite steep – before it levels and swings left around Flint Hill. It later curves right to crest the watershed into the Upper Ryburn Valley where there is a junction of paths by a water channel.

5. Go right here (a sign indicates Baitings Reservoir), continuing to skirt the hill on a good, level path. After a mile (1.6km), watch for a fork marked by a wooden post and bear left, gradually descending towards Baitings Reservoir. When you come to a wall corner, keep straight ahead, following the wall on your left. A developing track leads out to the lane. Go left and take the second right, reversing your outward steps to the car park.

Where to eat and drink
Take the opportunity to visit one of the oldest (it dates to the 14th century) and most delightful pubs in West Yorkshire. The Old Bridge Inn is tucked out of sight off the main A58 road, on a cobbled lane near the church, just beyond an old packhorse bridge. Real ale, picturesque surroundings and excellent food make the pub rather special.

What to look out for
The upland moors of the South Pennines are important Sites of Special Scientific Interest (SSSI), with sparse landscapes of heather, grasses, bilberry, cotton grass and crowberry, where birds such as merlin and golden plover still live. The only thing lacking, apart from trees is people and you can stride out across these moors for mile after mile without seeing another walker.

While you're there
The Ryburn Valley branches off from the Calder at Sowerby Bridge. Ripponden is a little straggle of a town that's well worth exploring. It was once an important weaving centre, known for its dark 'Navy Blue' cloth; at one time it was the sole supplier to the Royal Navy.

ALONG LANGFIELD EDGE TO STOODLEY PIKE

DISTANCE/TIME	9 miles (14.5km) / 4hrs
ASCENT/GRADIENT	1,821ft (555m) / ▲▲
PATHS	Good paths and tracks, several stiles
LANDSCAPE	Open moorland
SUGGESTED MAP	OS Explorer OL21 South Pennines
START/FINISH	Grid reference: SD936241
DOG FRIENDLINESS	On leads as sheep grazing throughout
PARKING	Car parks in centre of Todmorden
PUBLIC TOILETS	Brook Street, Todmorden

This walks starts at Todmorden – call it 'Tod' if you want to sound like a local – a border town, standing at the junction of three valley routes. Before the town was included in the old West Riding, the Yorkshire–Lancashire border divided the town in two. Todmorden's splendid town hall, built in an unrestrained classical Greek style, reflects this dual personality. On top of the town hall are carved figures which represent, on one side, the Lancashire cotton trade, and, on the other side, Yorkshire agriculture and engineering.

Stoodley Pike is a ubiquitous sight around the Calder Valley, and an unmistakable landmark. It seems you only need to turn a corner, or crest a hill, and it appears on the horizon. West Yorkshire is full of monuments built on prominent outcrops, but few of them dominate the view in quite the way that Stoodley Pike does.

In 1814, a trio of patriotic Todmorden men convened in a local pub, the Golden Lion. Now that the Napoleonic War was over, they wanted to commemorate the peace with a suitably grand monument. They organised a public subscription, and raised enough money to erect a monument, 1,476ft (450m) up on Langfield Edge, overlooking the town. Construction was halted, briefly, when Napoleon rallied his troops, and was not completed until the following year, when he was finally defeated at the Battle of Waterloo.

This original monument was undone by the Pennine weather. Ironically, it collapsed in 1854, on the very day that the Crimean War broke out. Another group of local worthies came together (yes, at the Golden Lion again) to raise more money. The Stoodley Pike we see today is this second versions: 121ft (37m) high and built to commemorate the ending of hostilities in the Crimea. It remains visible for almost every step of this exhilarating ridge walk. As well as being a favourite destination for local walkers, the Pike is visited by walkers on the Pennine Way.

Remember to pack a torch for this walk. By climbing a flight of unlit stone steps inside the monument, you emerge at a viewing platform offering wonderful panoramic views over Calderdale and beyond.

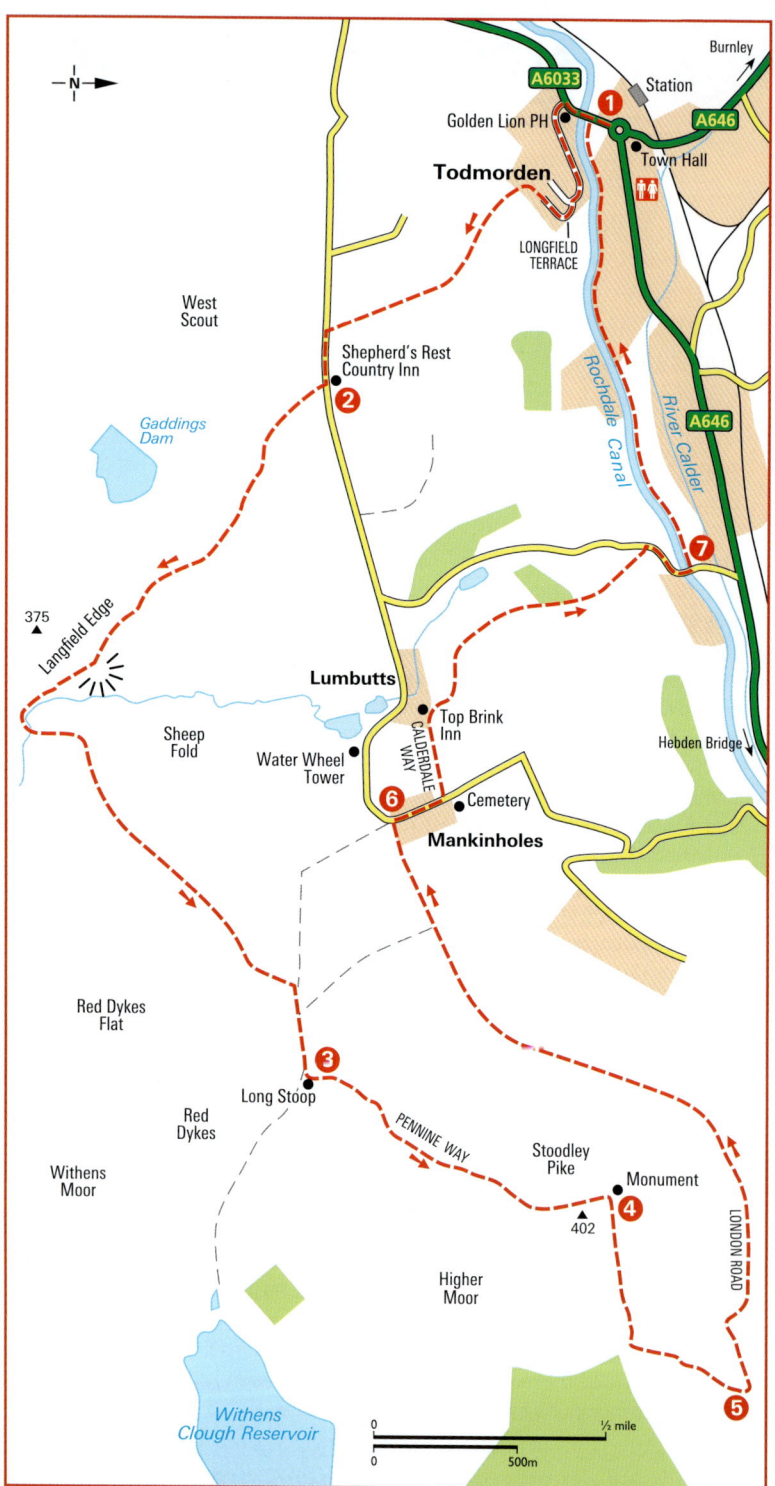

1. From the town hall in the centre of Todmorden, take the Rochdale road (A6033), cross the canal, turning left and immediately left again around the Golden Lion pub to walk up Longfield Road. Keep ahead as the main street veers away to new houses, but then swing right with Longfield Road up to Longfield Terrace at the end. Just before the row of houses, bear left on a track climbing between the fields behind. When the track forks, keep left to a farm, from where you will get the first glimpse of your destination – Stoodley Pike – on the horizon ahead. Continue along the farm track to a road. Go left, to find a pub, the Shepherd's Rest Country Inn, in splendid isolation.

2. Opposite the pub, take a track leading through a gate, uphill, onto Langfield Common. Keep ahead past a waymark along a distinct and well-graded path that rises across the steep hillside below Langfield Edge. Levelling at the top, it is joined by another path to round the head of the clough. The way runs on above the edge, eventually intersecting a broader path, the Pennine Way. Go left towards the distant monument.

3. Passing a stone seat, the path falls to a junction. Climb ahead past the leaning ancient waystone of Long Stoop. The way soon levels for the final stretch to the tower, 0.75 miles (1.2km) further on.

4. From the monument, swing right, walking down to a wall stile. After a few paces cross a second stile in the adjacent wall, from which the path drops more steeply to a lower track, London Road.

5. Follow the track left in a long and gentle descent to come out onto a lane. Go right, into the hamlet of Mankinholes.

6. After 0.25 miles (400m), opposite a cemetery and former Wesleyan Sunday school, turn off left along a walled path, signed the 'Pennine Bridleway'. It winds between fields to the Top Brink Inn at Lumbutts. Turn right between houses and continue at the field edge along a causeway path. Passing through a squeeze gap into the third field, bear half right across the slope. Keep going beyond a broken wall, the path shortly closing beside a high fence. Meeting a farm track head downhill to emerge by cottages. Follow the lane right, and swinging in front of a converted mill to a bridge spanning the Rochdale Canal.

7. Drop right to the tow path and follow the canal back under the bridge into the centre of Todmorden.

Where to eat and drink

The isolated Shepherd's Rest Country Inn is near the beginning of this walk, while the Top Brink Inn at Lumbutts is towards the end. Back in town, the Golden Lion serves Thai food and has regular live music, and Todmorden has plenty of other food outlet options.

What to see

London Road, the fancifully named track you follow from Stoodley Pike down into Mankinholes, was a 'cotton famine road'. When the cotton trade suffered a slump, mill owner John Fielden of Todmorden put some of his men to work on building this road, so he could ride his carriage up to Stoodley Pike. Fielden also built Dobroyd Castle, its castellated turrets on a hill overlooking the town.

43 HARDCASTLE CRAGS AND CRIMSWORTH DEAN

DISTANCE/TIME	5 miles (8km) / 2hrs 30min
ASCENT/GRADIENT	1,359ft (414m) / ▲▲
PATHS	Good paths and tracks, plus open pasture
LANDSCAPE	Woodland, fields and moorland fringe
SUGGESTED MAP	OS Explorer OL21 South Pennines
START/FINISH	Grid reference: SD987293
DOG FRIENDLINESS	Keep dogs on leads near livestock
PARKING	National Trust pay-and-display car parks at Midgehole, near Hebden Bridge (accessible via A6033, Keighley Road)
PUBLIC TOILETS	Just before car parks at Midgehold

Hebden Bridge, just 4 miles (6.4km) from the Yorkshire/Lancashire border, has been a popular place to visit ever since the railway was extended across the Pennines, through the Calder Valley. But those train passengers weren't coming for a day out in a little mill town; the big attraction was the wooded valley of Hebden Dale – usually called Hardcastle Crags – just a short ride away. Here were shady woods, easy riverside walks and places to spread out a picnic blanket. To people who lived in the terraced streets of Bradford, Leeds or Halifax, Hardcastle Crags must have seemed idyllic. The steep-sided valley became known as 'Little Switzerland' – at least to the writers of tourist brochures. The only disappointment, in fact, was the crags themselves: unassuming gritstone outcrops, almost hidden by trees.

The Industrial Revolution created a huge demand for water: for mills, factories and domestic use. To quench the thirst of the rapidly expanding textile towns, many steep-sided valleys, known in the South Pennines as cloughs, were dammed to create reservoirs. Six of these lie within easy walking distance of Hardcastle Crags. They represented huge feats of civil engineering by the hundreds who built them, around the end of the 19th century, with picks and shovels. The men were housed in a shanty town, known as Dawson City, and both men and materials were transported to the work sites by a convoluted steam-powered railway system that crossed the valley on an elaborate wooden viaduct. Hardcastle Crags escaped the indignity of being turned into a reservoir, but three times during the last 60 years (the last time was in 1970) plans were drawn up to flood the valley. And three times, thankfully, wiser counsels prevailed and the plans were turned down.

Lord Savile, a major landowner in the area, once owned the valley. It was he who supplemented the natural woodland with plantings of new trees, particularly pines, and laid out the walks and the carriage drive. In 1948, he donated Hardcastle Crags, and the nearby valley of Crimsworth Dean, to the National Trust, so now the future of this delightful valley looks secure and local people will be able to continue to enjoy this valuable amenity.

Hardcastle Crags are a haven for wildlife. Look out for pied flycatchers, woodpeckers, jays, sparrowhawks and the ubiquitous dipper – which never strays from the environs of Hebden Water. In spring, there are displays of bluebells, in summer, the woods are filled with birdsong, and the beech woods are a riot of colour as the leaves turn each autumn.

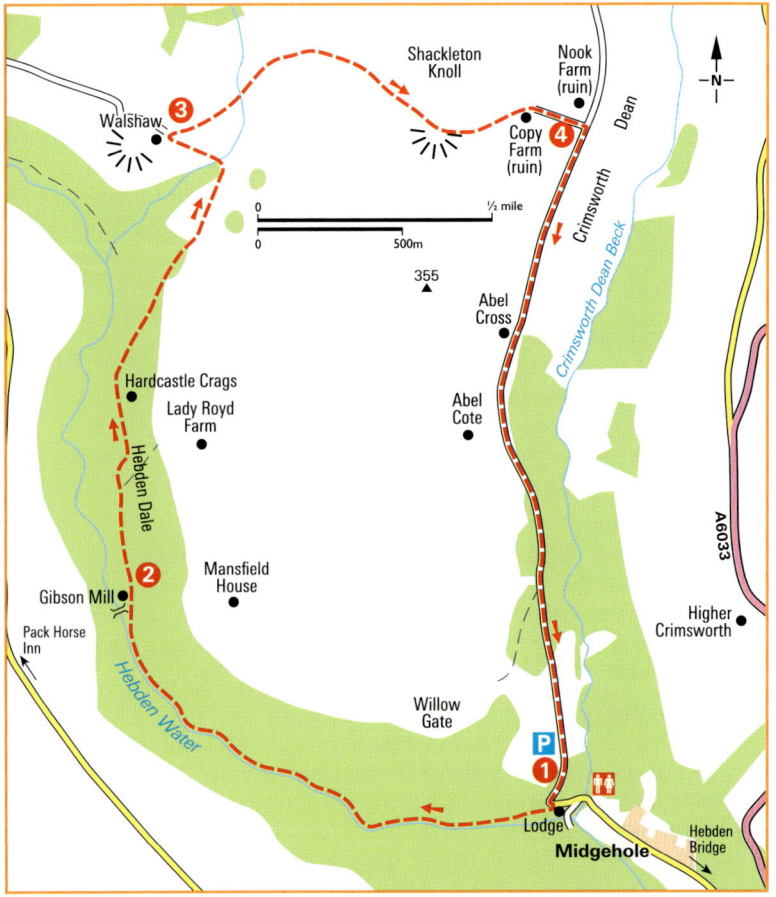

1. From the car park at Midgehole, walk back to the main drive. Go left towards the lodge but, just past the information board, immediately double back right on a path falling to a picnic area beside the river. Keep left whenever there is a choice of paths and continue upstream for a mile (1.6km) to reach Gibson Mill, occasionally climbing above the river where it becomes constricted between rocky banks.

2. Joining the main drive, follow it left beyond the mill, soon passing the crags that give the woods their name. Keep right at a later fork, shortly emerging from the trees and the National Trust estate to join a rough metalled drive. It runs left to the farm and adjacent cottages at Walshaw, which enjoy a terrific prospect along the Hebden Water valley.

3. Just before you reach the houses – when you are opposite some barns – turn sharp right through a gate onto an enclosed track (signed to Crimsworth Dean). Running on as a field track, it peters out beyond another gate to follow a wall over the shoulder of Shackleton Knoll. Approaching the watershed, the path slips through a gate to continue on the wall's opposite flank. Developing as a track, it later turns through another gate and drops into Crimsworth Dean, ending at a junction beside the ruin of Nook Farm. Running the length of the valley, the rough way is the old road from Hebden Bridge to Howarth and is a great walk to contemplate for another day.

4. For now, however, turn right along this elevated track, passing a farm on the left. You can make a short detour right at the next fork to see Abel Cross, actually a pair of old waymarker stones standing beside the track. Return to the main track and continue down the valley, soon re-entering the woodland of the National Trust estate. Keep left at successive forks, eventually returning to the car park at Midgehole.

Where to eat and drink
The Pack Horse Inn can be found on the road between Colden and Brierfield, just beyond the wooded valley of Hardcastle Crags. It is one of many solitary, exposed pubs to be found in Pennine Yorkshire, which existed to cater for the drovers and packhorse men. It remains a favourite with travellers, but is closed Mondays and Tuesdays.

What to see
Hebden Water rushes picturesquely through the wooded valley of Hardcastle Crags. These upland rivers and streams are the perfect habitat for an attractive little bird called the dipper. Dark brown, with a blaze of white on its breast, the dipper never strays from water. Unique among British birds, it has perfected the trick of walking underwater.

While you're there
Walk the old road from Hebden Bridge to Haworth (it's marked on the OS map) that includes the section of track through wooded Crimsworth Dean. The old road is never hard to find, and offers easy walking with terrific views all the way.

WADE WOOD AND LUDDENDEN DEAN

DISTANCE/TIME	1.5 miles (2.4km) / 40min
ASCENT/GRADIENT	300ft (91m) / ▲▲
PATHS	Wood and field paths, quiet lanes, several stiles
LANDSCAPE	Valley bottom woodland and cobbled lanes
SUGGESTED MAP	OS Explorer OL21 South Pennines
START/FINISH	Grid reference: SE036278
DOG FRIENDLINESS	Dogs should be on lead when not in the woodland
PARKING	Jerusalem Farm car park, Luddenden Dean
PUBLIC TOILETS	Campsite toilets at Jerusalem Farm

Luddenden Dean is a tranquil gem, tucked away in a corner of Calderdale with only limited road access. Despite the valley's small population – a few scattered farms and cottages, and the picturesque hamlet of Saltonstall – its remote Cat I'th Well pub is rarely quiet.

Wade Wood is a Site of Special Scientific Interest and among its many trees and plants are species that suggest this could be ancient woodland, looking much as it would have in the wake of the last ice age 12,000 years ago. Jerusalem Farm is a 32-acre (13ha) nature reserve, and the converted farm buildings offer facilities to school groups, with Calderdale Council's Countryside Service running educational workshops. The farm has its own tents-only campsite, set above Wade Wood.

At the valley head stands an ornate gateway, the entrance to the old Castle Carr estate. There are no public rights of way through the estate, however, occasionally, guided walks led by The Ramblers, or local walking festival events, are granted permission to enter the grounds and such excursions are worth keeping an eye out for.

The estate was established by Captain Joseph Priestley Edwards in the mid-1800s. Long driveways led to a coach house for half a dozen carriages. Beyond a Norman archway – complete with portcullis – was a huge banqueting hall. The grounds were even more impressive: laid out around a series of reservoirs, their focal point was five fountains, the highest of which flung water 130ft (40m) into the air – said to be the highest in Europe.

Edwards died in a railway disaster in Abergele in 1868, before the house was finished. Successive owners found the estate too expensive to maintain and the house, which fell into ruin, was demolished in the 1960s. When guided walks pass through the estate, however, the ornate fountains are occasionally brought back to life, as great a spectacle today as they ever were.

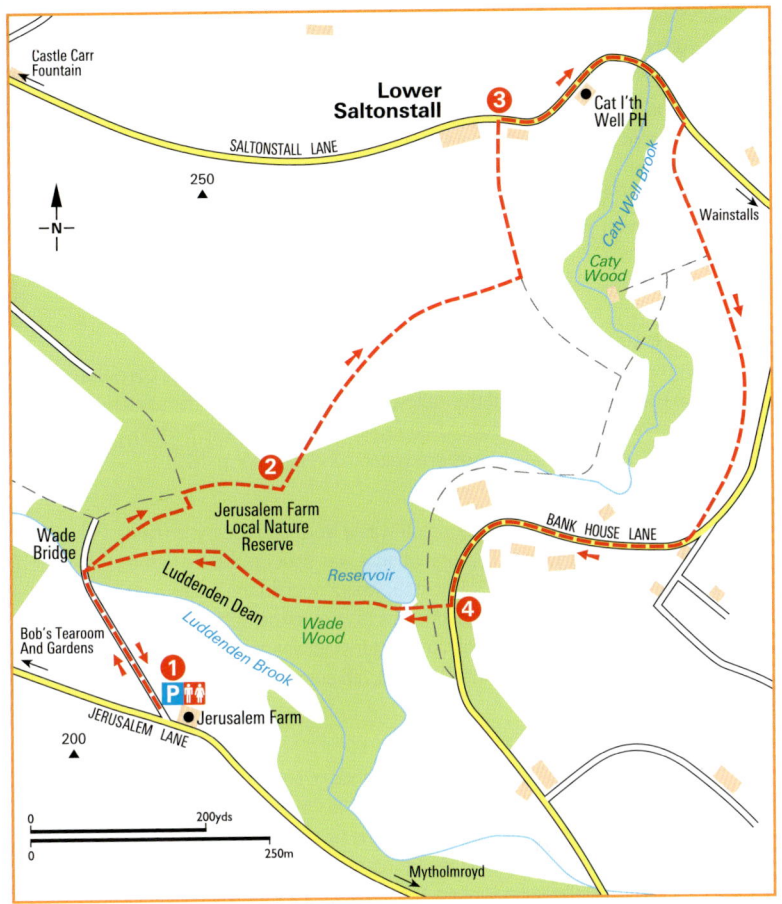

1. Pass through the stile at the bottom of the car park and descend the walled lane beyond, to cross Wade Bridge over Luddenden Brook. Several routes diverge from the opposite bank: take the broad, timber-edged path that climbs gently ahead-right. At a junction, bear left on the ascending Calderdale Way. At a second junction, head up steps to your right, signed 'Saltonstall', onto a well-worn earthy path that ascends to a gate through a fence in a field corner. Through this bear slightly right for 20yds (18m) to climb a stile, being careful not to dislodge loose wall stones.

2. Cross the next field diagonally to its top-right corner. Pass through the gate there and maintain direction across the next field, to pass through an open gateway. Walk parallel to the top-left wall through the next field to a wooden gate in its top corner. After that and the stile beyond turn left, ascending the final field, to exit through a small gate in the top-left corner. Ascend a rough driveway to a metalled road.

3. Turn right, down the quiet lane, past the Cat I'th Well pub. Cross Caty Well Bridge over Caty Well Brook and climb the lane for 60yds (55m), to take a surfaced track off to the right signed 'Public Footpath'. Through a wooden gate at the end pass to the left of a cottage and take a gate beyond a strip of grass.

Bear right on a 330yd (302m) field-edge path and back into the lane at its far end. Turn right, downhill, past a row of cottages known as Jowler.

4. In 90yds (82m) beyond the cottages, where a sign points to Jerusalem Farm, pass through a gap in the wall on your right and descend steps, kinking left at the bottom on a cinder track for 10yds (9m), then right, down more steps. Pass through a kissing gate and cross a bridge over the outflow of a small pond. Around 100yds (91m) past an area of woodland art, the path forks. Bear left, descending your outward path back to Wade Bridge and the track to the car park.

Where to eat and drink
Pictures on the walls in the Cat I'th Well pub show life at Castle Carr, the large estate at the head of the valley, in the days before its demolition. The pub serves food Wednesday to Sunday, including child-size portions, and offers pie and peas daily. Dogs are welcome in the beer garden.

What to look out for
The tiny hamlet of Upper Saltonstall was a Norman vaccary, or cattle farm, until the early 14th century when it was split up and let to the peasant farmers of Lower Saltonstall, who ploughed the pastures to grow oats. One of the first such lets, or assarts, was to the Saltonstall family, who grew wealthy. In 1597 Richard Saltonstall was made Lord Mayor of London, while his nephew also Richard, led some of the first colonisers of New England, in 1629.

While you're there
Clogs – the footwear worn by the thousands of people who worked in West Yorkshire's mills – are still produced in Calderdale. Walkley Clogs, of Mount Pleasant Mills, Mytholmroyd, is the last place where British clogs are entirely handmade, from the cutting of the leather to the carving of the beech sole. The shop is open Tuesday to Saturday, when visitors are welcome to watch the manufacturing process.

VISITING EAST RIDDLESDEN HALL

DISTANCE/TIME	5 miles (8km) / 2hrs
ASCENT/GRADIENT	623ft (190m) / ▲▲
PATHS	Field paths and canal tow path, several stiles
LANDSCAPE	Arable landscape and canalside
SUGGESTED MAP	OS Explorer 297 Lower Wharfedale
START/FINISH	Grid reference: SE098419
DOG FRIENDLINESS	Keep on lead near livestock. Dogs not permitted in East Riddlesden Hall
PARKING	Roadside parking in East Morton, opposite Busfeild Arms pub
PUBLIC TOILETS	None on route

Now hidden away in the suburbs of Keighley, East Riddlesden Hall is one of West Yorkshire's architectural gems. This gaunt, gritstone manor house is the work of James Murgatroyd, a wealthy yeoman clothier from Halifax. He built it in the 1640s on the site of an even older hall, but of this earlier building only the great hall remains.

Above the battlements of the hall's bothy, James Murgatroyd had two heads carved in stone: a bewigged Charles I and his queen, Henrietta Maria of France accompanied by the legend Vive le Roy (Long live the king). This was a dangerous time for such strong expressions of allegiance, for the country was divided by civil war and many Royalists were deprived of their possessions for far less. Despite its remoteness from the seats of power in London, the north was quickly drawn into the conflict and many in this part of the country supported the Parliamentarians. Nevertheless, Murgatroyd offered one of his other houses, Hollins at Warley near Halifax, to his king's forces for the storage of weapons. Inevitably, it was attacked and fell after a short but fierce battle, in which even the tiles of the roof were ripped off and used as missiles. Although 44 men were taken prisoner, Murgatroyd appears to have got away and managed to complete his building works at East Riddlesden by 1648.

Though surrounded by houses today, East Riddlesden Hall was a farm and there used to be a medieval mill beside the River Aire. By the hall, the huge 17th-century tithe barn is one of the finest examples in the north of England.

The Hall is remarkable in that it has remained largely unaltered, due to the fact that it was let to tenant farmers during the 18th and 19th centuries. Although the surrounding land was gradually sold off, the Hall was bequeathed to the National Trust in 1934 and is one of their must-see properties in the area. Striking features are the rose windows over the entrance porches at the front and back, which are typical of the 'Halifax' houses found in this part of the South Pennines. Oak-panelled rooms and mullioned windows provide a sympathetic setting for the collections of domestic utensils and Yorkshire oak furniture that date from the 17th and 18th centuries.

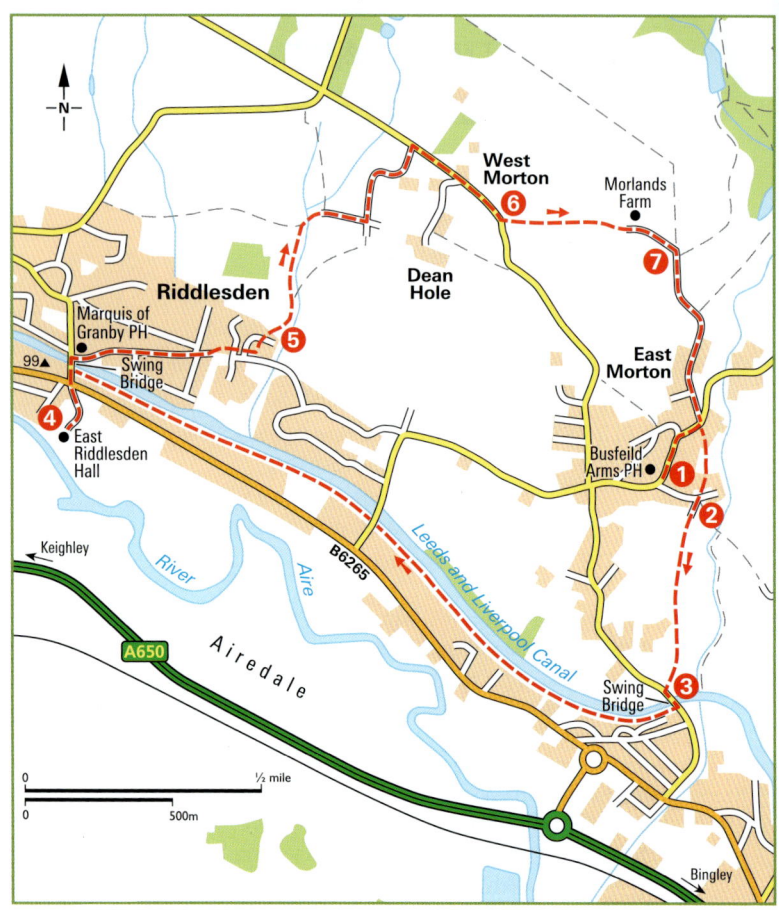

1. Follow the main road northwest past the Busfeild Arms. After 150yds (137m) at the crest of the hill, turn right down Little Lane. Go through consecutive gates beside the bottom cottage and continue along a walled path that leads out to a street, Cliffe Mill Fold.

2. Turn right and then left into Hawthorne Way, crossing a stile at the end of the cul-de-sac into a field. The path follows the right-hand wall into the next field, but as the wall later curves right, keep ahead to a squeeze gap in the lower boundary. Carry on down through trees and then along a fenced path between paddocks to emerge over a stile onto a road by the Leeds and Liverpool Canal.

3. Cross the swing bridge and follow the tow path to the right for 1.5 miles (2.4km), passing beneath a stone bridge to arrive at the next swing bridge. Leave the canal there and follow the lane left to the B6265, crossing beside the traffic lights to East Riddlesden Hall opposite.

4. Having looked around the hall, retrace your steps to the canal and cross the swing bridge. Immediately turn right in front of the Marquis of Granby pub along Hospital Road. At the end, carry on along a path immediately left of the old gates to the former isolation hospital. Continue ahead along the edge of

a housing development, across two streets. Around 15yds (14m) beyond the second street, turn off through a gap stile in the left wall. Follow a paved walkway up through the estate and out between houses at the top to a stile.

5. Cross a small paddock to a second stile and continue at the field edge beside a beck. Beyond a gate, stick with the ongoing track, which soon swings over a bridge and into a farmyard. Walk on past cottages to meet the bend of a lane. Turn left and follow it up to a junction at the top. Go right and walk for 0.25 miles (400m).

6. Just past the cricket green, where the lane bends right, leave through a squeeze gap by a gate on the left. Walk along by the right wall, keeping ahead through a gate into a second field. Over a stile in the next corner, continue to a squeeze gap on the left from which a walled track leads to Moorlands Farm.

7. Skirt the buildings and leave along its access track. Lower down, bear right past a junction and carry on to meet a lane at the bottom. Go right along Main Road to return to East Morton.

Where to eat and drink
The Busfeild Arms (named after a prominent local family) at the start of the walk in East Morton, offers good food, if eccentric spelling. The Marquis of Granby, just over the canal from East Riddlesden Hall, offers refreshments at the halfway point.

What to look out for
East Riddlesden Hall is blessed with a cast of ghostly characters. The most famous is the Grey Lady, the wife of a previous lord of the manor, said to wander from room to room

While you're there
As well as visiting the National Trust's East Riddlesden Hall, take a little time to explore the neighbouring mill town of Keighley (say 'Keithlee'). There are still some fine Victorian buildings intact which give an indication of the wealth the textile industry brought with it. There is also an excellent indoor market.

WARLAND AND ALONG SALTER RAKE

DISTANCE/TIME	6 miles (9.7km) / 2hrs 30min
ASCENT/GRADIENT	902ft (275m) / ▲▲
PATHS	Good paths and tracks throughout
LANDSCAPE	Open moorland, reservoirs and canalside
SUGGESTED MAP	OS Explorer OL21 South Pennines
START/FINISH	Grid reference: SD943204
DOG FRIENDLINESS	Keep on lead throughout the walk, especially around sheep
PARKING	Parking area 300yds (274m) north of Warland Gate End on A6033, by the Riverside Centre
PUBLIC TOILETS	None on route

Salter Rake is an old packhorse road which, as the name suggests, was used particularly for transporting salt from the Cheshire salt mines across the Pennines. When these trading routes were first established, the Calder Valley was largely undrained. The teams of packhorse ponies, laden with pannier bags, would keep to the drier high ground, only descending into the valleys to cross rivers on the narrow stone bridges that are so typical of the area.

Most of these causeways (or 'causeys') were paved with stones. More than three centuries after they were laid, these stones still fit snugly together as the pieces of a jigsaw. To judge from the way they are deeply 'dished', the stones have seen heavy use over the years by countless horses' hooves.

Gritstone rocks and outcrops are familiar features throughout the South Pennines. The Basin Stone, an oddly-shaped rock looks – from one viewpoint, at least – like a fishtail. It is a prominent landmark high on Walsden Moor and was one of the many sites used by travelling Methodist preachers when they delivered their open-air sermons, well away from the watchful eyes of the local authorities.

Like many of the reservoirs you will encounter whilst walking in the South Pennines, the one passed on this walk – Warland, and its near neighbours, Light Hazzles and White Holme – were built to supply water for a canal. The Rochdale Canal was built to link Manchester to the Calder and Hebble Navigation at Sowerby Bridge. By the 1920s, there was very little commercial traffic still using it, so the reservoirs were converted to an alternative use and joined the complex of water supply systems built to quench the thirst of East Lancashire's mill towns.

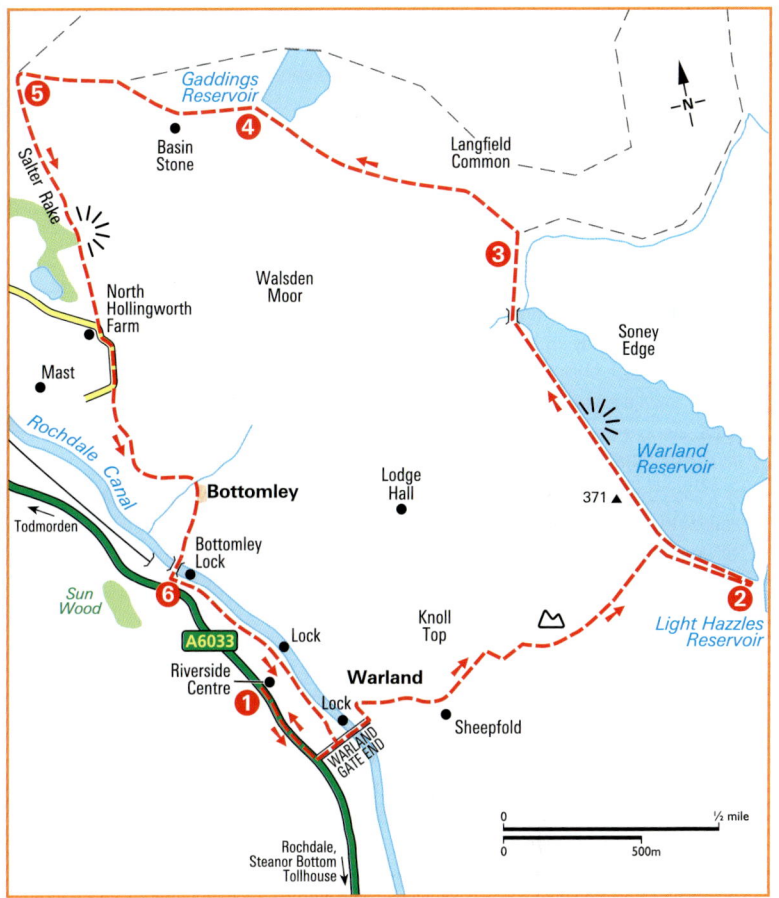

1. Walk southeast along the road for 300yds (274m) to take a track on the left past cottages, Warland Gate End. Cross the Rochdale Canal on a swing bridge and follow the track over a stream to zig-zag steeply up the hill. Where the track later forks, keep right through an ornamental gate towards Calflee House. Turn right when you reach a T-junction. Approaching the house, go through a second gate and swing left on a track that leads up to another house. Pass around the back of the building to find a field gate and continue across the open moor on a rising rough track. As you approach the retaining embankment of Warland Reservoir, follow the track to the right, which slants upwards to reach the reservoir.

2. Double back left along the top of the dam, from which there are terrific views over Calderdale and East Lancashire. Cross a bridge at the northern end of the reservoir, and keep on the track as it follows a drainage channel.

3. When both track and channel wheel to the right, go left in front of a stone bridge, to follow a flagged path in the direction of another, smaller lake, Gaddings Reservoir. It supplemented water supplies for the textile mills in the valley disrupted by the construction of the canal. There are two windfarms on the distance, built to take advantage of the winds that sweep the Pennines.

4. Bear half left at the far end of the reservoir, down stone steps and continue along a clear path that soon passes close to the curiously shaped outcrop called the Basin Stone. Shortly you come to a meeting of paths, marked with a small waymarker post.

5. Turn left here, on a path that's soon delineated by causeway stones; you are now following Salter Rake, the old packhorse road. Enjoy excellent views over Walsden as you make a gradual descent, still across open moorland, then accompanying a wall. Eventually, leave the moor through a gate and continue to a junction opposite a mullion-windowed farmhouse. Bear left to pass a second house, Hollingworth Gate, walking through a gate back onto the moor. Immediately branch right off the track on to a causeway path, marked as the Pennine Bridleway. It later swings above another farmhouse and before long, winds across a beck to reach the tiny hillside settlement of Bottomley. Go right here, down a metalled track, but then bear immediately right again, through a gate, along a cobbled, walled path heading directly downhill, which takes you to the Rochdale Canal.

6. Cross the canal by the side of Bottomley Lock, and walk left along the canal tow path. An easy stroll of about 0.5 miles (800m) takes you back to the swing bridge straddling the Yorkshire–Lancashire border over which you set out. Go right to the main road and right again back to your car.

Where to eat and drink
Todmorden, 3 miles (4.8km) away, has various cafés and pubs including the White Hart dating from 1728. In the early 1800s, a 'Court of Petty Sessions' was established at the inn, and it was reached by a flight of steps on the outside of the building. In 1935, the old White Hart was replaced by the present mock Tudor-style building.

What to look out for
Steanor Bottom tollhouse is a small hexagonal building dating from the 1820s. You will find it on the main A6033 road south of Warland Gate End, at a junction with a minor road. Tolls were collected here from any travellers wishing to use the new turnpike road. The tollhouse has been restored and retains its notice board presenting the tariff for all the different kinds of traffic, from sheep to carts.

THE BRIDESTONE ROCKS FROM LYDGATE

DISTANCE/TIME	6.25 miles (10.1km) / 3hrs
ASCENT/GRADIENT	1,615ft (492m) / ▲▲
PATHS	Moorland and packhorse paths, some quiet roads, several stiles
LANDSCAPE	Steep-sided valley and open moorland
SUGGESTED MAP	OS Explorer OL21 South Pennines
START/FINISH	Grid reference: SD923255
DOG FRIENDLINESS	Keep on leads along lanes and near grazing sheep
PARKING	Roadside parking in Lydgate, 1.5 miles (2.4km) out of Todmorden, on A646, signposted to Burnley
PUBLIC TOILETS	None on route

The Long Causeway, between Halifax and Burnley, is an ancient trading route, possibly dating back to the Bronze Age. Crosses and waymarker stones helped to guide travellers across the moorland wastes, though most of them have been lost or damaged in the intervening years. Amazingly, Mount Cross has survived intact: a splendid, though crudely carved, example of the Celtic 'wheel-head' design. Opinions differ about its age but it is certainly the oldest human artefact in the area, erected at least 1,000 years ago.

The hills and moors to the north of Todmorden are dotted with gritstone outcrops. The impressive piles of Orchan Rocks and Whirlaw Stones are both encountered on this walk. But the most intriguing rock formations are to be found at the Bridestones. One rock in particular has been weathered by wind and water into a teardrop shape, and stands on a base that looks far too slender to support its great weight.

Further along the edge to the northwest, and well placed to catch the winds funnelled along the valley, are the tall turbines of Coal Clough Windfarm. With a capacity of around 9.6 megawatts, enough to power around 5,500 homes, it was opened in 1992 and was one of the first such schemes to be commissioned in this country.

The Cliviger Valley links two towns – Todmorden in West Yorkshire and Burnley in Lancashire – that expanded with the textile trade, and then suffered when that trade went into decline. The valley itself is narrow and steep-sided, in places almost a gorge. Into its cramped confines are shoehorned the road, railway line, the infant River Calder and communities such as Portsmouth, Cornholme and Lydgate that grew up around the textile mills. The mills were powered by fast-flowing becks, running off the steep hillsides. The valley is almost a microcosm of the Industrial Revolution and full of character. This area is particularly well provided with good footpaths, some of them still paved with their original causeway stones.

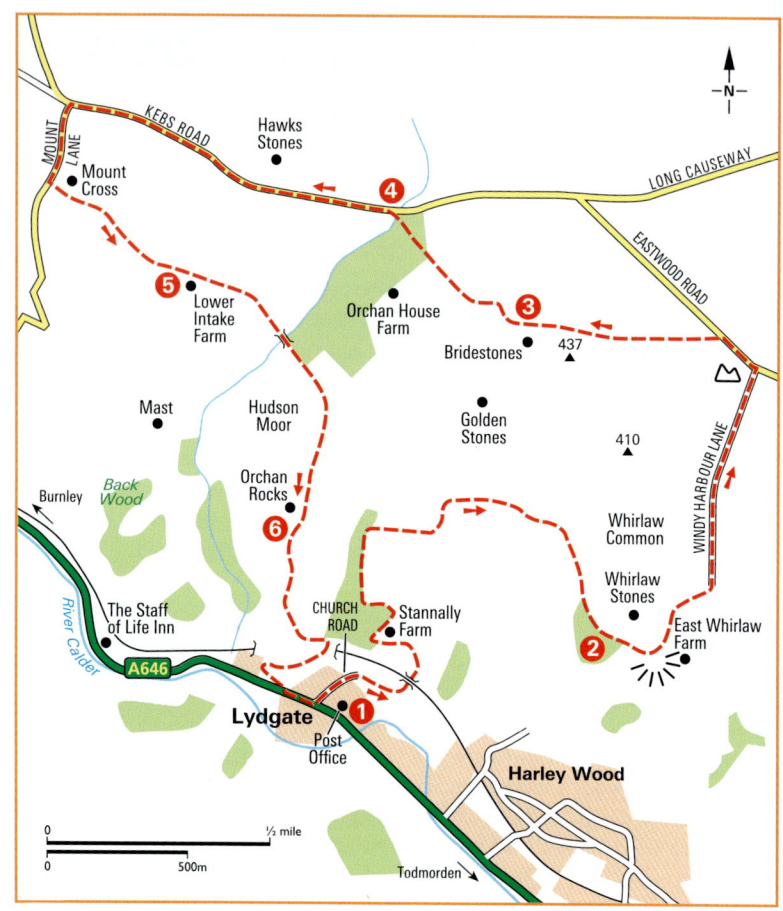

1. From the post office in Lydgate, take Church Road. At the end go right into Owlers Walk and continue along a contained path. Meeting a track at its end, follow it beneath a railway bridge and up to Stannally Farm. Walk past the buildings and swing right as the track zig-zags steeply up the wooded hillside. Eventually breaking out onto the edge of open moor, it swings right towards a farm. Pass on the left of the farmhouse and then bear left up a narrower walled track. When you meet another walled track, go right towards a rocky outcrop on the first horizon. Beyond two gates, the path crosses onto the rough common that aprons Whirlaw Stones.

2. A causeway path skirts the base of the outcrop, giving panoramic views of the Cliviger Valley, Todmorden and Stoodley Pike. Keep going through gates until you reach a junction above East Whirlaw Farm. There turn sharp left along a stony track that winds up beside the outcrop to meet the end of Windy Harbour Lane. Carry on up the lane, which shortly leads to Eastwood Road. Go left for just 150yds (137m). Where the wall ends, take a kissing gate on the left. A grassy path leads you to another fascinating collection of rocks, known as the Bridestones.

3. Continue past the Bridestones across a landscape of scattered boulders. Keep ahead, dropping to cross a ruined wall. Continue ahead past waypoints, the path curving above the edge and eventually falling to a gate and stile. Follow a track right out to a lane.

4. Go left, along the road for 0.75 miles (1.2km), passing below the Hawks Stones on the right and a handful of houses, until you come to a minor road on the left. This is Mount Lane, signed to Shore. Walk down for 300yds (274m) before turning left onto a broad bridleway. Look out for Mount Cross, which stands a short way along, over the wall in a field to your left.

5. Bear left past Lower Intake Farm on a path that soon resumes as a track. Cross an intersecting track and, later, a bridge spanning a stream before reaching a stile, 250yds (229m) further along on the right. Ignore the stile, but take the adjacent track, which drops alongside a wall past another gritstone outcrop, Orchan Rocks.

6. Where the wall bears left, beyond the rocks, follow it downhill to a stile. You now join a farm track that makes a serpentine descent through woodland back to Lydgate. Reaching a large building, turn sharp left heading downhill on a path back to the main road.

Where to eat and drink
The Staff of Life Inn on the main A646 at Lydgate is a cosy real ale pub offering a warm welcome to walkers. The bar has rotating guest beers and locally produced organic beers as well as a range of ciders.

What to see
In geological terms, the South Pennines are largely made up of millstone grit and coarse sandstone. Where the gritstone is visible, it forms rocky crags and outcrops, like those encountered on this walk. The typical landscape is moorland of heather and peat, driven by steep-sided valleys.

While you're there
If you continue along the Long Causeway, you'll soon come to Coal Clough Windfarm. These huge wind turbines can be found on the crest of many South Pennine hills, attracting strong winds and generating energy.

JUMBLE HOLE AND COLDEN CLOUGH

DISTANCE/TIME	6 miles (9.7km) / 3hrs
ASCENT/GRADIENT	1,831ft (558m) / ▲▲
PATHS	Good paths, many stiles
LANDSCAPE	Steep-sided valleys, fields and woodland
SUGGESTED MAP	OS Explorer OL21 South Pennines
START/FINISH	Grid reference: SD991271
DOG FRIENDLINESS	Keep on leads near livestock and roads
PARKING	Pay-and-display car parks in Hebden Bridge
PUBLIC TOILETS	Hebden Bridge and Townfield Lane, Heptonstall

This walk links the little town of Hebden Bridge with the old hand-weaving village of Heptonstall, using sections of a waymarked walk, the Calderdale Way. The hill village of Heptonstall was, in its time, an important centre of the textile trade and at the hub of a complex network of old trackways, mostly used by packhorse trains carrying wool and cotton. Heptonstall's Cloth Hall, where cloth was bought and sold, dates from the 16th century, when Hebden Bridge was little more than a river crossing on an old packhorse causeway.

Heptonstall prospered when textiles were still a cottage industry, with spinning and weaving undertaken in isolated farmhouses. As the processes became mechanised during the Industrial Revolution, communities sprang up wherever a ready supply of running water could turn waterwheels to drive the new machinery. Heptonstall was literally left high and dry and a new settlement grew down in the valley at the confluence of two fast-flowing rivers, the Calder and Hebden Water. There, large mills enabled the textile processes to be developed on an industrial scale. At one time, there were more than 30 mills in Hebden Bridge.

With Hebden Bridge hemmed in by hills, and the mills occupying much of the available land on the valley bottom, the workers' houses had to be built up the steep slopes. An ingenious solution to the problem was to build 'top and bottom' houses, one dwelling on top of another – best viewed on the last leg of the walk. Today, Hebden Bridge has reinvented itself as the 'capital' of Upper Calderdale, a place to enjoy a day out. The town is known for its excellent walking country, narrowboat trips along the Rochdale Canal and its popular summer arts festival.

Jumble Hole Clough is a typical South Pennine steep-sided, wooded valley. Though a tranquil scene today, this little valley was once a centre of industry, with four mills exploiting the fast-flowing beck descending to the River Calder. You can see remains of these mills, and some of their mill ponds, on this walk.

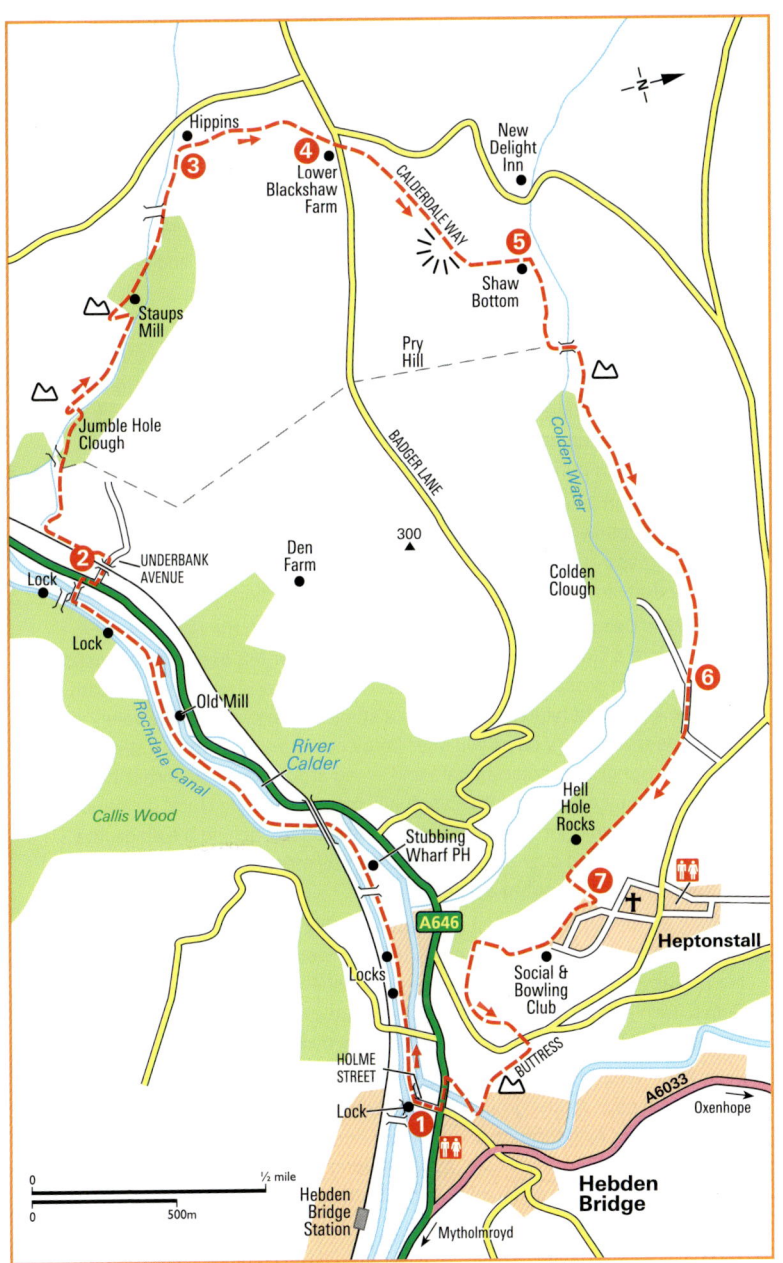

1. Begin along Holme Street, off the main A646 just east of the bridge, to the Rochdale Canal. Go right to follow the tow path beneath two bridges, past the Stubbing Wharf pub and beneath a railway bridge. Carry on for another 0.75 miles (1.2km) before turning off before the next bridge to follow a track to reach the A646.

2. Cross the road and turn right for 75yds (69m) to take Underbank Avenue, on the left. Walk beneath the railway and go left again, past houses, to where another road comes through the viaduct. Go sharp right on a track past a mill, and follow the beck up into the woodland of Jumble Hole Clough. Where the track later swings sharp right, leave across a stone bridge onto a track rising steeply through a hairpin. Higher up as it wheels left, take the narrow path ahead to continue above the beck. Ignore a later intersecting path and climb beyond to a stile. Join another path down to Staups Mill. The climb resumes beside the ruin to reach a footbridge. Scale the opposite bank and go left in front of a signpost by a gap in a wall to come out at Hippins.

3. Join the Calderdale Way, turning right up a track between farm buildings to a stile. Follow a path to the next stile and on beside a wall. Cross a track at Apple Tree Farm and continue over a couple of stiles on a causeway to a row of cottages. Pass the end of the terrace, crossing more stiles and a rough pasture to a kissing gate. Follow the onward causeway to a farm, there following a track out to the lane at Blackshaw Head.

4. Cross to a small gate almost opposite and bear half right across the field to a stile, then follow the right edge of the next field. Continue on a diagonal line across successive fields, eventually reaching a walled track. Walk down to Shaw Bottom and bear left beside the house to a junction.

5. The New Delight Inn is to the left, but the route lies to the right, the way degrading to a stony track. After 200yds (183m), bear left beside a waypost on a stepped path dropping steeply to cross Colden Water. Take the rising path, but then keep right higher up to follow a stone causeway along the valley side above the trees. Carry on as you later break out into a field. Over a stile at the far corner, ignore the adjacent gate and swing around the wall corner to pick up the continuing flagged path. Eventually meeting a rising track, go left to a junction and turn right on a tarmac drive. Bear off left behind a cottage, the causeway resuming over a stile beyond. Shortly meeting an intersecting track, go right and follow it out to a lane.

6. Walk up the hill, leaving just before a bend through a gap in the right-hand wall. From here, your path meanders through woodland (it's a bit of a scramble in places). Emerging from the trees, continue above the edge to Hell Hole Rocks. Turn away from the viewpoint along a walled path between gardens. Cross a street to the ongoing path, which shortly meets a track behind houses.

7. Go right, emerging opposite the Social and Bowling Club. Turn right on a contained path. As the ground falls away, curve left by the boundary, eventually dropping through a wall onto a crossing path. Walk left to meet a track and go right to a junction. Bear left along the lower, main road, doubling sharply right after 50yds (46m) onto the Buttress, an old packhorse trail that drops steeply back to Hebden Bridge.

Where to eat and drink

As you'd expect, Hebden Bridge is full of walker- and dog-friendly pubs, cafés and restaurants.

AROUND SALTAIRE VILLAGE

DISTANCE/TIME	3 miles (4.8km) / 1hr
ASCENT/GRADIENT	195ft (60m) / ▲
PATHS	Roads, woodland paths and canal tow path
LANDSCAPE	Urban streets, woodland and waterways
SUGGESTED MAP	OS Explorer 288 Bradford & Huddersfield
START/FINISH	Grid reference: SE139379
DOG FRIENDLINESS	Dogs can exercise in the woods and on the canal tow path
PARKING	Pay-and-display car park at corner of Victoria Road and Caroline Street, Saltaire
PUBLIC TOILETS	At car park at start

'I hope to draw around me a population that will enjoy the beauties of this neighbourhood – a population of well fed, contended, happy operatives'. So said mill entrepreneur Titus Salt, embarking on a scheme to build an idealistic village around his giant mill on the banks of the River Aire. Salt was born in Morley in 1803 and left school to learn the skills of buying and selling wool. As the trade expanded, his father moved the family to Bradford, where Salt's career took off. He soon owned five mills around the city and made his fortune when he spotted the potential for spinning alpaca wool to produce a fine quality worsted cloth.

Salt was one of a handful of textile barons who sought to better the lives of their workforces. In the mid-19th century, the majority of Bradford's textile workers endured appalling conditions. The boom in the industry had seen a migration of people into a city that lacked the infrastructure to support them. Salt realised the benefits of a happy, healthy workforce. He began by taking his workers – up to 2,000 of them – on day trips into the Yorkshire Dales. But he had a greater vision in which his mills would be consolidated into one, at the heart of a new community.

He chose his site specifically for its proximity to the waters of the Aire, needed for production, and the Leeds and Liverpool Canal, for distribution. Construction began in 1851 and when it opened on September 20, 1853 – Salt's 50th birthday – most of the 3,500 guests were employees.

Salt next set his architects to designing an entire village for his workforce. Albert Terrace was first to go up and the building of good quality housing continued for another 15 years. Salt provided shops, a church, schools, a club and institute for social and educational use, an infirmary... everything a town might need, other than pubs, which he saw as a source of social evil.

On his death at his mansion at Crow Nest in Lightcliffe, near Halifax, in December 1876, his body was borne by procession to the family mausoleum at Saltaire Congregational Church. It's estimated that 100,000 people lined the route.

Today, the village is a UNESCO World Heritage Site and the regenerated mill is home to shops, an art gallery devoted to the work of Bradford artist David Hockney, and many more attractions. Saltaire Mill, renamed Salt's Mill, is a remarkable memorial to a remarkable social pioneer.

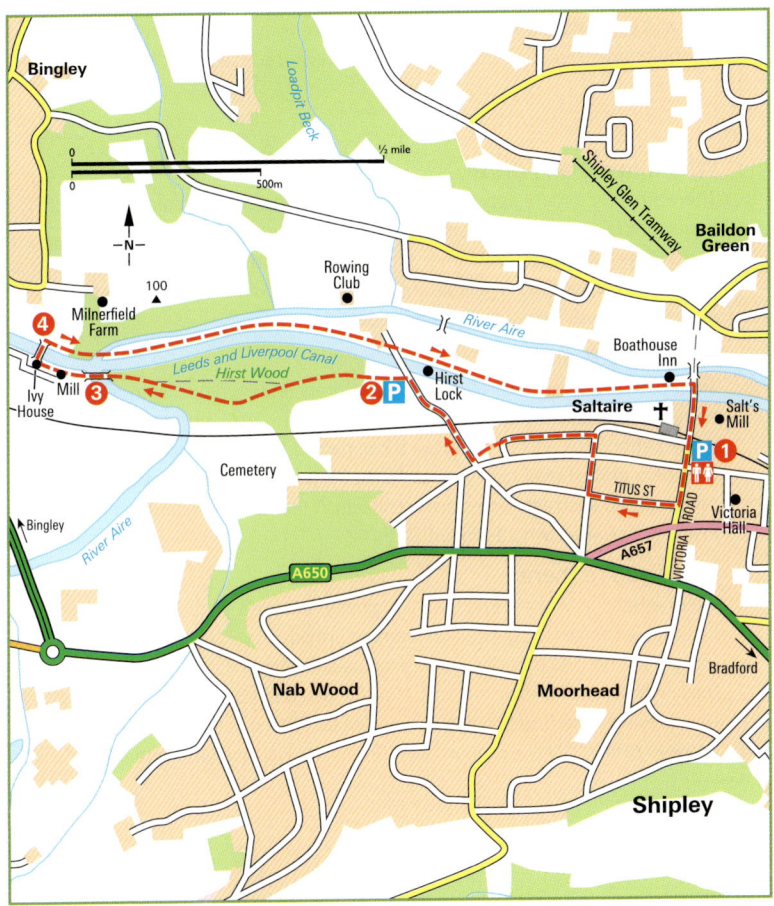

1. Head up Victoria Road and turn right along Titus Street. Turn right at the end, down Albert Road, turning left near the bottom along Albert Avenue. At the far end, take the footpath across the recreation ground, then turn right down Hirst Lane, crossing a railway bridge. After passing a coffee shop, head through the Hirst Wood car park.

2. Pass through a metal kissing gate into woodland. Keep left when the track forks after 100yds (91m), ignoring lesser paths that stray off to either side. When the trail branches in three directions, stay with the central option. Various tracks eventually converge and gently descend to a junction, where you turn right, to the canal tow path.

3. Turn left, over an aqueduct, after which the path drops to the left, then right, to run between walls past a converted canal warehouse and cottages, where it

becomes a roughly surfaced track. After rounding Ivy House, bear right to cross a canal bridge.

4. Bear right along the tow path, canal on one side and the River Aire on the other, for 1.4 miles (2.25km), until you reach Saltaire, where Titus Salt's Congregational Church, his final resting place, stands on the opposite side of the canal. Leave the tow path by an Airedale Greenway information board and cross the bridge over the canal, continuing up Victoria Road back to the start of the walk.

Where to eat and drink
There's hardly a more appropriate place to refresh yourself after the walk than within Salt's Mill. On the second floor, you'll find the contemporary Salt's Diner, which serves high-quality hot meals and light refreshments. Children's portions are available. Titus probably wouldn't approve but the diner also serves wines and bottled beers.

What to look out for
Titus Salt and his wife Caroline had 11 children, and each has a street named after them in the village that Titus built. This walk visits the streets named after Titus and Caroline but those named for their offspring, and members of the Royal family, await further exploration and discovery. Also remembered in street names are architects William Mawson and Henry Francis Lockwood, who designed Salt's Mill.

While you're there
Victoria Hall, on Victoria Road, was originally Saltaire's Victoria Hall and Institute, a centre for culture and learning provided by Titus Salt for his villagers. It housed libraries, games rooms and even a dance hall. Among those who spoke here were Prime Minister Benjamin Disraeli and explorer David Livingstone. The building serves similar functions today and is also home to Britain's only Victorian Reed Organ and Harmonium Museum.

THE WOODLANDS OF HARDEN BECK

DISTANCE/TIME	2.5 miles (4km) / 1hr
ASCENT/GRADIENT	246ft (75m) / ▲
PATHS	Woodland paths and tracks, field paths, several stiles
LANDSCAPE	Deciduous woodland and arable land
SUGGESTED MAP	OS Explorers 288 Bradford & Huddersfield, OS Explorer OL21 South Pennines
START/FINISH	Grid reference: SE088378
DOG FRIENDLINESS	Can be off lead in woodland
PARKING	From Harden, take Wilsden Road to roadside parking at bottom of hill, just before bridge and the Malt pub
PUBLIC TOILETS	None on route

Today, the unassuming valley enclosing Harden Beck and Goit Stock Woods is a quiet backwater, little visited except by locals. But this wasn't always the case, for by the beginning of the 19th century, there were at least three textile mills processing silk, cotton and worsteds crowded within its narrow confines and taking advantage of the fast flowing stream to power the spinning and weaving machines. The buildings of two have survived: Harden Bridge, which is now used by light industry and Bents Mill at Hallas Bridge, higher up the valley, which has been converted for housing. And the terraced cottages, built nearby to house the mill workers, are still lived in.

Times change, and by the beginning of the 20th century, despite being converted to steam, the relative isolation of Goit Stock Mill left it uneconomic. By then, however, the inherent beauty of the valley, its woods and the bonus of a modestly spectacular waterfall began to draw visitors. With railways serving both Bingley and Cullingworth, the 'Happy Valley' soon became popular and part of Goit Stock Mill was converted to a ballroom and café. Crowds flocked to this quiet spot and reports say that the 1927 May bank holiday drew 20,000 people. However, it turned out to be a tragic day, for that evening a fire destroyed both the famous dance floor and the instruments of the Wilsden Brass Band, who were providing the entertainment. All that remains today is the chimney of the old steam engine, standing on the hillside above the residential park home.

Cloaked in deciduous woodland, the valley has become a haven for wildlife, supporting birds such as jays, tree creepers, woodpeckers and many small songbirds that build their nests amongst the trees and bushes. You might even see a dipper probing the pebbles of the sparkling beck for insects.

Goit Stock falls themselves were created by the differential erosion of a band of soft shale underlying the gritstone rock, which, as it is worn away, eventually causes the hard rock to collapse, leaving the lip of the fall.

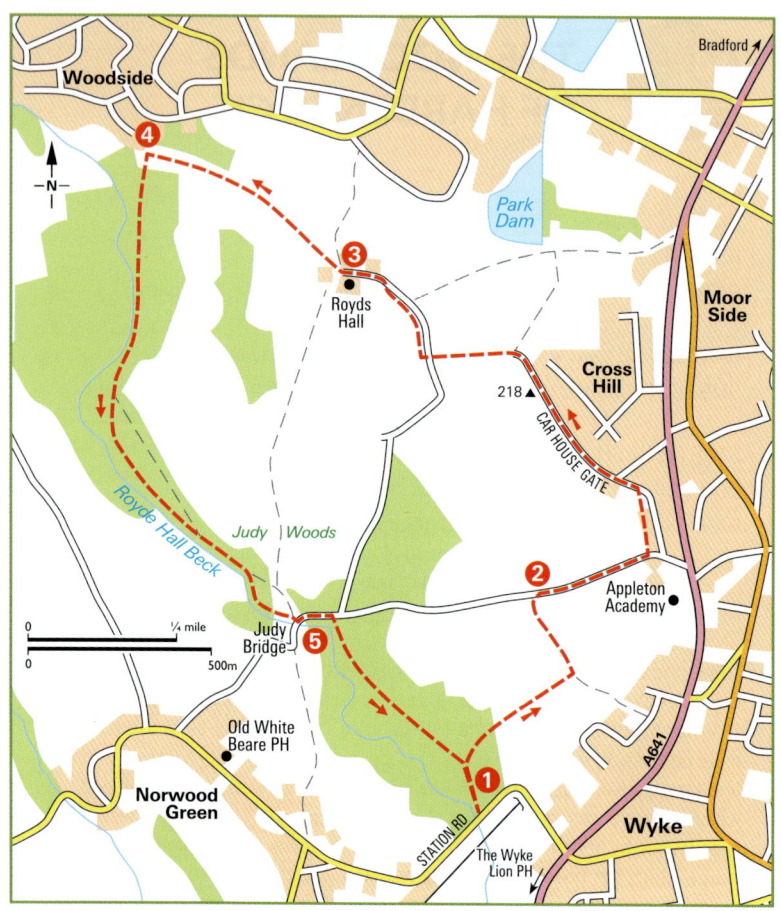

1. From the parking area, walk downhill to take, just before the bridge, the second turning off on the right into Goit Stock Lane. Beyond a terrace of cottages, built for the workers at Harden Beck Mill, the ongoing rough lane crosses a cattlegrid and soon joins the stream along the base of the valley below Crag Wood. The track later crosses a bridge to run between a residential park home and its parking spaces. The Goit Stock Mill lay towards the top end of the park home site, its tall chimney still standing.

2. At the far end, keep ahead to pass Calgary Lodge and enter Goit Stock Wood. Ignore the path off left and walk forward above Harden Beck along the Millennium Way for some 0.25 miles (400m) to reach the first and largest of the two waterfalls. The continuing path clambers up the rocks beside the fall; and although a handrail has been installed, care is required as the rocks can be slippery. Carry on past a second, smaller cascade and cross a plank bridge, soon emerging onto a crossing bridlepath above Hallas Bridge by the third of the valley's mills built in this short stretch of valley.

3. Turn left up the hill, going left again in front of a terrace of stone cottages. At the end of the street, climb steps to a stile and walk on at the left edge of successive pastures above the wood. At the far end of the fifth field, the path slips through a gap stile to continue within the upper fringe of the wood. Soon joined by another path from the left, keep going across another stile to then leave the trees behind. Follow the field edge past another row of cottages to emerge over a final stile onto Wilsden Road.

4. Go left past a garden centre, where there is a café. As the road then bends right, keep ahead down a steep, narrow lane, Mill Hill Top. Rejoining the main road at the bottom, walk left past The Malt to the parking area.

Where to eat and drink
The Malt is a handsome 16th-century pub with mullioned windows, close by the bridge over Harden Beck. Homemade traditional food is served every day, with a specials board to add variety to the menu. If the weather is kind, you can eat in the large, beck-side beer garden. If you're looking for more choice, it is a short drive down into Bingley, where there are many more options available.

What to look out for
One unexpected pleasure in West Yorkshire is to find so much broadleaved woodland. Elsewhere, too much ancient woodland has been supplanted by the ranks of conifer trees, which offer little to wildlife. Goit Stock is one of many delightful and deciduous woods that make welcome green oases, supporting a great variety of animals, birds and plants.

While you're there
The little stone village of Harden is next to the Bingley St Ives Estate. This walk through Goit Stock Wood would make an ideal morning stroll, followed by a leisurely exploration of the wooded hillside of St Ives. You may also like to explore the group of villages that occupy the high land between Bradford, Bingley and Keighley. Wilsden faces Harden across Harden Beck, Cullingworth lies higher up the valley. A delightful network of old lanes link up with Denholme and the historic conservation village of Thornton where Charlotte, Emily, Anne and Branwell Brontë were born. There is a Village Trail around Thornton's cobbled streets, centred on the Brontës' birthplace.

Explore the UK at RatedTrips.com

AA